THE TOP FIVE OF *ALMOST* EVERYTHING

AS HEARD ON **talkSPORT's**
DRIVE SHOW WITH
ADRIAN DURHAM AND **DARREN GOUGH**

talkSPORT

THE TOP FIVE OF ALMOST EVERYTHING

talkSPORT Limited
1 London Bridge Street
London SE1 9GF

www.talksport.com

First published by talkSPORT in 2021

2 4 6 8 10 9 7 5 3 1

Edited by Bill Borrows at Vondot Media Ltd.

Sub-editor: Richard Purvis

Cover by Neil Jamieson

Design by Igloo

Thanks also to: Elizabeth Stephenson, William Hall, Andrew Downie,
Joshua Law, John Mahood, Will Varney, Liam Fisher, Joe Amphlett,
Andrew Jolly, Ryan Clancy, Nicola Young, Lee Clayton, Adrian Durham,
Darren Gough, Andy Goldstein, Max Rushden, Sam Matterface,
Jamie O'Hara, Perry Groves, Darren Bent, Dean Ashton, Troy Deeney,
Andy Townsend, Jamie Carragher, Gabby Agbonlahor and the
rest of the brilliant talkSPORT production team.

ISBN 978-0-9563284-2-7

Printed and bound by
CPI Group (UK) Ltd, Croydon, CR0 4YY

All cover photographs supplied by Getty. All inside photographs
supplied by Getty with the exception of the following supplied by News
Licensing: David Beckham (p34); Keeley Hawes (p62).

FOREWORD

In March 2020, COVID-19 hit the UK and we went into lockdown, and sport stopped. I was asked the question: "What will you talk about on *Drive* with no football?" My reply was that we had a duty to entertain our listeners, lift their spirits in these difficult times, and we would have to be creative to do this effectively.

People love lists, they love a Top 10 or a Top 5, and they love comparing lists, and discussing, debating and arguing about what has been included and what has been left out.

So the producer Patrick D'Angelo and I decided to make the Top 5 a daily feature. Another member of the team had the idea to do it at 5pm, and hence the "Top FIVE @ 5" was born; simple, but very popular.

The ideas were endless, and the joy of this feature for us was in the research, and the telling of the stories behind our picks. We had so many trips down memory lane, reminiscing about music, TV, films, talkSPORT moments, free kicks, goals, players, other sports – it was all so positive and magical.

Goughie and I occasionally clashed – he didn't like Queen, I'd never watched a war film – but it was all good-natured, and we both plunged into it to make the feature work. I actually watched 8 war films over a weekend so I could come up with a Top 5!

This book goes over the best Top 5s from that time, and throws in some others as well.

Reading through it has been a fantastic experience. It took me back to that time: with the backdrop of our country in the midst of a horrific crisis, we found a way of making a meaningful, positive connection with our wonderful listeners, and if our Top 5s brought a smile to their faces, what could be better than that?

Adrian Durham

CONTENTS

TOP FIVE @ 5

TOP FIVE @ 5: MOST DIFFICULT OPPONENTS

HOW TO USE THIS BOOK

Each TOP FIVE @ 5 features two presenters, usually Adrian Durham and Darren Gough, who talk about and discuss their choices in each category. The avatars below show who is speaking. When one of them wants to comment on the choice of another, their contribution and initials are in bold. For example...

I'm Adrian Durham and you can hear me on *Drive* with Darren Gough. **DG: That's me interrupting here.** Now this is me again. Let's get cracking...

AD

Adrian Durham
The Disputatious Don of *Drive* and King of Saturday afternoons has 20 years of debating and an encyclopaedic knowledge of all things sport.

DG

Darren Gough
Drive stalwart, England cricketing legend and Strictly champion. He now ducks Adrian's bouncers rather than bowling them.

AG

Andy Goldstein
Landlord at the *Sports Bar* and regular Friday host on *Drive*. He loves Man United, snooker and Oasis. Don't get him started on any of those subjects!

MR

Max Rushden
Host of *The Warm Up* and *Drive* supersub. Obsessed with ex-NCFC defender Ian Culverhouse, but then aren't we all?

SM

Sam Matterface
talkSPORT's Chief Football Commentator who also turns out for Dancing On Ice on ITV. Likes the sequins, apparently.

JO

Jamie O'Hara
"I loved every minute of it." The Celebrity Big Brother star also played for Spurs and appears as 'Chunky' on *Breakfast*.

PG

Perry Groves
Cult hero with over 150 appearances for Arsenal. One of Herbert Chapman's favourites at Highbury back in the day.

DB

Darren Bent
England international with record for the number of times he has seen Ben-Hur. Scored goals wherever he went.

DA

Dean Ashton
West Ham and England striker forced to retire at 26. Claims to have copied that Van Basten goal. In a gym somewhere.

TOP FIVE @5 SPORT FILMS

When your research for a big section of the show is watching sports movies, I mean, what's not to love? I got up extra-early and watched or rewatched three of them this morning. Our first Top Five is sporting films. So let's get cracking...

5 COOL RUNNINGS

I'm going to kick us off with Cool Runnings. **DG: I forgot that one.** I've got a massive confession to make: the first time I've ever watched it was this morning. I was thinking I can't do a top five sports films if I haven't watched *this*, and you bet it gets in the top five. Made in 1993. If you haven't seen it, why not? I've been asking myself that question. It's about the Jamaican bobsleigh team at the Winter Olympics in Canada and is very loosely based on a true story. There are some lovely messages through the film about going for your dreams against the odds. It always resonates with me, that kind of message. It's good fun to watch, a real feel-good movie. On a very serious level, there are certain moments where it challenges some racial stereotypes, but overall my main takeaway is that it's a really good, fun movie. You cannot help but enjoy Cool Runnings.

4 FEVER PITCH

This film is about an Arsenal fan during the season they won the league at Anfield with virtually the last kick of the season. The film sums up how football fans are: their team means everything, but then there's a moment where something happens that means you can't be as close to your club, even though you still love it. And that is the beauty of this movie. The other little thing about it? My wife is in the film. **DG: Is she?** Yeah, she's an extra in the last scenes outside Highbury, which is great for her because she's an Arsenal fan. **DG: Were you there?** I absolutely was not. **DG: Secret Gooner?** No, but the shots of Highbury remind you what a fantastic old stadium it was. The only problem with the film is that Arsenal fans drink Holsten Pils in it, and I guarantee you that no Arsenal fan would drink Holsten Pils at that time because they'd been a sponsor of Spurs.

5 HAPPY GILMORE

My number five is a film that starred Adam Sandler and it's called Happy Gilmore. **AD: Another one I should have seen, by the way.** It follows on from all the other films like Caddyshack and is basically a story about a hockey player who can hit a golf ball nearly 400 yards but can't do anything else. He doesn't rock up in typical golf kit, he wears a shirt that's untucked. No golf etiquette whatsoever. And he really takes the mickey out of the 'stiff upper lip' golfing world. And that's what I find funny about it, because that kind of thing has put me off playing golf in the past. Sandler's character has a serious, serious anger issue. There are great quotes throughout the film and it's well worth the watch.

4 SLAP SHOT

I think you like this one, actually; I've heard you mention it before. It's Slap Shot. It's set in a hard-working town, Charlestown. Their team, the Chiefs, have had years and years of being absolute rubbish and they want to have a chance of being brilliant. And that's mainly down to Paul Newman, who plays the part of Reggie Dunlop, a bloke who's been around the leagues and his career's coming to an end but he wants to put a team together to give it one last shot. The Hanson brothers are the stars and just want to fight absolutely everyone. **AD: Aren't there three of them?** What, Slap Shots? **No, Hanson brothers.** Yes – Jeff, Steve and Jack. It's a brilliant film to watch as long as you don't mind lots of fighting, violence and blood. This was old-school ice hockey. I mean, the fighting does happen now but not as much. I remember this film so well, growing up watching it.

3 THIS SPORTING LIFE

My number three is a very old film, from 1963. The main character is called Frank Machin, who is described by the leading lady as "a great ape on a football field". It's a rugby league film, but if you don't have a lump in your throat when he walks past the kids at the end then you're too hard-boiled for life. In some sport films the action scenes on the field are a little bit forced but this has the best action shots from any sports movie I've ever seen... and they had to be because Frank Machin is a working-class hero, a loose forward who spills blood for the rugby league cause. He excels at the blood and thunder on the rugby field but can't cope with anything that life throws at him and he's a tragic character because of it. It's a long film, but absolutely terrific.

3 RUSH

I'm going for a film called Rush next. It's about the rivalry between James Hunt, who's played by Chris Hemsworth, and Niki Lauda, played by Daniel Brühl. This is the story of two drivers who each went about their business in a totally different way: James liked drinking and women, partying and the glamorous lifestyle of F1... and then you go to Lauda, who was a bit quieter, very professional. They admired each other and were friends from the Formula Three days but the film is mainly about their rivalry in 1976. It was a battle right to the end and included that terrible crash that Lauda experienced in Germany, where his car caught fire. Can you believe that he raced on six weeks later in Italy, only to lose the title by one point? Fantastic film.

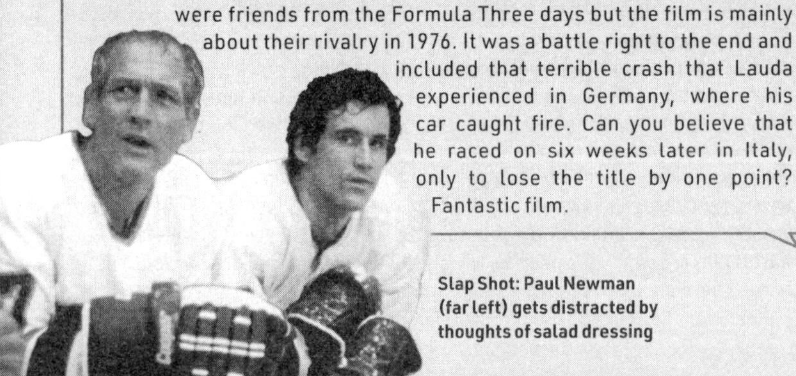

Slap Shot: Paul Newman (far left) gets distracted by thoughts of salad dressing

2 FIELD OF DREAMS

You know what? My number two could easily be my number one. If you don't know it, Kevin Costner plays Ray Kinsella – he's a farmer, hears voices in his cornfield, rips it up to build a seemingly pointless baseball field. There are ghosts involved as well. I won't give you anything else but what I can tell you is that I watched this film when I was about 21 and it completely changed my life – the lesson to be learned is that you have to go for it. And even if the outcome isn't what you expected, or originally hoped for, then the journey, the experience and where it takes you are what life, striving to fulfil your dreams, is all about. So if you buy into the movie, you'll get all that out of it. If you don't buy into the movie, you'll think it's a bit weird. I absolutely loved it. It's one of my favourite films ever. What's your number two?

2 ESCAPE TO VICTORY

It's about a group of POWs in Germany who are challenged to an exhibition football match by their captors, and see it as a possible way to stage an escape attempt. Sylvester Stallone is the goalkeeper and not very good, but luckily there are plenty of great real-life footballers – like Ossie Ardiles, Bobby Moore and Pele – to make up for it. I must have watched it 20 times now... **AD: All the Ipswich lads were in it as well but Alan Brazil had gone on holiday to America and missed out. I wonder if he'd have stayed if he'd known it was to become a piece of genuine sporting film history?**

1 ROCKY

Sylvester Stallone again. It's a great underdog story that's over 40 years old and has stood the test of time. Stallone is an average heavyweight boxer who lives on the breadline, he's kind of a debt collector for a local loan shark, not very bright, but as the Italian Stallion he gets a shot at the title. So he punches meat in the local butcher's to get fit and runs up the steps [at the Philadelphia Museum of Art]. It's an iconic moment. **AD: I've done that. I made it to the top too.** The film will lift anyone, and it'll even make you want to go and train – the soundtrack is perfect for the gym.

1 THE DAMNED UNITED

Michael Sheen as Brian Clough, Stephen Graham as Billy Bremner, and Colm Meaney gets Don Revie off to a tee. David Peace wrote the original book, which is brilliant, and the film has a superb '70s feel to it. It's about Clough's 44 days in charge of Leeds United, so they got a little bit lucky with the stadium for the time [*because Elland Road had changed so little*] but it is just truly superb. **DG: A lot of people complained when it came out, said it was sightly twisted – but that doesn't matter, it's a brilliant story.** Peace said it was a work of fiction based on facts, he makes that very clear and I have no problem with that whatsoever. A thoroughly, thoroughly enjoyable movie... and those are our top five sporting films.

TOP FIVE @ 5 FREE KICKS

We've put in hours and hours of free kick watching. It's not a bad job, to be fair. There are so many that could have been in here, everybody has their favourites, but here are our Top Five free kicks. So, retreat the full ten yards and here we go...

5 MARCUS RASHFORD v Chelsea (2019)

This was 30 yards out – he showed unbelievable technique. Rashford had already scored a couple of top free kicks for Manchester United but this is the best of the lot for me. It was a shoelace strike that gave the goalkeeper no chance whatsoever. He hit it at pace into the top corner to the keeper's right. It was a terrific showcase of skill. **AD: It's Caballero in goal – it's a knuckleball, which means it goes with such power but he can still control the height of it. Amazing!** He has scored a couple of beauties but this one beats them all.

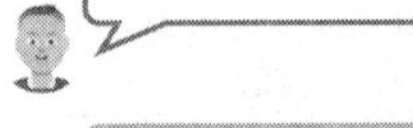

5 SHUNSUKE NAKAMURA v Manchester United (2006)

What decided this for me is who's between the sticks: Edwin van der Sar is in goal for United – you are not talking about some mug. Nakamura is some way out and left-footed; he lifts it over a jumping wall and into the corner of the net. Celtic Park absolutely erupts. And that's how it finished – Celtic 1, United 0. I think if you ask Celtic fans, that free kick will easily be in their top ten moments of all time, because of the magnitude of the opposition and the quality of the goal itself. **DG: What about the one he scored against Kilmarnock to lift the title?** He scored some belters.

4 ROBERTO CARLOS v France (1997)

I know you're not a big fan and I've also included it in my best goals, but I still can't believe this went into the net and it has to be in here. It was in France in 1997, Roberto Carlos was 30 yards out, he charged at it like a rhino and hit it with the outside of his left foot. He smashed it. It looked like it was going 10 yards wide... and I still don't know how it went in. I've seen balls curl and I've seen them go both ways through the air but this one curled back right into the corner. The keeper had no chance whatsoever. I know you will come back and say the keeper was in the wrong position and he's not moved, but no one moved, not even his own teammates – they thought he'd absolutely fluffed it and it was just going to go into the crowd. But it curled back. What a goal! **AD: I understand why people like this goal but it is 'bloke curls ball' and that happens every single Sunday morning in parks up and down the country.** What, with the outside of the boot? How many people have you seen do that? **AD: I know the wall's there for a reason but Fabien Barthez should have covered his post.** Leave it. It was a brilliant goal and I am having it. **AD: Well, when it comes to former Real Madrid players and brilliant free kicks, my number four takes some beating...**

4 DAVID BECKHAM v Greece (2001)

I love this free kick and what it meant to the country, so no apologies for including it in this Top Five. Alvin Martin's pure passion as he was commentating was something else – he could not help himself. I was sitting alongside him and England had been terrible that day. It was supposed to have been a formality but the Greeks didn't even have to play that well. England were hopeless. Beckham took a load of free kicks and nothing really happened. And then came that moment in injury time to make it 2-2... I've seen this many times and studied the keeper on this free kick because he is convinced it's going to go the other way. And Beckham had this gift, a real gift to just disguise what he was doing. And somehow he managed to persuade the keeper with his body shape, maybe the shape of his boot as well, that he was going to go for the other corner. And then he put it to the keeper's right. And the keeper was caught flat-footed and barely moved. It is probably more the moment than the free kick itself. **DG: I could have easily had this in but I knew you'd include it. But of course it was a massive free kick in terms of what it meant for England.**

3 MATT Le TISSIER v Wimbledon (1994)

We all know he was brilliant at set pieces. He only ever missed one penalty – scored 47 out of 48 taken – but this free kick in 1994 for Southampton against Wimbledon is my number three. It was on the edge of the box, just outside the D. Everybody thought Le Tissier was just going to strike it but Jim Magilton rolls it back to him and he flicks it up casually, no rush, calm as anything, and then volleys it into the top corner. It was inventive, rather than just a blast into the net which we see a lot with free kicks. He never ever attempted to do that again, which I find amazing. Just felt like doing it there and then. **AD: Isn't that strange? Maybe he thought every keeper would be on their guard after that... but this was a footballer capable of pure genius, no question.**

Gazza, basically hoofing it

3 PAUL GASCOIGNE v Arsenal (1991)

It was a North London Derby at Wembley, Spurs v Arsenal, an FA Cup semi-final – and for the first 10 minutes he absolutely ran the game. Gascoigne was at his imperious best, and five minutes in Spurs get this free kick and he's 30-odd yards out. **DG: He just blasts it!** Right into the top corner. He hits it so hard and with such accuracy, Seaman gets his hand to it but can't keep it out. It is amazing. **DG: Not for me, this one really.** What? **DG: Gazza's celebration was a thing to enjoy but I've seen loads of free kicks like that.** Spurs went on to win the Cup but that was an iconic free kick and so was the commentary from Barry Davies [*"That is schoolboy's own stuff, I bet even he can't believe it. Is there anything left for this man to surprise us?"*].

2 CRISTIANO RONALDO v Spain (2018)

David de Gea in nets for Spain gets nowhere near this one – and that was at a time when he was generally regarded to be one of the top keepers on the planet. Cristiano Ronaldo at the Russia World Cup, 2018. What I really love about this is that, as he bends it around the wall and right into the corner, it completes the hat-trick. And you have to factor in the importance of the game: for Portugal to lose would have been unthinkable, and Ronaldo really dragged his team up to a level which they hadn't played at until that point. A quality free kick – he was asked to deliver something really special and boy, did he deliver.

2 DAVID BECKHAM v Everton (2003)

I did have to have one from this guy – and it is a beauty. United were losing 1-0. It was on the right-hand edge of the box, which was a ridiculous position. And the technique, the pace – an in-swinging curler into the far corner. What makes it special is that it was in Beckham's last match for United before his move to Real Madrid and his last goal for the club. **AD: It was a real contender for my Top Five.**

1 ERNIE HUNT v Everton (1970)

My number one was a free kick taken the year I was born! It's Ernie Hunt in 1970 for Coventry. It was called 'The Donkey Kick' and they banned it at the end of the season – if you've not seen it, watch it on YouTube. Willie Carr stands over the ball at the edge of the box and, secretly, while they are sorting the wall out, grips the ball between his ankles and flicks it up to Ernie Hunt, who blasts it into the net on the volley. Great technique, great power. It was also the first goal shown in colour on Match of the Day, and it won Goal of the Season. **AD: I did not know that!**

1 DAVID BECKHAM v Malaga (2003)

This free kick has always stuck in my head. It's for Real Madrid at Malaga; Roberto Carlos, Luis Figo and David Beckham are all over the ball. Beckham rolls it to Figo, who puts his foot on the ball. He still has the option of a pass to Carlos or taking the ball on himself but he leaves it dead and Beckham wraps his right foot around it. It looks like he will obviously try to put it to the keeper's left. In the meantime a defender comes firing out of the wall like a ball from a cannon and completely misreads it because there's so much confusion going on... and Beckham bends it to the keeper's right. The deception is absolute genius – the keeper can't keep his balance. It lands in the inside netting.

One of Becks' many great hairstyles (and free kicks)

TOP FIVE @ 5 SPORTING SHOWMEN

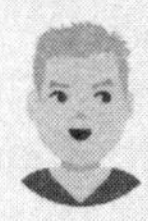

What makes a great sporting showman? That is the question. We've come up with our own set of criteria: Someone you watch not just for their sporting ability; someone who gets you on the edge of your seat; and someone with an element of the maverick about them who creates front and back page news.

5 DENNIS RODMAN

You, Ade, tend to like basketball more than most but this guy was a true entertainer. He had five NBA titles. He dated Madonna. He styled his hair in all different colours. He's one of the few basketball players I know whose dress sense would fit right in now; it probably didn't back then. He turned up in a wedding dress for his book launch, he promoted his autobiography by sitting in a coffin and he is mates with Kim Jong-un, the leader of North Korea. He's an absolute born entertainer, completely on the wild side and creates news wherever he goes. There are better basketball players but this guy is exactly what a maverick showman is! **AD: It's a terrific shout.**

4 DIEGO MARADONA

Now, it pains me to say he's this far down my list, but I've gone with Maradona. Even celebrating the 'hand of God' goal and then calling it that was him being a showman. Even in the warm-ups, you couldn't take your eyes off him – he was putting on a series of tricks his whole life. Sections of his life have literally turned out to be a show: see Maradona In Mexico on Netflix, where he goes to manage a second division Mexican club. It's unbelievable, some of the stuff he gets up to there. And it's all for show. For me, I mean, he could have easily been number one, but you'll have to wait to see who my top three are. But Maradona is my number four.

The queue to pay respects as Maradona's body lay in state was more than 1.6km long

5 NEYMAR

Since the World Cup in 2018, and with some of the things that have happened since, people seem to have gone off Neymar and I do understand why, but he is a great player who showboated so much in one game he got booked for it – PSG were 1-0 up against Montpellier, still in the first half, he did a rainbow flick, the referee didn't like it and so he booked him. Extraordinary. As a showman, even the rolling around on the pitch during the World Cup, that was him being a showman. He just wants to steal the limelight all the time. Sometimes he does it with great football, other times he does it with ridiculous stuff, other times he does it by trying to be a pure entertainer. I don't think he'd be anywhere near the number one football showman, but he does make my Top Five. Are you having that one? **DG: Yeah, definite entertainer. Definite showman. Bit of a party boy.**

4 CHRIS GAYLE

There's Viv Richards, Shane Warne and Ian Botham in this category but I'm going to go with Chris Gayle. You can't leave him out. He has so much confidence. He wants to be known around the world – he's got a huge following on social media because of his personality. He plays cricket like he is playing in the back garden. He's played in all the T20 leagues around the world. He's hit sixes for fun, a world record number of sixes, he's had a double 100 in a World Cup and he's also got a triple 100 in Test cricket. He dances, he sings. He's called The Universe Boss, a name he gave himself. He has to be in it. **AD: Have you ever been to a party on a boat in the West Indies with Chris Gayle?** I've been to parties and Chris Gayle's been there. The things he gets up to I can't say. He's a great bloke. He does a lot of charity work as well, but he just wants to be known all around the world and he will not give in. **AD: He plays with a swagger. And that's an understatement, although he did get into trouble being the showman with female interviewer Mel McLaughlin [and asking her out for a drink on live TV].** Yeah, but that wasn't him being nasty, that was him being the Chris Gayle that he can get away with being because he's the King of the West Indies – but he fell short there and it still affects him now. I don't think he's been accepted back in Australia to play since. He's made mistakes but you only have to see the attention the guy gets in India. He gets more attention than any other cricketer.

3 RONALDINHO

I've gone for Ronaldinho. An immense array of skills but he was the king of them all – the flip-flap, no-look pass, stepover. He did them all at incredible speed as well. His skills made one of the world's best ever left-backs, Ashley Cole, look like a mug – or like me, even – in a World Cup quarter-final. And what about the toe-punt against Chelsea in the Champions League? Skill-wise he had it all. It was mad. Plus he topped it off every time with a dance to celebrate and a massive smile. **DG: He's got all the tricks. If you watch some of his training exploits, he loved putting the ball through his teammates' legs.**

Ronaldinho and his, er, massive smile

3 JOHN McENROE

You could not take your eyes off McEnroe. His tantrums... they had a bit of humour to them. They were mainly at the umpires' expense. "You cannot be serious" is one of the best lines ever. People love it. He was an incredible player and as confrontational as a human being can be, and he still is as a commentator. Tennis is not my sport, it's not something I really watch a lot, but when I watch it and listen to him doing the commentary it's fantastic.

2 SEVE BALLESTEROS

My number two is Seve. This is a guy who did genius things and achieved so much. He was respected throughout golf and that spirit of Seve just lives on: people are still talking about him. He wasn't the greatest player but what a character, what a personality, and when he played golf you wanted to watch every single shot. He would do something magic, be it getting out of the bunker, round the trees, he always managed to do something. That creativity, that imagination. It made him popular around the world and other golfers now use that inspiration when they're playing golf. You can see it an absolute mile off. **AD: He literally did things that other golfers wouldn't even dream of doing.**

Ballesteros used to sleep with a loaded .38 calibre pistol under his bed in case of intruders

1 GEORGE BEST

So let's do the big boys. I've gone for George Best. Tackled his own teammate, had a goal applauded by a referee it was so good, had a can of beer thrown at him while playing for Hibs and drank from it. He didn't mind showing off his skills and didn't mind embarrassing opponents all in the name of entertainment. His life was such a drama it led to countless books and films and we still talk about his life on and off the pitch even now, so my number one is Best. There will be never be another like him in terms of being a showman. **DG: A great number one.**

2 PAUL GASCOIGNE

The dentist's chair celebration, hijacking the England team bus... there are so many stand-out moments, but the one that does it for me is when he booked the referee. Rangers were 2-0 up against Hibs. Gazza had just missed a sitter and as he came back on the pitch he found a yellow card the referee had dropped so he picked it up, ran up to the ref Dougie Smith and waved it at him, ref-style. The ref was so annoyed he actually booked Gazza, which was an unbelievable decision. Rangers went on to win 7-0. That Rangers team, with Brian Laudrup and Gascoigne, you'd have paid some money to see those two run games. So it's Gazza for me in so many ways. An absolute showman of sport.

1 USAIN BOLT

I'm going to go with someone from athletics. Again, it's another sport I've no real interest in but everybody in my household went to the London Olympics and we watched this athlete going at it. Bolt is an absolute genius. He showboated before the race, showboated during the race and again when he broke the 100m World Record. That trademark pose has been done by so many other sportspeople. He's a must-watch. Thirteen individual golds – seven at the Worlds, six at the Olympics – plus five World Records, and the highlight for me was when he shot onto the scene in 2008, the Olympic 100m and 200m, both with World Record times. Incredible.

Bolt helpfully points the way to the next page

TOP FIVE @ 5 OLD-SCHOOL GAMES

We decided in our house during lockdown that at 8 o'clock every night we'd play a boardgame, so last night we got out Frustration – and now I know why it's called that. It annoyed the hell out of me. It was going to be in my Top Five but it was getting me so frustrated I've kicked it out. So, our Top Five old-school games...

5 BATTLESHIPS

I'm going to go for Battleships to start off with. It reminds me of being young. I used to have one with the noises as well, Computer Battleships, so that was the better one. It's about guessing the grid coordinates and you've got to target your opposite number's ships. I think there are five ships of all different sizes. **AD: Do you remember the advert for this game? A family are playing and the mum's battleship gets sunk and she shouts, "You've sunk my battleship!" in the strangest accent ever. It stuck in my head.**

Battleships: whoever took this photo was cheating

4 CLUEDO

For number four I've gone for Cluedo. I've got a Midsomer Murders version of Cluedo. It's a household must-have. **AD: No, not for me. I'm not into those sorts of games.** Any old version of Cluedo will do but the Midsomer Murders version is the best.

5 TEST MATCH CRICKET

This was unbelievably brilliant. This game actually fuelled my interest in cricket – I wasn't really into it before I played this. All the fielders had a little space and a little bowl between the legs where the ball could go. The ball used to get bowled down a chute and you used to be able to control the bat in the batsman's hand. **DG: With a string! And you let it go, then a ball-bearing used to run down and you'd have to get the timing right to hit it.**

4 CONNECT FOUR

Well, I'm going for a very, very simple game and it's making a huge comeback on social media. Connect Four. You get red and yellow discs; when one player gets four in a row vertically, horizontally or diagonally they win the game, and then you just press a button on the side, the discs drop, you separate them and start again. And you can keep going and going and going. But for some reason everybody always wants their first piece to go right in the middle. **AD: I don't mind Connect Four but it is over in a flash. Have you seen the massive ones in shopping centres? I want one of those for my garden.**

3 CASDON SOCCER

I've gone for a football game and it's not Subbuteo. Casdon Soccer. **DG: Never heard of it.** I was in love with this game as a young boy and played nothing else for years. There's a plastic football pitch, goals at either end, and the players are planted in the pitch. They're all in their own little section and it's all curvy. You have a knob in each corner and each knob controls three or four different players; a little bat at the bottom of each player hits the ball when you twist it. I think Bobby Charlton endorsed it. I'd play it for hours and hours on my own. It was so noisy I had to play in the kitchen while my mum was in the living room watching telly.

3 OPERATION

Operation is my number three. What it comes down to is hand-eye coordination. It was always the wishbone that was the hardest one to get. **AD: It was impossible, mate. I just couldn't play it.** Put it this way, if I ever had any thoughts about being a surgeon, they went totally out the window before I was a teenager because I killed everybody I operated on.

2 HUNGRY HIPPOS

Hungry Hippos! **AD: Quality.** It's addictive. Each hippo is attached to a lever and you tap on it to open the hippo's mouth; the quicker you press that lever, the more pieces your hippo's going to eat. If your hippo eats the most you win the game. A brilliant game. It's been around for years and years and has stood the test of time.

2 SCRABBLE

You're going to find this really boring – my number two is Scrabble. **DG: Oh dear.** I'm sorry. In fact, I make no apologies for Scrabble. I love the English language. I love words, I love books and Scrabble is right up my street. This is a proper test of your vocabulary. Actually, Scrabble played a little role in bringing me and my wife together. We used to share a train back home after work every evening and we'd play online Scrabble. We must have played it around 300 or 400 times over the course of a few years and she won once. I'll take you all on when it comes to Scrabble.

1 KERPLUNK

This will always be my favourite. It's the suspense when you're pulling the straws out of the holes and wondering how many marbles are going to drop down. **AD: It's the unpredictability of it for me.**

1 CHESS

I think you're going to find my number one very, very boring. **DG: Chess.** It is chess. **DG: I know you too well.** There's no better game. It's a metaphor for life. If everyone played chess the world would be a calmer place. It's about strategies, taking your time, thinking. It's about sitting there and watching, understanding your opponent, understanding the board. I taught myself to play. I'm no grandmaster but I wasn't bad as a kid and I still love playing it now. I have about 30 books on chess in my library, mate.

TOP FIVE @ 5 INDIVIDUAL SPORTING RIVALRIES

Remember the fight between Bowyer and Dyer? That was just one player not passing to another one and then a fight breaking out, so it doesn't go down as a legendary sporting rivalry. There are plenty to choose from, however – and a few among talkSPORT co-presenters over the years! Here's our Top Five individual sporting rivalries...

5 MARTINA NAVRATILOVA v CHRIS EVERT

First one up, Navratilova and Chris Evert, or Chris Evert Lloyd as she was for a time. They faced each other so often – each time I watched tennis growing up those two tended to be playing each other. Eighty times they played each other. Navratilova won 43 and Chris Evert won 37, so pretty close there. Fourteen Grand Slam finals they played against each other but Martina came out on top – she actually won 10 of them. And that rivalry went on from 1973 to 1988. **AD: Wasn't there a TV show where the two of them spent a weekend together chatting through all of their history? A proper sporting rivalry.** It was total respect for each other but it was almost that dread: oh no, not her again!

Ronaldo, pictured expressing the depth of his love for Messi

5 JOEY BARTON v SCOTT BROWN

This didn't last long in terms of the two of them playing against each other, but it became a massive thing and is still ongoing. When Joey signed for Rangers he did an interview on talkSPORT and said, "People keep talking about Joey Barton and Scott Brown. He ain't in my league. He's nowhere near the level I am as a player. He can't get to me. If I play well, Scott Brown doesn't stand a chance." So of course, Barton's first Old Firm game is his last game for Rangers... and they lose it 5-1. And Brown has not been able to let this go. In his book, Barton says, "To be honest, I don't get the reverence with which Scott Brown is treated, but I owed it to him to front up after the 5-1 defeat. I didn't catch what he said as he ran past me during the game but I purposely sought him out at the final whistle... I told him I have to come and shake your hand. That gesture of professional respect was the least that he deserved." It was not quite reciprocated. A couple of years later, in 2018, in an interview on the Celtic website, Brown claimed that Barton was still in his pocket. **DG: Well, he was in that game! When you get rinsed like that there is no hiding place. You just have to take it on the chin.**

4 JAMIE CARRAGHER v EL HADJI DIOUF

Diouf called Carragher out, saying that he was a right-footed player with two left feet and if he wasn't a Scouser he wouldn't have had the career he did. Carragher called Diouf the worst teammate he ever had, claimed he was the last pick whenever they did five-a-side in training. Remember that at school? There's always somebody who was last pick and it turned out to be me. **DG: I was never last pick.** Of course you weren't. But Diouf was always the last pick, apparently. And Carragher said he would have walked to Man City to get Nicolas Anelka back to replace him. He even said to Gerard Houllier's face that Diouf was absolutely terrible. Diouf has hit back many, many times. It's just two footballers who didn't like each other, didn't rate each other.

3 BJORN BORG v JOHN McENROE

I have gone for another tennis rivalry at number three and that's McEnroe and Borg. They've even made a film out of it. If you consider how good Borg was when he came on the scene as a young player... he was good-looking, cool as anything with the headband, and he wore a great fashion brand called Fila. McEnroe was the angry man. They played 22 times against each other and won 11 each, so you couldn't split them. Remember that five-set thriller at Wimbledon in 1980? Borg won that but McEnroe won the year after. Borg won five consecutive Wimbledons, but in the Majors they played each other four times and McEnroe won three of them. **AD: There was such a contrast of characters. One was so calm and the other just let rip whenever he wanted to.**

4 ALEX FERGUSON v ARSENE WENGER

Alex was already having success after success at United and Wenger came to Arsenal to try to stop him. He said in an interview in 1997 that the problem with fixtures in the league over here was that they favoured United, and this is when the rivalry started. Fergie's reply was that Wenger was a novice and should keep his opinion to Japanese football. This carried on throughout their respective tenures, fighting for the title and cups every year, and would spill over in a press conference, on the touchline, or even through their players falling out. It was an incredible rivalry and there was only one winner, let's be honest about it. **AD: You are bang-on! It was ferocious.**

3 LIONEL MESSI v CRISTIANO RONALDO

Now, in his book about Messi, Guillem Balague claims Ronaldo calls Messi a very rude word in private. That's the allegation. There's a football rivalry between them obviously because they are going for the Ballon d'Or every year and they want to win the Champions League every year... but I think the extent of the personal rivalry, we won't know until they're both finished. When they were recently interviewed together by our own Reshmin Chowdhury, Ronaldo said, "I'm sure at some point in the future we can have dinner together." And Messi replied, "If I get the invitation, then why not?" So it could be that after all these years of rivalry on the pitch, they end up becoming buddies.

2 SEBASTIAN COE v STEVE OVETT

Coe and Ovett just didn't want to face each other unless it was the Olympics or a World or European final. They turned up event after event and made sure they weren't running the same distance: if one ran in the 800m the other ran in the 1500m and that's the way they went about their business. They'd only raced each other once before the Moscow Olympics in 1980. They traded the mile record back and forth but made sure that they didn't meet on the track. Eventually they won three Olympic gold medals, two silvers and a bronze between them and broke a total of 14 middle-distance records. They are mates now. **AD: Amazing rivalry that evokes so many memories of fantastic middle-distance running by British athletes back in the day.**

2 ROY KEANE v ALF-INGE HAALAND

It's a bit naughty but that's what makes it so brilliant. In 1997 when Leeds were playing Manchester United, Alf-Inge Haaland leaned over an injured Roy Keane and sneered at him. Roy had done his cruciate ligament. That's a brief backstory. Four years later Haaland was playing for City and it was a derby match... Keane saw his opportunity. We've all seen that spine-chilling challenge. Roy was suspended and fined. He said later that Haaland was "an absolute bleep to play against" and admitted getting him back had been at the back of his mind. **DG: It was a shocking challenge.** But there is a killer line that Roy delivers: "There are things I regret in my life and he's not one of them."

1 MUHAMMAD ALI v JOE FRAZIER

I could not miss this one out. I've watched all their fights and they absolutely hated each other. They are two greats in any era, both unbelievable boxers with big mouths. They traded it three times. The first bout, called the 'Fight of the Century', was given to Frazier. This was Ali's first defeat as a pro. They had a rematch in '74 that Ali won on a decision and the third one was the 'Thrilla in Manila' in '75. Ali won that one – Frazier retired in his corner with one round to go. This is a proper, proper sporting rivalry.

Frazier and Ali in rehearsals for Strictly

1 JOSE MOURINHO v ARSENE WENGER

Now, the war of words started in the mid 2000s when Wenger suggested Chelsea under Jose were negative. Jose responded by calling Wenger "a voyeur" and then it all kicked off. Jose later apologised but the damage was done. Mourinho claimed he had a 120-page file filled with comments Wenger had made about Chelsea. He also called Wenger a "specialist in failure." Remember that? In 2005 Wenger came out with a belter: "He is out of order, disconnected with reality and disrespectful. When you give success to stupid people it makes them more stupid sometimes."

TOP FIVE @ 5 GOALS

I thought this was a great idea... but the more I've thought about it, the more I've became convinced it's one of the worst ideas I've ever had. The Top Five goals in football, of all time? I became so bogged down in it I almost quit. My list was endless, but I have got it down to five and I'm probably going to upset a few...

5 WAYNE ROONEY v NEWCASTLE [2005]

I've picked Wayne Rooney's volley for Manchester United against Newcastle, towards the end of his first season with the club, as my number five. And if you remember, he's berating the ref as Manchester United are going down the left-hand side and then he storms forward. The Newcastle defender Peter Ramage heads it, not particularly well, but straight into the path of Rooney – and he volleys perfectly and thunders it past Shay Given. There's a number of Rooney goals you could pick from but this one stuck with me.

5 DALIAN ATKINSON v WIMBLEDON [1992]

Atkinson scored some screamers that season, but here he picked the ball up in his own half with some serious challenges flying in from the Wimbledon players. He showed strength, close control, everything you want from a footballer. And then to finish there was a slight pause, the keeper came charging out and he just chipped it over him. There was everything in that goal. **AD: He is sadly missed. Everyone remembers the celebration as well: he's carrying Dean Saunders on his shoulders and Dean has an umbrella because it's chucking down.**

4 PAUL GASCOIGNE v SCOTLAND [1996]

Paul Gascoigne's solo goal against Scotland in Euro 96 – are you having a bit of this? **DG: Brilliant.** Let me paint the picture. Everybody's seen the goal but there is a little bit before that, because England were one up and David Seaman saved a Gary McAllister penalty. Tony Adams brought down Gordon Durie in the box, so we get McAllister's penalty (and there is a story about Uri Geller making the ball move), and it's only 90 seconds later that Gascoigne is through on goal. And when you watch the goal over and over again, it just gets better and better because it's a long ball up from Seaman but Darren Anderton plays this lovely lofted pass to him. Gazza has left Stuart McCall for dead in midfield and races onto the ball, and then there's that lob over Colin Hendry. Honestly mate, leaving Hendry on the floor and then the volley past the keeper... people talk about the celebration but the goal itself needs to be focused on because that is pure magic, isn't it? **DG: It was a massive goal.** Yeah, just a terrific goal and an important one as well, because England were one up, the penalty had just been missed so Scotland might have been pressing... and he just seals the deal. And it's against his club keeper Andy Goram as well!

4 ROBERTO CARLOS v FRANCE [1997]

My number four, also my number four free kick, is Roberto Carlos in 1987 at the Tournoi de France. It was ridiculous – 35 yards out. Everybody was amazed. What is this bloke doing? It's a free kick, he runs straight at the ball at speed and then with the outside of the left boot he smacks it. It looks like he's mis-kicked it and it's going to hit the corner flag but it boomerangs into the goal. **AD: I'm not that impressed with this one. The goalkeeper didn't move. He just had to stick his left arm out to save it.** I have watched it 50 times, man. You are not going to take away the power with which Roberto Carlos hits it. You've lost the plot.

3 DIEGO MARADONA v ENGLAND [1986]

It actually hurt me to put this in. My number three is the good goal Maradona scored against England in '86. It was a huge occasion. The pressure on him as an individual from a whole country was massive. There was political pressure given what had happened between the two countries going to war in '82 but on the pitch, for that goal, he kept his poise. Beautiful balance, speed on the ball, control of the ball, making fools of defenders. I hated it but loved it at the same time... and as time has gone on, the pain of that has gone and you can now just watch it and just admire the sheer genius of Diego Armando Maradona. **DG: I agree with you, but one of the England midfielders should have put a boot through it.** Terry Fenwick was on a yellow. Peter Reid can't get near him because Maradona is just quicker and don't tell me Maradona didn't know that by that stage in the game. This is all clever play.

3 MARCO VAN BASTEN v SOVIET UNION [1988]

Marco van Basten admits he did have little bit of luck with this one – he said he could hit that ten times and probably not even hit the target in nine – but the technique, the skill was unbelievable. It was the European final against the Soviet Union. An Arnold Muhren cross comes in from the left, slightly long, over Van Basten. He comes around it running sideways and gets his right boot around it to hit it on the volley. Even the manager, Rinus Michels, was overcome by it. He put his hands over his head. He just couldn't believe what had happened. **AD: Oh yeah!** It was like he was in shock – he didn't celebrate. And they won the Euros. If you consider that Van Basten had been struggling with injury and form going into that tournament, it was an absolute belter.

2 LIONEL MESSI v GETAFE [2007]

A Messi goal is number two for me. The one's against Getafe, in the semi-final of the Copa del Rey. He was only 19 and this was right out of the Maradona playbook. He picked the ball up just inside his own half and went straight past players at serious, serious speed. It's almost like they weren't there. Then he passed three more, overtaking the same player twice! The control of the football, the skill, the balance... he finally reached the goalkeeper, dummied him one way, went the other and then right-footed it calmly into the net with half the opposition chasing the ball and trying to stop it going in as it rolled over the line. It was an absolute beauty of a goal.

2 JACK WILSHERE v NORWICH CITY [2013]

I've gone for more of a team effort here. Let me tell you about the goal. It breaks my heart a little bit because this is another example of what Jack Wilshere could have been. It starts on the edge of the Arsenal box, Wilshere picks it up around 25 yards out and surges forward. He plays it out to Gibbs, then it goes to Cazorla, Wilshere, Cazorla, Giroud, Wilshere, Giroud, then Wilshere with a brilliant finish. **DG: Great goal.** It was beautiful football, probably the best Premier League goal I've ever seen.

1 ZLATAN IBRAHIMOVIC v NAC BREDA [2004]

This was the start of the whole Ibrahimovic thing and it was while he was at Ajax. He actually scored the greatest goal probably of his career here, and he scored some beauties by the way – especially overhead kicks. But this one put him on the map, it really did. He was moving to Juventus so the fans were booing him that game before he scored this goal, and it was remarkable. Starting 30 yards out he dribbles left and right, past half of the Breda backline, before an unreal finish, almost a dummy finish. He joked to go with his right foot and then he decided to hit it left-footed. It was an unbelievable goal and you've got to watch it. It is an absolute pearler. **AD: I can see why that's your number one.**

1 LARS RICKEN v JUVENTUS [1997]

The 1997 Champions League final. Dortmund are 2-1 up against a Juventus side with Zidane, Deschamps, Vieira and Del Piero when Lars Ricken comes on as a substitute with 70 minutes and 11 seconds gone. Four seconds later his teammate Andy Möller plays the most perfect defence-splitting pass into the Juve half. Ricken races onto it and, with his very first touch of the ball, eight seconds after coming onto the pitch, lobs Angelo Peruzzi – the ball sails over his head and into the back of the net to make it 3-1. That secured the first ever Champions League trophy for Borussia Dortmund. He was a German international from Dortmund, only played for Dortmund in his career and he scored a wondergoal in their only Champions League success to date. I just loved that goal. It's a perfect finish, but his first touch eight seconds after coming on? You couldn't make it up!

Ricken: didn't really contribute much in his first seven seconds

TOP FIVE @ 5 PIECES OF SPORTING MEMORABILIA

When I was told we'd be doing Top Five pieces of sporting memorabilia, it posed a problem as I'm not really one for collecting stuff or getting things signed – so I had to scratch around to find my five. I suspect Goughie's are a bit more professional...

5 NELSON MANDELA'S AUTOBIOGRAPHY

I'll start off with a book but it's a special book. It's by a very famous man, and one of the nicest people you could ever meet. I was shaking when I met him. It's Nelson Mandela's autobiography: a signed and dated first edition that makes it extra-special, and that's why it's so valuable. He inspired a generation of people in South Africa. **AD: How is that sporting memorabilia?** Of course it is! I was playing cricket for England in Soweto in South Africa and he came to the game and signed it. Sport is the only reason I've got the book! There is a sporting connection.

4 A SIGN FROM HIGHBURY

Thinking about it, this might be worth a couple of bob – although I think it technically belongs to my wife. It's an original sign from Highbury, Arsenal's old ground. It's hand-painted, it's wooden and it's a beautiful work of art... and it features in the film Fever Pitch, believe it or not. We only realised a couple of weeks ago when we watched the film and saw it in the background. **DG: When teams move grounds they often auction off little bits and pieces for old times' sake.** For those who used to frequent Highbury, it's block Z numbers 161–188. It is a thing of beauty from my point of view. A shame it's Arsenal!

5 BOJAN'S STOKE CITY SHIRT

This is slightly more quirky than Darren's and probably worth a little bit less too... there's probably only one item in my Top Five that's worth anything and technically it doesn't belong to me. My number five is a Stoke City shirt and I'm not even joking; it's a fairly modern one from maybe about five years ago. My mate Steve sorted this out for me and there's a little story behind it... This Stoke City shirt is signed to me by Bojan. I'm not a Stoke fan and he probably won't go down as one of their legends of all time anyway, mainly because injury robbed him of that opportunity, but I have a signed Stoke City shirt dedicated to me by Bojan Krkić. He picked up that there was this guy on the radio who was a massive Bojan fan, and I am – I've always been a big fan of his and Steve put in a request for this, so Bojan signed the shirt, signed it to me, and it's hanging right next to me: a traditional red and white striped Stoke City shirt with the words: "Dear Adrian, best wishes Bojan". I love it – but who would have thought a signed Stoke shirt would be in my Top Five of sporting memorabilia? **DG: Took me by surprise.**

4 FRANK LAMPARD'S ENGLAND SHIRT

A Frank Lampard England shirt with the number 8 on the back is next. My son has got it because he's a Chelsea fan. Frank sent it to me when he heard I was retiring – it's the actual shirt he wore in the England v Croatia game, 21 November 2007. It is match-worn and personalised to me. It says: "Goughie, legend of a player. Top man. The best of health for the future. Frank Lampard." **AD: Brilliant. That's a proper dedication.**

"Look up there, a story about me!"

3 CHRIS GAYLE'S WEST INDIES SHIRT

Number three for me is a signed Chris Gayle shirt that he wore in his last Test match against India. The legend that is Chris Gayle... and he gave me the shirt and it's signed by him, Brian Lara and Shivnarine Chanderpaul. I think there's about 30,000 Test runs just on those three. And then, also on the shirt, there are three Indian legends in Virat Kohli, Sachin Tendulkar and MS Dhoni. Now, there's probably another 30,000 runs there. So that is one shirt. And it's the most runs you'll ever get on one shirt, let me assure you. Six signatures. It's magnificent. It's framed. It's six absolute legends of the game. **AD: That sounds superb.**

Gayle hit a 30-ball hundred for IPL team Royal Bangalore Challengers in 2013

3 PETERBOROUGH UNITED V SHREWSBURY TOWN MATCH PROGRAMME

This is a very personal one – I've got this framed and hanging in the house. It's a programme from the first game I ever went to, and that was 24 April 1976. It's in fantastic nick. It was from Peterborough against Shrewsbury and I'm very proud of it, to be honest, because that's the game that gave me the love for my club. That was the day it all started. I went to the game and they won, but it was the atmosphere there – I just got intoxicated by it. It doesn't matter how big the club is that you support, the passion is the same. So there may be more Man United fans than Mansfield fans but a Mansfield fan's passion for his club is exactly the same as a United fan's. And that was the day it happened for me. That was the day I was inflicted with supporting Peterborough United. It's a great memory – I've got some very, very vivid memories of that day. And you know, there were no fences up at the time. Policemen used to wander around the perimeter. My legs were hanging over the side and I felt really close to the goal. We were right behind it and I could hear the ball rippling into the net. It finished 3-2 to The Posh... and every time I look at that programme it reminds me of that day and some of those memories from so long ago! I bought it off eBay. We finished mid-table and the game really was nothing special, but picking up that programme and framing it meant the world to me.

2 PAUL COOKE'S CHALLENGE CUP SHIRT

I've got a match-worn shirt from the scorer of the winning try, Paul Cooke, for Hull FC in the Challenge Cup final of 2005. It was their first cup win since 1982. We'd been waiting for a long, long time. I ended up writing his book. I am going to give the shirt back to his family because he's got three daughters and it really should stay in the family. So, in due course, that will go back when they're of an age to look after it. But in the meantime, I am very comfortable looking after that particular shirt as it is a little bit special.

2 INTERNATIONAL CRICKET CAPS

My number two is a presentation of national cricket caps. I've got the West Indies one signed by Viv Richards and the Pakistan cap signed by Wasim Akram. Viv's signature is on the peak of the West Indies cap; the Pakistan one is signed inside. I've got Dave Houghton's Zimbabwe cap, Nathan Astle's New Zealand one and Daryll Cullinan's from South Africa, so that's five of them and this presentation has got mine in there as well. So there's six caps framed.

1 ENGLAND CAP AND SWEATER

It's cricket again for my number one: an England cap and sweater, mine, and an Australian cap, the baggy green, and sweater. They're framed together because that for me is the biggest Test of all. My best series of all. Those two caps and sweaters representing each country, framed, is one thing that'll never leave my house. **AD: Terrific.**

1 JAMIE CARRAGHER'S ENGLAND SHIRT

My number one is a match-worn England shirt from the 2006 World Cup – and this is from a moment in my career. I was at that World Cup, I was at this game – England beat Ecuador 1-0. And this was Jamie Carragher's match shirt. He signed it to me as well. There's a little bit of a story to it, though. A year after that World Cup, Carragher quit international football and I called him a bottler on air so he phoned into the show. One of his challenges to me was to go to Liverpool and say it to his face. So I did. And we arranged it all and we were in the bar he owned at the time in the middle of Liverpool, and he walked in through the door and we were right there at the entrance... and he literally threw this carrier bag at me, full force, and it had this shirt in and I was completely blown away. It was a little joke. I brought him a framed picture of him lying on the ground in an England shirt after he had been left for dead by Ronaldinho. It's just a great picture! There's a little bit of sarcasm in there but a lot of people have been left like that by Ronaldinho. But I think he appreciated the fact that I'd gone up there. The shirt was genuinely worn in a World Cup game and they kept a clean sheet. He came on as a sub for Joe Cole after 77 minutes. It is framed and hanging up in the house. So that's got to be the number one for me, really. It's about that moment in my career, which is still an iconic moment in talkSPORT history.

TOP FIVE @ 5 CARTOONS

Oh, this is a good one. Cartoons. Both my parents went out to work so I stayed at my grandma's during the day, and if I couldn't play outside with a football I was in front of the telly watching cartoons. And they're still a big part of my life now! Here are our Top Five cartoons...

5 MR BENN

It's got to be Mr Benn. It was 1971 when it started and it's just an ordinary bloke who wears a bowler hat. He goes to work every day and lives at 52 Festive Road, an ordinary suburban street. But whenever he tries on an outfit in a mysterious costume shop, he steps out into a different time and place wearing the costume to match – whether it be as an astronaut, a pirate or a Native American – and then he returns to normal life. And there's always a clue as to where he's going to be going on his way to the shop. I Love Mr Benn. **AD: That's part of our childhood, isn't it?**

5 FOGHORN LEGHORN

My number five is Foghorn Leghorn. And he is brilliant – this always made me laugh out loud. A big chicken, a leghorn rooster, hence Leghorn. And he's got a mouth like a foghorn, hence Foghorn Leghorn. So, a big chicken with a southern American accent. He had a big rivalry with the barnyard dog. They basically play pranks on each other, blowing each other up with dynamite and whacking seven bells out of each other. And it's that voice that just makes you laugh. The character is so brilliant. At least 12 different actors have voiced Foghorn Leghorn since he first appeared in 1946. **DG: I've got all the DVDs.**

4 HONG KONG PHOOEY

He's Penry, the mild-mannered janitor who jumps into the bottom drawer of a filing cabinet and comes out of the top drawer – which is usually stuck, and Spot the cat helps him get out – and he's dressed as a kung-fu character. He then goes bumbling around solving crimes by accident. I have these DVDs as well. **DG: Where do you put all these DVDs?** I have lots of shelves.

4 THE FLINTSTONES

Fred Flintstone is a classic and Andrew Flintoff got his nickname from the character. There's Fred, Wilma, and their friends Barney and Betty Rubble. He is basically just a normal bloke from the Stone Age with a family who are best friends with their neighbours. It started in 1960 and ran for years in America. There have been TV spinoffs and films. A great theme tune too.

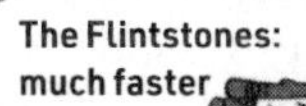

The Flintstones: much faster downhill

3 THE PINK PANTHER SHOW

The Pink Panther was, would you believe, a panther that was coloured pink, and just got into all sorts of japes. The opening was a real kid driving a real car – which was the Panthermobile – and then a cartoon Pink Panther and Inspector Clouseau emerged from it. It was on Saturday evenings after all the football results had come in. Saturday evenings were all about The Pink Panther for me.

2 TOP CAT

There are no confidence issues with my number two. Top Cat is a cat with a confidence like you wouldn't believe. He lives in the dustbin in an alley with loads of his friends and Officer Dibble, the local policeman, is on their case. I liked it so much the first cat I got I called Top Cat, a ginger. No longer with us, sadly.

1 POPEYE

Who else? Such a brilliant cast. Do you remember J Wellington Wimpy, who always had a burger in his hand? That was the nickname I gave to Moose [*talkSPORT's Ian Abrahams*]. Popeye is supposed to be a bit of a weakling, although he has got bulging arms with tattoos. He smokes a pipe and has a squint. But as soon as he eats spinach he gets superhuman strength. He started as a character in a comic book in 1929. **AD: Not one of my favourites.**

3 SCOOBY DOO

It is Scooby Doo for me at number three. It first came onto our screens in 1969 and is still going strong. The stars of the show are Scooby and his mate Shaggy, who isn't the brightest but everyone loves him. There's always a Shaggy character and in cricket it was Shaun Udal. There's also Fred, Thelma and Daphne. And I liked Scrappy Doo, the cheeky little dog. **AD: I stopped watching when Scrappy joined. I thought he was totally unnecessary.** Obviously Scooby and Shaggy are the stars. **AD: Did you fancy Daphne?** For a cartoon character I think she is pretty fit. **AD: Most boys had a crush on Daphne.**

1 FAMILY GUY

I absolutely love this. There's Peter Griffin, head of the family, his wife Lois and their kids. But the real star of the show is Brian the dog. He's absolutely magnificent. If you want an introduction to Family Guy, watch episode 17 from series 8. You've never seen anything like it in your life. Stewie the toddler and Brian get locked in a bank vault all weekend. They drink, they try piercing Stewie's ear, they talk about depression, and I won't tell you what Brian eats but it will make you retch. It's dark, clever and very funny. It took cartoons to a different place. It's also very un-PC.

2 DAFFY DUCK

There's something about ducks... I do like them, and I got plenty of them when I was playing cricket. I love Donald, but Daffy Duck from Looney Tunes is my favourite and my number two. He's a very insecure duck. **AD: Are you psychoanalysing a duck?** He is complicated. He talks with a lisp and he gets bullied by a smarter character in Bugs Bunny.

TOP FIVE @ 5 CHARACTERS FROM TV SITCOMS

We were going to do our Top Five comedy TV shows and then we thought, let's nuance it a little bit. **DG: Just to warn you, I am stuck in the era when I was growing up and obsessed with sitcoms.** Here we go...

5 CAPTAIN EDMUND BLACKADDER [BLACKADDER GOES FORTH]

Blackadder was iconic. It went through different eras of history. Blackadder Goes Forth, the final series, was the most excellent and Rowan Atkinson as Captain Edmund Blackadder was magnificent. The last series was set during the First World War and focused on the futility of it all. It was incredibly funny. Baldrick and Percy played their parts as well. It left you in shock and awe at the end. The whole series ended with a very serious slow-mo of all of them leaving the trenches and going over the top, hurtling towards certain death. All the way through the series we'd been laughing our heads off at some of their escapades, and the one-liners from Blackadder, and it ended the best way it could and the most appropriate way it could. It was thought-provoking but incredibly funny, and Blackadder as a character was just hilarious.

5 GEORGE ROPER [GEORGE AND MILDRED]

I have gone for a character in a show called George And Mildred. George is my number five. He is the archetypal miserable, put-upon husband. He's played by an actor called Brian Murphy and he doesn't have to say anything, his looks say it all. Hilarious. **AD: Is that the one where he had a motorbike and a sidecar?** Yes. In the opening titles he pulled onto the estate and she came out and got into it – all the neighbours were watching. The bike pulled off without the sidecar and she was just sat there in the sidecar going nowhere. I got a serious laugh out of that.

4 FRANK SPENCER [SOME MOTHERS DO 'AVE 'EM]

Number four is Frank Spencer in Some Mothers Do 'Ave 'Em. You know how "Ooh, Betty!" was his catchphrase? He only actually said that in one episode. **AD: That can't be right.** Series 2, episode 2. It was that good it actually returned in 2016 just for a one-off. Frank's character, played by Michael Crawford, is a very accident-prone human being. Everything he does turns into a disaster. He cannot hold down any job. And it's all done in such a funny, simple way. The comedy is right up my street. **AD: Fantastic.**

Frank Spencer: with the FA rulebook as new chief of VAR

4 RICK [THE YOUNG ONES]

I was a teenager when The Young Ones was on telly in the '80s and this was the show that took me to another level. Rik Mayall played Rick (with a silent 'P') who thought he was cool, but he wasn't. He thought he was intelligent, but he really wasn't. I could easily have picked Vyvyan, played by Adrian Edmondson, who I thought was magnificent; but it was a brilliant series, perfect for its time as well. Darren, please tell me you've watched The Young Ones? **DG: Of course I have. My favourite was Neil.** "Neil, Neil, orange peel!"

3 ALF GARNETT [TILL DEATH US DO PART]

My number three is a proper working-class man: Alf Garnett, played by Warren Mitchell in Till Death Us Do Part. He's always complaining that he has worked all his life but is forever on the poverty line. He's a Conservative but won't support Thatcher because she is a woman and "women should be in the bloody kitchen". You would not get away with his humour in this day and age. **AD: He is definitely old-school and his comedy wouldn't be acceptable now.** When I rewatch it now some of it is cringeworthy, but everyone loved it back then. **AD: Big West Ham fan.**

3 ALAN PARTRIDGE [THE DAY TODAY]

Alan Partridge started out on the radio but got into TV when he was the sports presenter on a programme called The Day Today, which was a spoof news programme in the '90s. It was comedy news. The foresight they had back then – wow! But he was hilarious, saying stuff like "a foot like a traction engine" and then singing a medley of all the ABBA songs where he just can't reach the notes. It's worse than you and me singing. Just horrendous but hilarious at the same time. Steve Coogan is an absolute comedy genius.

2 DEL BOY [ONLY FOOLS AND HORSES]

Del Boy is my number two, played superbly by David Jason. It's such a great character, pretending to be a wealthy businessman when really he ain't got a pot. **AD: My favourite scene is the chandelier one when they're waiting for Grandad to smack the bolt holding it to the ceiling but they're waiting under the wrong one. Genuine slapstick comedy.**

The all-time British record TV audience for a sitcom is 24.35 million for the Christmas episode of Only Fools And Horses on December 29th 1996, when the Trotters chance upon an 18th century watch and finally become millionaires

2 MARK CORRIGAN [PEEP SHOW]

I recently watched all of Peep Show from start to finish – all nine series! It started in 2003 and went on to 2015. I found it innovative and funny. Mark Corrigan is one of the main characters and there is something funny and sad about Mark. David Mitchell is brilliant in this role. Mark is in his thirties, lives in a flat in Croydon, has a rubbish job as a loan manager at JLB Credit that is going nowhere and a series of disastrous relationships. **DG: I've not seen it.** The scripts are genuinely funny.

1 WILL McKENZIE [THE INBETWEENERS]

Ah, Will McKenzie from The Inbetweeners. I've watched all three series about five or six times and absolutely love it. It's still as funny and fresh as it ever was. All the characters are great but Simon Bird as McKenzie the swot just about sneaks it for me.

1 VICTOR MELDREW [ONE FOOT IN THE GRAVE]

My number one is Victor Meldrew from One Foot In The Grave. Victor is played by Richard Wilson. It ran for 11 years. It's an absolutely brilliant, brilliant programme. Victor is a very grumpy retired security guard and his poor wife, Margaret, has to put up with him every single day. Great catchphrase as well: "I don't believe it!" **AD: The best scene is when he gets home and goes to his bathroom and finds a tree planted in his toilet! Fantastic.**

Alan Partridge, preparing to smell someone's cheese

TOP FIVE @ 5 DAVID BECKHAM MOMENTS

Love it! A global icon – there's plenty of moments on the pitch and plenty off it, good ones and bad ones... and I think our selection reflects the mix that's on offer. My wife thinks I'm better-looking than Beckham, she genuinely thinks that. **DG: Really? I don't believe you!** So, Top Five Beckham moments...

5 THAT SARONG

Here was David Beckham trying to be on trend and failing. A fashion victim. It was 1998 and he was going out with Victoria. He still says to this day he would wear it now, but we have never seen him in a sarong since. If he thought he looked so great, why have we not seen him in one since? **AD: A great question. Would you consider wearing one, Darren?** I have thought about it but I couldn't carry it off. Absolutely not!

Where did it all go sarong?

4 JOINING REAL MADRID

My number four is when he signed for Real Madrid. Most people leave United and they are on a downward spiral, but not Beckham. He'd had a great career at United, but going on to play for Real Madrid, the biggest club in the world, was a real moment. He played four seasons with them and won the Champions League. And just look at some of the players he played with there – Zidane, Raul, Ronaldo, Figo and Roberto Carlos. He became the world's most famous footballer during his time there. When he was unveiled at Real Madrid, 500 journalists turned up. **AD: Incredible.**

5 THE BOOT INCIDENT

It was an FA Cup fifth-round tie against Arsenal at Old Trafford in 2003. United lost 2-0 and for the second goal Beckham was jogging back and wasn't tracking Sylvain Wiltord, and Fergie thought, "I'm not having that." He laid into him in the dressing room. Sir Alex Ferguson says in his book that Beckham is one of those players who does not let his mistakes fester. He just cracks on and doesn't even acknowledge them. **DG: That's the best way to do it.** So, Fergie had a right go at him in the dressing room. David wasn't that impressed and started to talk back. There was a row of boots between the pair of them and Ferguson just launched one of the boots with his foot, and it hit Beckham's head, right above the eye. He didn't apologise. Beckham went to have a go at him and some other players held him back. Fergie said, "Sit down, you've let your team down." That was the death knell for David Beckham at United. It was a key incident in his career, without a doubt.

4 THE GOAL FROM THE HALFWAY LINE

It was the first game of the '96-'97 season when he scored from the halfway line in open play for Manchester United against Wimbledon. He wasn't even playing for England then. They were 2-0 up and the game was won and this was in injury time, but he still had the imagination to do it. Gary Neville revealed afterwards that he used to practise that all the time in training – and it takes me back to that age-old thing of these Man United players from that era, that class of '92. They spent so much time on the training ground, they worked so hard to improve every single aspect of their game. That's how they all managed to reach the level that they reached. And David Beckham, despite everybody thinking he was a celebrity, was no exception. That goal wasn't a fluke. He saw the keeper off his line and thought he'd have a go. An iconic goal. And the Wimbledon goalkeeper, Neil Sullivan, kept watching that goal on VHS to see if he could have done anything differently. In the end, he'd had enough of it. He got bored and taped over it with EastEnders.

If Beckham had missed *that* shot, Alex Ferguson was going to sub him "for showboating"

3 THE MOHICAN

Beckham's mohican (and other haircuts) will always be a thing. This was just one of many different haircuts that he had... and Sir Alex Ferguson made him shave it off. He was in the dressing room, an hour to go before kick-off, and Fergie saw it and told him to get rid of it. He said no at first, then Fergie's face changed very quickly, so he went and shaved it off in the toilet. So the mohican didn't last very long. It was an extraordinary haircut for Beckham but nothing new. He had a sponsorship deal with Brylcreem, didn't he? **DG: That was supposed to be my contract! I was all set to sign it – he got a million pounds, my offer was nowhere near that, let me assure you. But it was Posh Spice and what do you think was going to happen? Originally they wanted a cricketer and I was man of the moment at that time, but then Beckham came along and scored that goal and was going out with Victoria and that sealed the deal!** When he shaved it off he nearly lost the gig! I was doing news at the time and it was a massive news story. I went to the press conference where they announced he was the new face of Brylcreem.

3 LONDON 2012

He was part of the delegation that travelled to Singapore in a bid to bring the Olympic Games to London, and did a speech that came from the heart. He didn't need a script. He just talked about the area he knew and what it would mean to the people there. He deserves a knighthood. He brought the Olympic torch to the stadium.

2 REDEMPTION AGAINST ARGENTINA

This is the penalty against Argentina in the 2002 World Cup, after Mauricio Pochettino blatantly fouled Michael Owen – a lot of people forget about that and he still claims he never touched him – but it was pure redemption because four years earlier Beckham had been sent off against Argentina in the 1998 World Cup for brushing his leg against Diego Simeone while he was on the floor. He had to keep his cool, and did. It went straight down the middle and the relief was so evident in his face. I remember feeling so happy that England had scored but more happy that David Beckham had got that little bit of redemption that a lot of us felt he deserved after the farcical red card four years earlier.

2 WINNING THE TREBLE

David Beckham being part of the Manchester United treble-winning team of '98-'99 has to be right up there. They were the first English club to do that and he was such a huge part of the team that season. He scored nine goals and got one in the final match against Spurs. He was brilliant in the Champions League final too – he had to play more of a central role because of the suspensions to Keane and Scholes. **AD: Great shout.** People forget how good a player he was for United.

When Beckham signed for Real Madrid, Raul was in possession of his favoured number 7 shirt so he chose 23 as a tribute to former basketball star and sporting icon Michael Jordan

1 BEING A SERIAL WINNER

On the same theme, he won four league titles in four different countries and that has to be my number one. It's not exactly a moment, more a culmination of achievements, but people don't realise this about David Beckham: he's a superstar around the world. In Milan, Madrid, Paris, England, America, they love him everywhere. He won six Premier League titles with Manchester United in England, La Liga under Capello in Spain, two league titles in America, that made it titles in three different countries. He didn't win one in Milan, but on deadline day in 2013 he signed for PSG, donated all his earnings from his final six months to charity because he just wanted to play for the love of the game, and won the title there. The first Englishman to win four in four different countries.

1 THE FREE KICK

This needs no introduction. "Can this be the moment that Beckham delivers?" as somebody asked at the time. That free kick at Old Trafford against Greece is my number one. When you do something that makes Alvin Martin scream – one of the calmest and most respectable men I've ever met in my life – when you make him scream you know you've done something special. And that free kick from Beckham to send England to the World Cup, right at the end of the game, was so, so special, wasn't it? **DG: That moment will be on everybody's list so I can't argue one bit. That was the moment that defined his career.**

TOP FIVE @ 5 AFRICAN PLAYERS

This Top Five is quite specific. It's not who you think are the best African players but who you enjoyed watching the most, your favourite African players. **DG: Some would be in the best of all time, some you might not have heard of.** This is open to interpretation and there are no right or wrong answers.

Yaya, from the Ivory Coast, which isn't really made of ivory

5 YAYA TOURE

It's everything about Yaya: the way he is, the way he carries the ball at his feet, that turn of pace. He's got skill and he's scored some great goals. To play at Barcelona and have some great times there and be part of that successful team, and then go to Manchester City and be part of that success, was impressive enough – but he was also African Player of the Year four times. What an amazing career, and he doesn't get the credit he deserves. He gets stick from a lot of people but I loved watching him play. **AD: It's a great shout because he was leading City on the pitch. The team was virtually built around him. Others got the headlines but he contributed in so many ways, both in defence and attack. He drove the team but seems to have been overlooked.** For a midfielder to score 20 goals in 35 games is astonishing.

5 MUSTAPHA HADJI

This player has been forgotten about because it was an earlier era of the top flight, but in that Coventry side of '99 to '01 he was immense. He was the same at Villa. Just the way he played football was a joy to watch. The way he caressed the ball, the way he passed the ball, the way he made things happen, the way he made things start and finish. I just thought he was absolutely amazing as a footballer and he's one who stuck in my mind. You know sometimes there are players – they won't necessarily win titles or cups or whatever it might be, they won't necessarily do all that – but this is just a player who stuck in my mind as a footballer who was a joy to watch.

4 RIYAD MAHREZ

Leicester paid £400,000 for Mahrez from a French Second Division side. He was plucked out of nowhere so their scouting system must be phenomenal. He goes to Leicester and wins the title there, then goes to Manchester City and wins the title with them and, what do you know, he then goes and wins the 2019 Africa Cup of Nations with Algeria as well! He's understated in a way. He gets more headlines for missing a penalty at Anfield than he does for the positive things... but when he really performs, he's an absolute genius. **DG: When he first went to City I thought it was a bad signing, but he has stepped up and improved even more.**

4 THOMAS N'KONO

You lot never give goalkeepers any credit. My number four is never mentioned in anything whatsoever when it comes to picking legendary African players but he inspired a generation. The guy is called Thomas N'Kono and he was the greatest African goalkeeper of all time. He played for Cameroon in three World Cups: '82, '90 and '94. He played for Espanyol for over 10 years, 300 games. He inspired no less a player than Gianluigi Buffon to be a goalkeeper. He is an absolute superstar and he doesn't get any credit whatsoever except from the Africans themselves. He was the African Footballer of the Year twice – as a goalkeeper, remember – in 1979 and 1982. Just think about that for a moment. He had to be on this list. **AD: That's a fair shout.** Just look at some of his saves for Cameroon. He was unbelievably brave. He was a very aggressive keeper. He'd want to charge out and want to punch the ball. You wouldn't want to be a centre-forward or a midfielder coming on to a cross in his penalty area, let me assure you.

3 LUCAS RADEBE

My number three is a defender... but he's more than a defender. I'm not going to say much – the quote from Nelson Mandela is that Lucas Radebe is his hero. What do you do after that? **DG: He is huge in South Africa. I know he's huge in Leeds as well, but in South Africa he's an absolute legend.**

2 ROGER MILLA

For a time he was the most famous African player in the world. Roger Milla played in three World Cups for Cameroon and became the oldest player to score at a World Cup in 1994. I think we all remember him dancing at the corner flag at Italia 90. An iconic World Cup image. **DG: How old was he?** He was 38 in '90 and so 42 at the World Cup in America. **DG: What!?** African Player of the Year twice... not just a footballer with clout but a pure entertainer as well. **DG: I still cannot believe he was playing at the highest level at 42. It goes to show the work he must have put in every single day.**

3 SADIO MANE

Wherever this guy's gone he has stepped up a level – he keeps getting better and better. For some reason we always compare him and Mo Salah. Salah is a tremendous footballer but I think Liverpool fans are starting to go down the route of thinking that Mane is the most valuable player for them. His commitment and the fact that he's an all-round good bloke helps. He's got everything that a footballer would want. His commitment to Liverpool has been outstanding. I thought he was great at Southampton but he's even better for Liverpool. He has had Champions League and Premier League success, and what he did to get Senegal to the final of the Africa Cup of Nations in 2019... **AD: I remember seeing him at Southampton when they beat Sunderland 8-0. I was lucky enough to be at St Mary's that day. He came on and he was superb.**

2 SAMUEL ETO'O

I'm sure a lot of people out there would have put this man as their number one and he was almost mine, but he comes in here just off the top spot. Samuel Eto'o is a four-time African Player of the Year and even has an Olympic gold medal from the 2000 games. He won the African Cup of Nations with Cameroon – twice, I think it was [*in 2000 and '02*]. He scored over 100 goals for Barcelona. He was part of a treble. Two Champions Leagues with Barcelona, scored in both finals. He won the Champions League with Inter as well. Do you need anything else? He came third in the Ballon d'Or in 2005, a fantastic player... I used to enjoy watching him putting the ball in the back of the net game after game after game. **AD: I can't wait to see who's at the very top of your list...**

1 GEORGE WEAH

Let me tell you why this guy is top of the tree. He tested himself around the world and had everything. He was 100% committed as a footballer – dribbling with the ball at his feet, he was fantastic to watch. He was a Ballon d'Or winner, the first African to win it back in 1995. He's now the president of Liberia, by the way. He played at Monaco, PSG, AC Milan, Chelsea, a little bit at Man City, Marseille. He scored goals all over Europe. There are some fantastic players missing off this list but, make no mistake, he had to be my number one.

1 SIPHIWE TSHABALALA

I have gone a bit leftfield with my favourite African player of all time. Siphiwe Tshabalala. I loved this guy. I loved that goal in the 2010 World Cup in South Africa. You'll remember this, we were there. **DG: I remember the goal, of course I do.** It was an historic occasion: the first World Cup finals on the continent of Africa, the first game of that World Cup and South Africa were playing against Mexico. When South Africa took the lead it was with a brilliant goal from Tshabalala – it hit the top corner, he absolutely lashed it with his left foot – and it felt like the noise from the stadium was not just from South Africa but the whole of the continent. **DG: He's from Soweto as well. To be born and bred in Soweto and play for your country is the dream... but to score, to be the guy who scored that first goal was massive.** The game finished 1-1 in the end and they didn't get out of the group, which was a shame, but if you go online and check him out playing for Kaizer Chiefs five years later he scores another worldie in the same stadium. This might not be one everyone agrees with but I don't really care.

Sadio Mane, wondering where Mo Salah is on this list

TOP FIVE @ 5 WAR FILMS

I've watched hundreds of war films. My dad is obsessed with them. He just watches them time and again, and growing up in a household where they were always on has kind of rubbed off on me. So this is the Top Five war films...

5 MIDWAY

You might not have heard of Midway. **AD: Isn't that an old film?** I'm talking about the original one from 1976 [*also known as Battle Of Midway*], although there was a remake in 2019. I love the graphics, it's like being in a game. I watched it on a plane going out to South Africa. Normally I would fall asleep but there was not a chance while this film was on. It educates, informs and entertains. It's about the historic battle that changed the course of World War Two and it's got some real battle scenes. It's all about the American and Japanese hostilities, and it revolves around the Pearl Harbor attack in December 1941... and then the Americans' revenge. It all came to a head at the Battle of Midway in June the following year. A fantastic film.

The cast of Midway includes four Oscar winners: Charlton Heston, Henry Fonda, James Coburn and Cliff Robertson. Heston turned down the role of Ambassador Robert Thorn in The Omen to appear in the film.

4 ATONEMENT

I do get emotional during films and I cried probably about three or four times during this. It qualifies as a war film as it's set around World War Two, and stars James McAvoy and Keira Knightley, who is utterly fantastic in it from start to finish. It's a heartbreaking tale of love and passion and misunderstanding and deceit. I'm not giving anything away but it should end with Cecilia and Robbie, the two main characters, living happily ever after... but it doesn't. And therein lies the tale. It won an Oscar and was nominated for six others. It's a truly emotional film. I absolutely loved it but it left me in floods.

5 THE HURT LOCKER

This film won six awards at the Oscars, including Best Picture. The Hurt Locker is an important film on every single level. Jeremy Renner is the main actor and his performance is stunning. He plays a bomb-disposal sergeant on duty for the US Army in Iraq. His work takes him to the brink – it takes him to the edge of danger, to the edge of death itself, so much so that he can't cope with civilian life. He has to leave his wife and kids behind to go on another 365-day tour of duty. It's a stunning exploration of the way war can damage you beyond recognition. A chilling film in many ways, but it's just brilliantly, brilliantly done. I thought it was spectacular. **DG: Good pick!**

4 THE GREAT ESCAPE

It was released in 1963 and Steve McQueen is in it. There were loads of famous actors in it but everybody remembers the scene where they're trying to escape and McQueen is on a motorcycle, and he's trying to jump over the barbed wire. It became such an iconic scene that Triumph [*Motorcycles*] brought out all that kit – Steve McQueen's replica outfit – and I've got the jacket, plus the T-shirt with Steve McQueen and Triumph. **AD: Have you?** Absolutely. The film is about a mass escape by Allied prisoners of war from a German PoW camp, which was actually in Poland in real life – because it is based on real events. That's what I like about it as well. They intended for 250 men to escape, but the guards uncovered a couple of the tunnels so only 76 got away. But then that's where the story really gets harrowing. I mean, it just gives you an idea of war. Fifty were killed by the Gestapo, and only three escaped. Only three people escaped out of 76.

3 THE ENGLISH PATIENT

This one is set at the end of World War Two. It's one of the saddest films I've ever seen. Nine Oscars, three other nominations. The acting is brilliant. Everyone was banging on about it when it was released but it lived up to the hype. You must remember? It was mid-'90s. When I heard it was 2 hours and 40 minutes long I couldn't be bothered to go and see it – in the end I relented and I'm so glad I did. Wow, what a film. If you haven't seen The English Patient you have missed out. **DG: It is a good film, I can see why you'd like it. You like the tear-jerkers, don't you, with the love interest running through them?** Yeah, sorry, I don't mind a tear-jerker. Some people might be a bit surprised to hear that but it's a little bit of me.

3 GLADIATOR

I've gone for an unbelievable film that won five Academy Awards! It's Gladiator. **AD: Controversial.** I don't know why it's controversial. Russell Crowe plays General Maximus Decimus Meridius, commander of the armies of the north. The fight scenes are spectacular! **AD: But he's a gladiator, and so therefore this is not technically a war film.** It starts off with war, he's a General! So in my mind it is a war film.

"Hey, maybe we'd be less conspicuous if we weren't wearing full RAF uniforms?"

2 THE BRIDGE ON THE RIVER KWAI

This was one of my favourite films growing up, probably one of my dad's too. It won seven Oscars. I've watched it on numerous occasions and it's another POW film. It's early 1943 and they've all arrived by train at a Japanese prison camp in Burma. There's an evil Colonel there, Saito, who's in charge. And he says no matter who you are, regardless of rank, you all have to work on this construction of a railway bridge on the River Kwai. **AD: I wonder what the film's called.** I'm trying to build up the suspense but OK, it's The Bridge On The River Kwai. And obviously the guy in charge of the English forces is so proud to be English, stiff upper lip and all that stuff. And he wants to finish that bridge and make sure it goes down in history as the best bridge ever built, but the problem is there are some escapees. In the end it becomes a struggle over what to do with the bridge, blow it up and play havoc with the Japanese war effort or give the men something to live for. It's a true story.

2 THE LIVES OF OTHERS

My number two is subtitled. **DG: I don't mind subtitles.** I find it quite tricky but this one had me gripped. It's called The Lives Of Others. I watched it a couple of weeks ago. It's set during the Cold War – the Berlin Wall comes down and a Stasi officer is assigned to spy on a writer in East Berlin, but starts to respect him and ends up saving him. Guess what I did at the end? Cried, of course!

1 BRAVEHEART

This is directed by and stars Mel Gibson as the Scottish legend William Wallace. His father and brother are killed fighting the English; he goes away to Europe to be educated and when he comes back he marries his sweetheart but it all starts to go downhill. She's captured and killed and this sends him over the edge. He wants to fight the English. He hates them. There are some great battles. Spoiler alert! He gets caught and executed. **AD: I've never seen it. It's on my list of ones to watch.**

1 CASABLANCA

There are so many lines that everybody knows from this film! Humphrey Bogart plays Rick, who's got a cafe in Casablanca. The Europeans are fleeing Nazi Germany through North Africa to get to the States. Victor Laszlo [*Paul Henreid*] is one of them. Ingrid Bergman is his woman but she used to be with Rick, so there's a love triangle that's just genius. The music is superb; everybody knows As Time Goes By because of this film. The best scene, though – and the one I cry most at – is when the German officers are singing this song in Rick's bar and Laszlo orders the band to play the French national anthem. The way they sing from their hearts is so powerful and passionate – I cry every time. I watched it again earlier today, just a little scene of it on YouTube, and I was crying again. And the most amazing thing about the film is that, even though it's set in World War Two, it was made in 1942. Right in the middle of the war. **DG: That's extraordinary.** It is right up there with my favourite films of all time.

TOP FIVE @ 5 'LEFTIES'

These are our Top Five lefties. It can be any left-handed or left-footed individual, or someone with left-leaning principles. Let's get to it...

5 PHIL MICKELSON

This man is an absolute legend and he's starting to get the recognition he deserves. For so long he was in the shadow of Tiger Woods. When Tiger was number one in the world Mickelson was the number two. At one point it looked like he was never going to win a Major but he's won the Masters three times, the PGA and the Open, so he's won three of the four. I'm desperate for him to do the Grand Slam. He has come second six times in the US Open. An absolutely wonderful talent – he plays some impossible shots – and a Ryder Cup legend. **AD: OK, but you do know he's right-handed, right?** He *writes* right-handed. **AD: He does everything right-handed apart from golf.** I do everything left-handed and right-handed, so what's your point? His nickname is Lefty! **AD: I think some people will take issue with you because he is naturally right-handed. He just copied his dad's golf swing in the mirror.** He plays golf left-handed, right? So he's left-handed! **AD: But he's right-handed.** He is a left-handed sports legend.

5 STUART PEARCE

He gives his right foot 2/10... but what he couldn't do with his right foot he more than made up for with his left foot. It's Stuart Pearce, of course. **DG: He was a tough, tough left-back.**

4 WASIM AKRAM

The master of reverse swing. He played for Pakistan and Lancashire. An absolute legend of the game – 104 Tests, 414 Test wickets at 23.6. And he wasn't bad with the bat either. He could smash it out of the ground. Wasim Akram. **AD: I consider him to be one of the greatest all-rounders.** He is a proper cricketer.

Phil Mickelson, pretending to be left-handed just to get on this list

4 TONY BENN

My number four was the best leader Labour never had and the best Prime Minister this country never had: the late Tony Benn. I didn't agree with all his politics, but I certainly wish every politician before and since had the passion and the sincerity that he had. I did politics at university and it was always my ambition to interview Tony Benn. So, as a postgraduate journalism student, I requested an interview – and his office agreed. I interviewed him in the basement study at his home in London. He took me on a book tour and made me a coffee. He even asked me to stick around after we'd done our interview so I could see how a professional did it... and that was Martin Bashir. Just a touch of class, which is so rare in politics and maybe rare in life as well. Politics is a poorer place without him.

3 LIONEL MESSI

Everybody knows how brilliant my number three is. The question is, why is Lionel Messi only at number three? Well, you'll only find that out when I do my number two and number one... **AD: Messi, what a player!**

You could've jumped, Shilts...

3 MANNY PACQUIAO

This was a difficult one. I wanted to put a boxer in here because there have been some fantastic southpaws – Marvin Hagler and Joe Calzaghe are two absolute greats – but I've gone for Manny Pacquiao. What a legend. He is the pound-for-pound king. The knocking-out of Ricky Hatton just about finished Hatton off. He had 71 fights and 62 wins. He has won at eight different weight classes and has fought some of the very best, and he is still fighting at 41.

2 DIEGO MARADONA

It's the left-handed Maradona, the left hand of God. I don't need to say anything more. What he did for Napoli and Argentina says it all. **DG: I'd have him above Messi too.**

2 RAFAEL NADAL

My number two is a tennis player. I've watched him twice in two finals at Wimbledon. Absolutely amazing tennis player. In an era that includes Novak Djokovic, Roger Federer and Andy Murray, the left-hander Rafael Nadal is just unbelievable. Yes, he plays with a two-handed back-hand, but he serves left-handed. He's won 20 Grand Slam titles: the Australian, the French – 13 French titles! – two Wimbledon titles and four US Opens. He's won the Davis Cup with his country five times. He has won Olympic gold at singles, won Olympic gold at doubles. During his career he's made over £120 million in prize money, which isn't bad. **AD: Your list is insanely good.**

1 BRIAN LARA

This guy is a remarkable human being. He scored a Test 300, a Test 400 and a first-class score for Warwickshire against Durham of 501. Would you believe it? To consider batting all that time! It's Brian Lara obviously. He got 375 versus England in '94. I didn't play in that game, thankfully. Matthew Hayden got 380 versus Zimbabwe in 2003, but Brian wasn't having that and reclaimed the record in 2004 with 400 not out in Antigua against England. He enjoyed playing against us. I wasn't playing in that game either, by the way! He was just out of this world and, having played against him on a few occasions, to see his skill up close was an absolute privilege.

1 ANEURIN BEVAN

Excuse the pun, but I've gone leftfield but topical for my number one. It is Nye Bevan, the son of a miner from the Welsh Valleys who founded the NHS. He saw health provision as an individual's right and thought it should be free for all. He was a man of conviction and compassion. We all fell back in love with the NHS during this pandemic; we shouldn't have fallen out of love with it in the first place. Let's hope this leads to a proper long-term funding plan for the NHS and proper salaries for all of those working in it.

Lara hitting out at the inherent inequities of the capitalist system

TOP FIVE @ 5 STARS WHO CHANGED THEIR SPORTS FOREVER

This is not a question of being the greatest, but they have to have had a huge impact on their sport. I've just stuck to football – no surprise there – but Darren has done all sports. Let's see where we've gone with it...

5 JUSTIN FASHANU

A black kid brought up by white parents in a rural English village in East Anglia – it couldn't have been a tougher start for Justin Fashanu and his brother John. They both became footballers, obviously, and Justin was a very good one until injuries ruined his career, but he's here because in 1990 he came out as gay in an article in The Sun newspaper. In truth, the paper had evidence to prove Justin was gay and so his hand was forced, and that led to him coming out... but he did it. He came out as gay and carried on being a professional footballer. It should have changed attitudes more than it did, but the world seemed to demonise him. Opposition fans felt fine at that time singing homophobic songs to him at games and eventually he was hounded out of the country because his private life was under so much scrutiny. He ended up killing himself. It's an incredibly tragic story but it could have been so positive for the sport of football. **DG: What he did was such a brave thing at that time, such a brave thing.**

5 ARNOLD PALMER

There was golf before Tiger Woods... and Arnold Palmer, aka The King, changed it forever. He was from humble beginnings and he helped take the sport from an upper-class pastime to one accessible to everybody. His career spanned over six decades. He won 62 PGA Tour titles from 1955 to 1973 and seven Majors. And then when the Senior Tour started, he was one of the first players on it. He captained the US Ryder Cup side twice. He bought the golf club in Pennsylvania where his dad was a member, the Latrobe Country Club. I think he's one of golf's top five money earners of all time. He made golf sexy.

4 WAYNE GRETZKY

My number four is a Canadian ice hockey player: Wayne Gretzky. He's also probably the only ice hockey player most people in this country have ever heard of – that's how big he was in his sport. When you look at how many records he broke over his career, the list goes on and on. He scored 92 goals in one season and had 163 assists in another. He had three consecutive 200-point seasons. Unheard of! And he did it four times. When he called it a day, all the clubs in Canada retired the number 99 shirt in respect for his record-breaking career.

Gretzky's famous number 99 shirt was retired league-wide in 2000

4 TONY ADAMS

This guy was so open and honest about his experiences with alcohol, it transformed English football. It was the beginning of the end of the drinking culture. And when I say that, I mean it was the end of heavy drinking being acceptable in English football. Tony Adams was so honest about the days he spent endlessly drinking, the bed-wetting, the blackouts, waking up to find he had taken a door off its hinges and had no memory of it. The drink-driving that led to a spell in prison. It woke up people in the game to the dangers of excessive alcohol indulgence. Tony goes into great detail in his book, Addicted. The Arsenal captain – a champion, a leader, an England hero – stood up two months after Euro 96 and told the world he was an alcoholic. It changed football's attitude, in my opinion, to alcohol in this country forever.

3 SHANE WARNE

I'm going to my own sport here. Shane Warne breathed life into the dying art of leg spin. He brought style, personality, good looks and fun. He had front and back pages throughout his whole career. He can't help himself – he's still doing it now! He was feared throughout the world of cricket and he's got an amazing cricket brain. When he first came onto the scene, spin was dying out of the game – not just leg spin, that had gone. But he really made people realise how important it is to have a world-class spinner in a side. There are Shane Warne clones all around the world now. He got 708 test wickets in 145 tests – ridiculous. And to top that off, 125 slip catches... and he slogged a few as well. He still influences the world of cricket from the commentary box. **AD: He transcended his sport. A genius.**

3 GEORGE BEST

Has any other player been as magnetic on and off the pitch? People flocked to George Best, to watch him play or just to get a glimpse of him. In the post-war era there was a stern dourness about English football. It needed to get out of this stupor. Winning the World Cup was part of it but even Bobby Moore said England didn't win it with style. By that time, however, Best was already weaving his magic for Manchester United. I believe his individuality and love of expressing himself on the ball led to the return of entertaining football to this country. **DG: People still talk about the games they saw Best play in.** He got kicked to ribbons every time he played.

2 BILLIE JEAN KING

Billie Jean King has been a huge campaigner for gender equality, and she was a decent tennis player too: 39 Grand Slam titles in singles and doubles. It all started when she won Wimbledon in 1968. She won 750 quid and the male winner got two grand. So she became a big campaigner for equal prize money. In 1973 she threatened to quit the US Open as the tournament didn't pay equal prize money to men and women, and she played against the male chauvinist that was Bobby Riggs in the 'Battle of the Sexes' in front of 30,000 spectators and a TV audience of 90 million. She won the match 6-4, 6-3, 6-3 – and that was massive for women's tennis.

2 BOBBY MOORE

Bobby Moore is my number two. What a guy! He was loved by everyone. His teammates wanted to be him and it wasn't just because he was a brilliant player. Bobby Moore knew how to make the most of his career and this is how he changed football forever. He always looked immaculate. He struck up deals. He started businesses and he knew exactly how to handle his contract negotiations as well. Shortly before the start of the World Cup in '66, his contract with West Ham was due to run out. The rules at the time stated no player could play for their country unless they were contracted to a club, so he ended up signing a one-month contract to see him through the World Cup and then cashed in, doubled his salary and got a three-year deal. Unheard of then. He set the standard in terms of monetising his talent and pursuing opportunities outside of football. He transformed it – and this isn't a criticism. He set the standard.

1 LIONEL MESSI

He is 5ft 6 on his tiptoes, doesn't show off great abs and never gives the impression he's always in the gym. And despite having growth hormone deficiency, Lionel Messi is my number one because he has become one of the best players of all time. The mantra in football was that footballers needed to be of a tall athletic frame rather than skilful. Messi has turned that on its head and has given fresh hope to so many talented but small footballers. Messi has changed the criteria of what you need to be a top footballer to what it should all be about. It should always have been about ability. In that sense he has transformed the game.

1 VIV RICHARDS

This guy was way ahead of his time. What Viv Richards did for one-day cricket and how it's played now is amazing. He has had so much influence over the game. He played in an era where a strike rate of 60 was good; his strike rate was over 90 in that era. He's an absolute legend, from his walk to the crease, the chewing of the gum, that swagger, swinging the bat round and round. And he played mind games with the opposition straight away. But he's in here for the way he played the game. **AD: Viv the visionary. He shaped the future of the game. It's a brilliant number one.**

Bobby Moore: he'd get a straight red for that nowadays

TOP FIVE @ 5 FOOTBALLS

This one couldn't be simpler: we're talking balls. It's our Top Five footballs...

5 MATCH BALL, JOHNSTONE'S PAINT TROPHY 2014

I've been a teeny bit self-indulgent. My number five is the match ball from when Peterborough won the Johnstone's Paint Trophy at Wembley in 2014. I have one of these. It is a Mitre ball, predominantly white but with little multi-coloured streaks on it and the Football League logo. Apart from the sentimentality, it's a beautiful-looking ball.

4 MITRE ULTIMAX

My number four is the Mitre Ultimax. It was the Premier League ball of the '90s. It was top of the range at the time with its out-of-this-world new technology, and was described as the world's fastest and most accurate football. This is going back to when I used to play a little bit and so I have good memories of it. **AD: Yeah, I've got to give you that.** It's a proper football.

5 ADIDAS JABULANI, WORLD CUP 2010

This is a bit hit-and-miss with a lot of people but I just love the design. It's the Adidas Jabulani World Cup football from 2010. I just like the look of this ball – I'm not bothered how it performed. The players hated it but to me it absolutely looks the part. It's got that 'grip and groove' technology that was supposed to give more control but the players said it made it unpredictable. I had one of these balls but I don't know where it's gone. It's probably been kicked into the neighbour's garden and their dog's had it! I love the colours on the ball: yellow, gold, green, black and white. It's a ball that's pretty. **AD: I didn't like it. This is the only World Cup ball I haven't purchased of all the World Cups I have been to. Different strokes for different folks.** You have just shot me down.

4 ADIDAS FINALE 13

This was predominantly white with deep red stars and I absolutely love it. The first time I saw the Adidas Finale 13 was when I was watching a Champions League game on telly. There was a close-up of the ball as a free kick was going to be taken and I had to pause the telly because I looked at that ball and thought, "Oh my goodness. Now that is a football!" I've always been terrible at football so whether the ball swerves or not I will still be rubbish. It's the aesthetics of a ball that appeal to me, not its capability on the pitch.

The Ultimax: a ball

3 WEMBLEY TROPHY

Everybody of a certain age will know this football. **DG: It looked like a basketball.** It's an orange ball, it's the Wembley Trophy. It was fairly hard without being painful unless it whacked you on the inside thigh on a cold day. You felt that sting for ages. In the '70s and '80s these were the closest thing you'd get to a leather ball. I'm sure the vast majority of football-loving kids had one of these back in the day. **DG: One hundred per cent.** It's not an official match ball, obviously, but in the playground these were used all the time.

3 MITRE DELTA 1000

This ball came out in 1986, before the Premier League. Yes, guys, there was football before the Premier League! Simple in design. Black and white. The Mitre Delta 1000 has got the highest accolades throughout the years. It ticks every single box, whether it be weight, circumference, roundness, bounce, water absorption, loss of pressure, shape and size retention... it is top of the tree! **AD: Another good choice.**

2 MITRE DELTA MAX

This is the ball I've got at home at the moment. The Mitre Delta Max is the *creme de la creme* of footballs. It's the pro-level Championship and FA Cup ball at this moment in time. It's got this outer material made of microfibre that provides consistency in performance so is more durable than the standard Delta. Most footballs scratch and scuff but this ball is high-quality.

2 ADIDAS BRAZUCA

I love this football so much. I own four of them, all different colours. It's the Brazuca from the 2014 World Cup.

1 ADIDAS AZTECA

My number one is the ball from Mexico '86. **DG: I was close to picking that but I went for something quite close.** The beautiful thing about the Adidas Azteca is the little Mexican patterns on it. It's got everything you would want from a World Cup football. It's black and white and it looks the part, but it's that little hint of Mexico in there that makes it for me.

1 ADIDAS TANGO ESPANA

I've gone for the football from the World Cup before, the official ball of 1982. It's the last World Cup ball to be made out of genuine leather. It's a classic-looking ball, with that black and white design, and it was strengthened from the World Cup in 1978 to be more water-resistant. I don't think it's as good as the Delta Max, but I was 12 years old when the Adidas Tango Espana came out and that is a very influential age. I saw that ball and thought, "Wow, I'd love to be kicking that around." **AD: I cannot argue with that choice. They're close to our heart, these balls.**

The Tango Espana: also a ball

TOP FIVE @5 MALE ACTORS

I do regret coming up with this one. It's a flipping good Top Five but so hard to narrow it down. So many names flood into your head - Adrian had 25 written down at one point and there will be those you hadn't even thought of, but here are ours...

5 LENNIE JAMES

I'm starting off with the star of Save Me and Save Me Too. He created it and wrote it as well. I'm not a fan of The Walking Dead, but he's in that and I'm told he's so good that he had a cameo to start with and they wrote him into the script with a bigger role. But I first spotted Lennie James in the first series of Line Of Duty and he was fantastic. I've kept an eye out for him ever since... and then Save Me turned up and I just think he's so brilliant. He is one of the best actors we've ever produced. So I'm gonna stick him in there.

5 TOM CRUISE

My number five is a household name - it's Tom Cruise. I used to pretend I was a fighter pilot after Top Gun came out. There was also Cocktail and Days Of Thunder, some of the early ones. Then he did the Mission Impossible movies and played Jack Reacher. He was also brilliant in A Few Good Men and The Firm. You've got to give him serious credit. He does a lot of his own stunts. Tom Cruise has to be in there, he really, really does. **AD: It's amazing he has never won an Oscar.**

4 MICHAEL CAINE

Great voice - he's done a lot of voiceover work too. I first came across Michael Caine in Zulu, which is an unbelievable film, and I reckon out of all his films I must have watched that one more than any other. He's won two Oscars and been nominated for six. His Oscars were way back: in 1986 he won one for Hannah And Her Sisters, then he won another in 1999 for The Cider House Rules. But I know him more for The Dark Knight Rises, Zulu, The Italian Job and Get Carter. **AD: Terrific choice.**

4 JAKE GYLLENHAAL

My number four came to prominence in Donnie Darko. He was utterly brilliant as the troubled youngster. You'll know him for Brokeback Mountain and Nightcrawler. It's Jake Gyllenhaal. A brilliant actor with a long career ahead of him.

3 TOM CRUISE

He was Darren's number five but I've got him at number three. It's Tom Cruise. He was sensationally good in Jerry Maguire, and Vanilla Sky is another favourite Tom Cruise film. He makes that film happen. **DG: We're both big Tom Cruise fans!** Indeed.

3 MORGAN FREEMAN

I love this actor. He played Ellis Boyd 'Red' Redding in The Shawshank Redemption, one of my favourite films of all time. It's Morgan Freeman. I've actually got the cinema poster signed, but it's at the framers' as we speak. **AD: Is there a big hole in your wall?** Haha! **You have to have seen the film to get that one.** He also plays a detective called Alex Cross in Kiss The Girls and Along Came A Spider, the films of the books by James Patterson. Freeman is also great in Seven and has been nominated five times for an Oscar; he's won one, Best Supporting Actor for Million Dollar Baby.

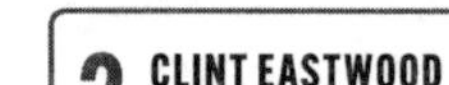

2 CLINT EASTWOOD

This guy is absolutely superb in Dirty Harry. Four Oscars, 11 nominations. He just keeps going and going. It's Clint Eastwood. I think he's got better and better as an actor as he's got older, and as a director as well. He's done everything from The Good, The Bad And The Ugly – which was when I first got into him – to war films, romances, historical dramas and sporting movies. **AD: I am not a fan but I can see why he'd be in many people's top fives.**

1 TOM HANKS

There are so many different films this guy's been in. Forrest Gump is one of my favourites. In Cast Away he's excellent because it's basically just him for the whole film and he's truly amazing. It's Tom Hanks. He really buys into the parts and does everything he can to make them realistic. For me he is one of the greatest actors ever. **DG: Can't argue with that. I've just bought a Tom Hanks-signed 'Wilson the ball' from Cast Away.**

2 MORGAN FREEMAN

Our lists coincide again. Seven is one of the films that I love and Morgan Freeman is my number two... but Gone Baby Gone is my favourite film of his. It has one of the most dramatic endings to a film I've ever seen and he is utterly brilliant in that particular scene. It's so emotional.

1 ROBERT DE NIRO

If I say Casino, The Godfather, The Deer Hunter, Heat, The Fan and, most chilling of all, Cape Fear, you'll know who I'm talking about. Robert de Niro. You are scared to death watching him on screen. He has that mean streak in him when he's in those films, the gangster movies, but he can also do comedy as he does in Meet The Fockers. Very funny. I loved The Irishman, recently, but his best one for me, and he got an Oscar for it, was his role in Raging Bull. **AD: How good was he in that?**

Morgan Freeman, asking where he can redeem his shawshanks

TOP FIVE @ 5 MOST UNDERRATED PLAYERS IN THE PREMIER LEAGUE ERA

There have been so many underrated players in this era, so many who haven't received the recognition they deserve from anywhere outside of their own football club. This has been a really tough one and some will miss out again, but here are our Top Five...

5 PETER BEARDSLEY

What a career this bloke had without really being the main focus up front. When people talk about Liverpool legends they talk about Rush, Fowler, Gerrard, Dalglish, Souness... Beardsley hardly gets a mention. When he played for England, Gary Lineker described him as the best partner he could ever have had. And at Newcastle (twice) he was outstanding – and how many players can go from Liverpool and then play for Everton? An absolutely fantastic player. Lovely skill. **AD: You're right, he doesn't get mentioned among the Liverpool legends and he should.**

4 DION DUBLIN

In the '97-'98 season this striker was the joint top scorer in the Premier League – think about that for a minute – and he could also play at centre-back. Dion Dublin had some terrible injuries yet he still came back. Unfortunately for him he missed out on a place in the England '98 World Cup squad. He should have been taken to that World Cup but Glenn Hoddle left him out, and I think that did for him in terms of where he is rated.

5 MARK ALBRIGHTON

Aston Villa decided this guy could leave on a free transfer so he went to Leicester City and played on the wing consistently well. Now, you might not think he's ever had many 10/10 or even 9/10 performances, but when did he ever put in a performance below 7/10 for Leicester City in their Premier League title-winning season? Never. Marc Albrighton was fantastic for them. He also scored their first ever goal in the Champions League. **DG: He was such a big player in that title season. And he's still such an important player.**

4 GARETH BARRY

He started off as a youngster at Aston Villa and could have left many times, but stayed loyal to them until City came in for him in his late 20s. He won trophies there before heading to Everton and, yes, he got 53 England caps but fans were always complaining that he shouldn't be in the team. I think Gareth Barry was never going to be appreciated before he finally hung up the football boots in 2020. He's a fantastic footballer who played in a record number of games. Such a consistent performer.

Guess who was born four miles away from Peter Beardsley...

3 **MATT HOLLAND**
A regular for Ireland when they qualified for tournaments, a midfield general for an Ipswich side that massively overachieved and for a Charlton side that stayed in the Premier League. Maybe he lacked a little bit of pace, but when Matt Holland hit one from 25 yards it usually arrowed into the top corner. He was a leader and captain everywhere he went. Managers loved him as well. And he knows how to have a laugh.

3 **JAMES MILNER**
A few years back there were loads of England fans moaning about this player being in the squad. Well, James Milner has proven to every single one of them how good he is. You don't play for Leeds, Newcastle, Villa, Manchester City and Liverpool at right-back and left-back, in midfield and as a winger if you're not any good! He is the perfect pro – the attitude, his fitness and versatility. And he's still going.

2 **DIRK KUYT**
He gets overlooked as an absolute high-quality player but, before you even look at his six years at Liverpool, Dirk Kuyt has 104 caps for Holland and played in five major tournaments for them. Only top players manage that. **AD: I didn't know that. That's amazing.** Exactly. He was another team player who could play everywhere.

Yep, it's the equally dishy Steve Bruce

2 **CHRIS BRUNT**
This guy is a West Bromwich Albion legend with a wand of a left foot, a thoroughly brilliant pro, and the things he could do with that wand I think went unnoticed by far too many. **DG: He got so much stick from fans but he was a fantastic player.**

1 **MICHAEL CARRICK**
Detractors say my number one never made it for England. Well, that was the fault of the England managers. Michael Carrick is the real deal. Doubters will still refuse to accept this but all those trophies he won with Manchester United speak for themselves. A terrific passer of the ball. Absolutely brilliant. **DG: To only get 30-odd caps for England when he was part of that of that super-successful United team was ridiculous.** He only played in one tournament game for England. That to me is a disgrace, but United benefited from it.

1 **STEVE BRUCE**
Here's another United player who never got the recognition, not even one cap for England. Can you believe that? **AD: Incredible.** He was the captain of Manchester United after Robson left in '93, and in the '93-'94 season he became the first Englishman to captain a club to a domestic double. He scored 51 goals and in '90-'91 was the club's second-highest goalscorer. As a centre-half. And, I'll say it again, he never played for England! Ridiculous. **AD: England flopped at Euro 92 and didn't even qualify for the World Cup in '94... so perhaps there's a connection there.**

TOP FIVE @ 5 ELVIS SONGS

It is incredible how many Elvis impersonators are out there – the Japanese tribute act has to be seen to be believed, he's supposed to be one of the best. We can't get enough of the King of Rock'n'Roll so here are our Top Five Elvis tracks...

5 VIVA LAS VEGAS

I needed to start with a real rocking tune so off we go with Viva Las Vegas... as, of course, featured in the film of the same name. And I just love this song. There was an old BBC drama called Blackpool and the actor David Morrissey was in it. He was singing it into a mirror thinking he was Elvis and I thought, "What a magnificent tune!" After that, I listened to the authentic version by the King and I was blown away. Such a great song and you can't help but jig along with it.

5 RETURN TO SENDER

My number five was the UK Christmas No.1 in 1962. It's Return To Sender. It only got to No.2 in the US charts as he couldn't knock Big Girls Don't Cry by the Four Seasons off the top spot. I think it's one of his best songs. **AD: Another one where you kind of have to sing along.**

4 SUSPICIOUS MINDS

This didn't get to No.1 in the UK. Can you believe that? Fine Young Cannibals did a cover version of it in the '80s. It is a super version. Roland Gift, the lead singer, actually said Elvis had come to him in a dream and told him he would make the greatest version of Suspicious Minds ever. Extraordinary. I think with this track, everyone knows the words. And it's got a brilliant crescendo.

4 ALL SHOOK UP

This is where you can really do the Elvis impression. All Shook Up was his first UK No.1 and it was there for seven weeks. Absolutely brilliant. It was No.1 for eight weeks in the US, it was No.1 in the R&B charts and the country charts as well. That just tells you how good it was. Rock'n'roll all day long. You should see me moving along to this – I turn into an animal when it comes on. **AD: I've just had a WhatsApp message asking for a video of Darren dancing along to Elvis... and it's all gone quiet.**

3 A LITTLE LESS CONVERSATION

There are so many hidden gems in Elvis's back catalogue. This one came out in the '60s during a pretty fallow period in his career and did nothing. Then it was used in Ocean's Eleven... then it was remixed by JXL, and was a massive hit in 2002 before being used for a World Cup advertising campaign by Nike. I just love it, and the subsequent releases put Elvis back out there.

Elvis received a writing credit on many songs but didn't actually write any of them

3 CAN'T HELP FALLING IN LOVE

This one's a beauty. You can do a lovely waltz to this. Can't Help Falling In Love was released in 1961 and was in the film Blue Hawaii. It got to No.2 in the American charts and made it to No.1 in the UK. And during the '60s and '70s he used this as the show finale in all his live performances. I could just close my eyes and listen to it all day.

2 (LET ME BE YOUR) TEDDY BEAR

I used to play cricket with Hugh Morris for England A and he used to sing (Let Me Be Your) Teddy Bear all the time. He really got me into it and it's still one of my favourites. It was No.1 in the summer of '57 for seven weeks. It also got to No.1 in both the R&B and country charts. It topped the lot, mate. What more do you want from a song? **AD: I'm surprised you've got it this high, but hearing you sing it, I cannot do anything but love it.** It's gold dust, the lyrics are brilliant.

1 THE LADY LOVES ME

We've already had the title song from Viva Las Vegas but this was also in it. It's a duet with Ann-Margret and it brings a smile to your face. It's funny and it's sweet, a terrific love song, and Elvis and Ann-Margret were actually having a real-life love affair at the time. There's a magical chemistry between them. They're at a holiday resort and he's following her around desperate to get a date and she's having none of it. She pushes him into the swimming pool and that's the climax of the song. I just love it. This is my number one by some distance.

1 JAILHOUSE ROCK

Another one from a film, one of my favourites. It's Jailhouse Rock and Elvis plays a convict. He was wrongly accused and gets out eventually and becomes a star. It's a beauty of a track and features some great dance moves as well from Elvis. It topped both the US and the UK charts. This is real Elvis – this is what Elvis for me is all about.

2 IN THE GHETTO

If this were a Top Five of sad songs, this would be number one. It's In The Ghetto and he delivers it beautifully. It was huge because he had been out of the picture but this single catapulted him back into the big time. There's a personal reason for this choice too: my mum was a massive Elvis fan, and the day we found out he died in 1977 she dragged the three of us out to buy every single newspaper. It was pelting it down that morning but she wanted all the newspapers on Elvis. When we got home she played this song on a loop for days. Oh, and another memory I associate with this song is Freddie Flintoff singing it during the Big Bash. **DG: What about when he was singing Elvis on finals day and was so into it he tripped and fell over? What a numpty!** Superb.

Elvis riding an invisible bucking bronco

TOP FIVE @ 5 AMERICAN SPORT STARS

The amount of grief I get on social media when somebody does not make a Top Five is unbelievable, but people are not listening to the words. These are not necessarily the best but they are our FAVOURITES, for the reasons we shall give. This will be fun: our Top Five favourite American sport stars...

5 WILLIAM PERRY

I'm kicking off with a 6ft 2in, 23-stone American footballer. His nickname was The Refrigerator, for obvious reasons. But he could play and he hit the NFL by storm in the 1980s. He was a defensive lineman and, even though he was massive, he could move and had a level of fitness. One of his famous quotes was, "Even when I was little I was big." He scored that touchdown in the Super Bowl in 1986 when the Chicago Bears thrashed the New England Patriots. The size of his Super Bowl ring is more than double the average size for a man. Since he quit he's had tough times with illness and alcoholism. I believe he's in a care home right now. But when those of us of a certain age watched NFL on Channel Four in the 1980s, The Refrigerator was a superstar. He certainly wasn't the best, he wasn't even the best on his team, but he was just an iconic figure. **DG: NFL was huge in the 1980s because it was on terrestrial TV on a Sunday evening and he was a huge part of that.**

The Fridge: big, cool, emits a constant low-level hum

5 CHRIS EVERT

My number five was an absolutely amazing tennis player. Chris Evert was the number one tennis player in the world. She won 18 Grand Slam singles championships and three doubles titles. She was in 34 finals overall. She was obviously up against some good opposition during that time, notably Martina Navratilova, but she managed to win all those Grand Slams. And when I was a young lad I had a huge crush on her – I didn't have any posters of pop stars or sport stars on my wall, but if I had done, the first one would have been of her. Happy memories.

4 CARL LEWIS

He won four golds in a single Olympics in 1984. I was 14 years old and I remember watching those Olympics and thinking, "Wow, this guy is serious!" Carl Lewis was in four Olympic Games and he ended up with nine gold medals: two in the 100m, one in the 200m, two in the 4x100m and four in the long jump. That's how talented he was. A great sprinter and a great long jumper. The long jump was where he was really the king, and he won the long jump in four consecutive Olympics. A proper athlete, Carl Lewis. He was on another level. **AD: Yep, he took those LA Games by storm.**

4 LEBRON JAMES

There have been certain basketball players who can just do things no others can... and that is LeBron James for me. It's not just because he is one of the greats of the sport; I don't think that's in doubt. I'm not saying he is the greatest of all time but he's certainly in the conversation. I got back into the NBA big-time when I was in the States a few years ago. I started watching the play-offs and I wondered why I had not stayed in touch with this sport. It was sensational. Golden State won it and they were fantastic; LeBron was terrific for the Cleveland Cavaliers at the time. I was watching the games in a bar in Boston and LeBron really caught my eye. I mean, he is a basketball superstar. His teams got to eight consecutive NBA Finals between 2011 and 2018. He's been a champ four times, the MVP all four times there as well. He has you on the edge of your seat. And the thing I like about him is that he's not afraid to have an opinion. **DG: I'm not a massive basketball fan but I've got into it since watching The Last Dance documentary.** A great film.

Lebron James and Tiger Woods share a birthday – December 30th. Woods is 9 years older.

3 MICHAEL JORDAN

As I said, I'm not a big basketball fan, but for the career he's had you have to admire Michael Jordan. He transcends basketball, he's a global superstar... and he played in an era without social media. Can you imagine if he had been in his pomp now, how big he would be? He was the sport's first billionaire. He's got his own brand at Nike – and if you watch The Last Dance, he didn't even like the brand at the beginning.

2 MUHAMMAD ALI

You've got to admire him as a boxer and you've got to admire him as a man. He had principles. He stood up against the Vietnam War and endured a lot of personal sacrifice because of it. But he came back to be World Champion again. Ali called himself the greatest of all time; I don't think anybody can really argue against it. **AD: I'd have an argument with you about him being the greatest but that's for another time – no argument about him being in your Top Five at all.**

3 ODELL BECKHAM JR

American football again. He's definitely not the best player at his sport and I'm not pretending he is; he's just one of my favourites. I grew up as a New York Giants fan. Odell Beckham Jr was there for a while but he didn't really do anything. I should have gone off him but he's still in my heart. He is box office. As I say, not the greatest player but capable of truly great moments. That famous one-handed catch – check it out on YouTube, it's just out-of-this-world genius. It's been the only good thing about following the Giants in recent years. I am gutted he's no longer in New York but he's a superstar beyond NFL and he has undertaken an incredible amount of charity work. If you want to be a sportsman, you probably want to be him. There's even a touch of the bad boy about him.

2 SERENA WILLIAMS

I've said many times on talkSPORT that this woman is unbelievable, literally unbelievable. She had a dad with expectations like you wouldn't believe and a big sister, Venus, who was world-class already. And yet Serena Williams wasn't fazed by any of that. She got on court and showed the world who's boss. She has beaten her sister seven times in Slam finals – that's seven out of eight finals since she lost the first one in the 2001 US Open . She has won an Open-era record of 23 Slams, winning the 23rd in Australia when she was in the early stages of pregnancy in 2017. I have nothing but admiration for Serena Williams and she's not scared to speak out as well. She'll wear what she wants, she'll say what she wants and she will win what she wants. Just an unbelievable sports star. **DG: Not going to argue with that one. Amazing athlete.**

1 TIGER WOODS

What an absolute superstar. My number one is one of the most famous athletes ever, known around the world. He has won 15 Majors – only Jack Nicklaus has won more. He has gone through lots of personal issues but Tiger Woods keeps coming back. He spent 281 consecutive weeks as the world number one... and then, after 11 years without a Major because of injuries and other difficulties, he comes back and wins the Masters in 2019! Black trousers, red shirt. What a star. **AD: He has a touch of the bad boy about him like Odell Beckham – there's literally everything going on in his career.** I followed him round when he played at The Grove in that World Matchplay and you can't get a view because thousands of people want to see him. Even when he is practising it's difficult to get a glimpse of him through the crowds! **AD: You need to become the talkSPORT golf correspondent and get on the other side of the ropes.**

1 JESSE OWENS

My number one broke three world records and equalled another in the space of just 45 minutes at a meeting in Michigan in 1935. I mean, that in itself is incredible. But it wasn't even the biggest moment of his career. The following year, Jesse Owens went to the Berlin Olympics... and this is in the era of Nazi Germany. He won four golds at the Berlin Olympics for sprinting and the long jump. But even more than that, the grandson of a slave had shown Hitler in his own backyard that the whites were not the superior race. And now in Berlin, near the Olympic Stadium, there's a street named after Jesse Owens. It's just an extraordinary story, isn't it? **DG: Absolutely. And Jesse Owens can go down both as your favourite and as one of the greatest. A game-changing athlete.**

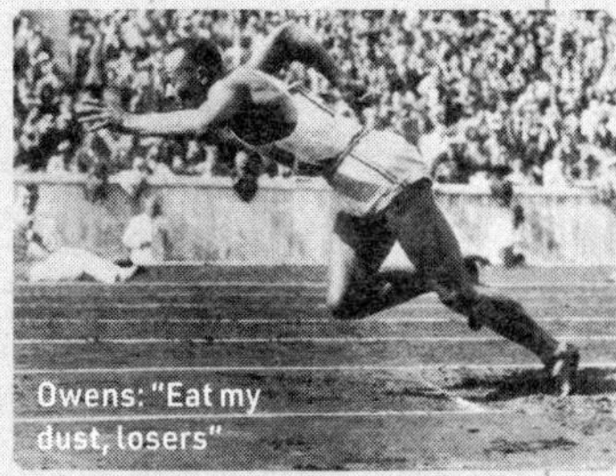

Owens: "Eat my dust, losers"

TOP FIVE @ 5 THINGS THAT MAKE BRITAIN GREAT

There's a lot to love about the Britain we live in today. We could bang on about some of the negatives if you like, but I don't really want to. The inspiration for these Top Fives is the people – but also the NHS, our sporting tradition and the things we see around us every day but maybe take for granted...

5 THE COUNTRYSIDE

I'm lucky enough to live in the countryside and I was out there again this morning, really early. Beautiful skies, breathtaking scenery... and wherever you are – whether you're in Dorset, the Yorkshire Dales, the Scottish Highlands – it's just beautiful to be out there and seeing all that beauty. You're never far from great scenery in this country.

4 RED PHONEBOXES

I've said red phoneboxes, but this really amounts to the symbols that are recognised all over the world as typically British: the Queen, red phoneboxes and postboxes, black cabs, red buses... and that's what I love about living here. I've got an old-fashioned red postbox in my village, at the end of the road. You don't see as many phoneboxes now. **AD: I didn't even think about things like that. Love it. I was in a village in Yorkshire a couple of years ago and there was a red phonebox that was full of books. If you took a book you had to replace it with another one. Amazing.** I'd love a red phonebox in my garden. **AD: It's iconic, isn't it?**

5 HISTORIC BUILDINGS

There was a shot of Tower Bridge on the TV yesterday and it just struck me what an incredible building it is. And we have so many castles, stately homes and cathedrals. The medieval architecture of the university towns is world-famous. Everywhere you look you can find awe-inspiring feats of engineering: from the world's first iron bridge to the Humber Bridge, there are so many historic structures and buildings in Britain.

The internal height of a phone box was originally to accommodate the wearing of a top hat

4 GOOD FISH AND CHIPS

I was torn over what to include and what not to include in terms of food, but I went for fish and chips. The thing is, they've got to get it right. **DG: So many don't, though.** Yes, and that's a massive disappointment. So that's why I've specified *good* fish and chips. It's so satisfying when you find one of those places that I just had to include good fish and chips!

3 THE HOUSES OF PARLIAMENT

Again, this is part of a bigger category and that is – to touch on what you mentioned before – the historic buildings around us. But it takes your breath away when you go in the Houses of Parliament. It's not just the benches and the viewing gallery that everyone knows, but the history stretching back to Westminster Hall and the 11th century. Incredible. **AD: I first went I when I was about 21 and it blew me away.**

3 VILLAGE PUBS

This is why I love Midsomer Murders – because there's always a village pub. It's not so much the show itself, because he is arguably the worst DCI in history – there are at least three murders before he works out who's doing it... **DG: We love a village pub. Your mum and dad would go and then it would be your first pub when you were old enough.** Some of the best pubs I've been to are in Oxfordshire, but also the Lake District.

2 THE ARMED FORCES

We mentioned the NHS earlier and these guys also have to be on my list: the armed forces. You only have to go back to the two World Wars to see how they protected us. You look at the ongoing wars throughout the world and they're still protecting us from other enemies. The SAS and SBS are two of the finest outfits in the world. We are very lucky to have such great armed forces.

2 SUNDAY ROAST

I must be hungry because I've gone back to food for my next selection – and this is the most British of the lot. For some reason the Sunday roast is frowned upon by the rest of the world, but it's so beautiful. You have to have gravy. You have to have roast potatoes that are done properly, crispy on the outside and fluffy on the inside. You have to have your Yorkshire puddings, and I'm not talking about those frozen ones. In terms of the meat, I know you're a chicken fan but I love a joint of beef.

1 SPORTING VENUES

FA Cup finals at Wembley, a Test match at Lords, Wimbledon, or when we held the Olympics here in 2012... This is not just stadiums like Wembley – although we have the best in the world here – but other grounds around the country where the local community can go and support their team, cricket grounds like Worcester with the Cathedral in the background. Perfect. **AD: Great shout.**

1 THE RAIN

My number one is the reason this country is so green. You know when you fly over Spain, for example, it's so arid and brown, but when you fly over England it's all different shades of green and beautiful, lush countryside? It's because it rains so much. That's the reality. **DG: I used to love playing football in the rain. And with cricket, as soon as rain stopped play we could go off and do what we wanted for five hours. I've got a lot of time for rain.**

TOP FIVE @5 FEMALE ACTORS

Before doing this I wasn't aware that you don't call females in the film business 'actresses' any more. **DG: They want to be known as actors. Let's move with the times.** OK, well we've done the Top Five male actors, so here we have our Top Five female actors...

Keeley: steely

5 KEELEY HAWES
In Ashes To Ashes she was absolutely knockout brilliant. The way her and Philip Glenister bounced off each other was fantastic. There's no better person to start off this selection than Keeley Hawes. She was incredibly good as Lindsay Denton in Line Of Duty too. She played the part of baddie in that but I just wanted to look after her. I've got a spare room, I'd have cooked for her...

5 CHARLIZE THERON
She won an Oscar in 2004 for her role in the film Monster but rose to fame in the film Devil's Advocate in 1997. She was magnificent in that. And then she did The Cider House Rules and that was another massive part. It's Charlize Theron for my number five. She sued Playboy because they put her on the cover in 1999 using pictures from an old modelling shoot. But she's done films like The Legend Of Bagger Vance alongside stuff like Mad Max and the Fast & Furious franchise. She's also incredibly beautiful.

4 KATE WINSLET
In 2009 she won a Best Actress Oscar for The Reader and I thought she would get an Oscar for her performance as Apple's marketing executive in the Steve Jobs film. I thought she was great in Revolutionary Road alongside Leonardo DiCaprio and she won a Golden Globe for that. But everybody really knows Kate Winslet from Titanic. She made it seem so real. She's one of very few to have won Academy, Emmy and Grammy Awards.

4 MERYL STREEP

She absolutely nailed it in the series Big Little Lies. She wasn't in series one but turns up in the second and absolutely steals the show – her fiery relationships with Nicole Kidman and Reese Witherspoon make it some of the most memorable TV I've ever seen. But Meryl Streep goes way back. She first came onto the scene in the late '70s with classics like Kramer Vs. Kramer. She was in Out Of Africa, Death Becomes Her, The Bridges Of Madison County, The Manchurian Candidate. I loved her in The Devil Wears Prada. She was also in a film called Julie & Julia which is a gentle film, about cooking actually, which is one of my favourite films and a life-changer for me. In Sophie's Choice she has to choose which of her children she has to leave with the Nazis – how do you begin even thinking how to act that role? What a performance! **DG: They are all brilliant in Big Little Lies.**

3 JODIE FOSTER

She won an Oscar for her part in The Silence Of The Lambs. She shot to fame as a young child actor in Bugsy Malone and was also in Taxi Driver in 1976, of course, playing Iris, a teenage prostitute. She subsequently took four years out to go to Yale University and then came back to acting. She has done some absolutely stunning films and is probably most famous for her role as FBI agent Clarice Starling opposite Anthony Hopkins in The Silence Of The Lambs... but I also love The Accused, and she got an Oscar for that. She was phenomenal in The Panic Room too. I like her in just about anything and actually feel bad for not having her higher up. **AD: She deserved the Oscars for Silence Of The Lambs and The Accused and was very much in my thinking for my Top Five, so I'm glad you've got her in.**

John Hinckley claimed he shot President Ronald Reagan to impress Jodie Foster

3 OLIVIA COLMAN

She played Sophie in Peep Show for 13 years and then went on to play the Queen! An unbelievable range of roles. It can only be Olivia Colman. Then throw in Broadchurch, and she's also done the voice for one of Thomas's friends on Thomas The Tank Engine. But I was a massive fan of Peep Show – and when you know her from that and the next time you see her she's reading out an acceptance speech at the Oscars, it blows your mind. She won for The Favourite, beating Glenn Close, who was supposed to be a shoo-in for The Wife. More recently she was superb in The Night Manager, but the fact that she's also been in Midsomer Murders secured her position in My Top Five.

2 JULIA ROBERTS

What can I say? Again, such a wide variety of roles and films to choose from. Julia Roberts first came to my attention in Sleeping With The Enemy, and I wanted to include a quote from that but they were all too dark. An Oscar winner as well. We all know her from Notting Hill and I'd be amazed if she's not in your Top Five, so I'll leave that there...

2 RENEE ZELLWEGER

Apart from the fact that she's had four Oscar nominations and won two, and was hilarious in Bridget Jones, not to mention being excellent in Jerry Maguire and Cold Mountain – and singing and dancing in Chicago – it's the way she played Judy Garland trying to make a comeback in London in the film Judy that gets Renee Zellweger my vote here. Amazing film, and she played her to perfection – looks like her, talks like her, it's an amazing portrayal. **AD: I think the Bridget Jones films are underrated, and the fact that she's from Texas but nailed the part of a 30-something singleton living in London was remarkable. Plus the fact that she was in the Texas Chainsaw Massacre sequel back in the early days makes your choice fine with me.**

Julia: pretty

1 JULIA ROBERTS

I think you second-guessed me here. I saw Pretty Woman when I was 20 years old and she just grabbed me in the role she was playing, as a call-girl hired by a rich businessman to be his escort. I think she's absolutely stunning and she's in here for her acting, for sure, for brilliant performances in films like Erin Brockovich and Sleeping With The Enemy... but I can't deny she was one of my crushes when I was younger. The thing is she can also do comedy – have you seen Runaway Bride? **AD: Yeah, absolutely.** She's hilarious in that, a very funny lady.

1 MARILYN MONROE

Is my number one the best at acting? No. Do I want to watch how she plays Sugar in Some Like It Hot on a loop for days and days and days? You bet I do. She just gets it right. She was in Gentlemen Prefer Blondes, Bus Stop, The Seven Year Itch. She won a Golden Globe for Some Like It Hot; she does comedy, she does sexy and she can sing. Whatever 'it' is, she had it – and if she were around today she'd be a cover star every week. Marilyn is a global icon above all others. **DG: Yep, she was on my list but didn't quite make the cut. No arguments, though. She was fantastic.**

Marilyn: itchy

TOP FIVE @ 5 ABBA SONGS

I've been looking forward to this one. They are great singalong songs. **DG: You will get people not admitting that, but can they really say they've not danced along to an Abba song at some point?** It's impossible to go through the Abba back catalogue and say you don't like any of them – there are some quality tunes in there. So let's get going...

5 SUPER TROUPER

Are you telling me that people listening in their car, when that came on, weren't tapping their foot on the floor? Super Trouper just gets you going. Great track and also the name of the album. It was a massive success: it was the biggest-selling album of 1980 in the UK. The single reached No.1 in the UK but only 45 in the US – it didn't have much success there. It was No.1 in 14 countries, their ninth and final one here. Sing it! **AD: It sounds alright but I must admit, it's not one of my favourites.**

A Super Trouper is a kind of spotlight used in large concert venues

4 SUMMER NIGHT CITY

Now this has got a Bee Gees feel to it, hasn't it? The Abba biography I've got describes Summer Night City as a dance track, a tribute to a hectic nightlife. Top-five UK hit but there's a bit of controversy with this one: as the song is fading out, it's alleged someone sings a rude word. It has always been denied but it sounds pretty clear to me. So much for Abba's squeaky-clean image! There is a bomb dropped right at the end of the song, just after three minutes or so. Abba didn't like the song: Bjorn called it lousy, Benny said it should never have been released, Agnetha said it wasn't very Abba. But I flipping love it! So I'm having it. **DG: Not for me, let's quickly leave that behind...**

5 LAY ALL YOUR LOVE ON ME

This is from the Super Trouper album too. Lay All Your Love On Me is my number five: an underrated track. Really like this one – it's got a techno electro feel to it. I love the variation in their work. It was a top-10 hit in the UK in 1981 and you can dance to it... and you know I'm a great dancer, mate. **DG: Don't mind the song, probably in my top ten, but not so sure about dancing to it.** Well, I'll leave that to you, you're the professional.

4 KNOWING ME, KNOWING YOU

One of the biggest-selling singles of 1977 – a huge hit but, by all accounts, it's written about the relationships within the group, which were very strained at this time. There is a hint of divorce in it. Knowing Me, Knowing You was No.1 in the UK, Ireland, Mexico, South Africa and West Germany. **AD: In this country Alan Partridge has totally transformed the image of it. "A-ha!" But when you boil it down, it's still a brilliant song.**

3 MAMMA MIA

I've watched this twice at the theatre and it is super – the audience are all up dancing at the end. I'm talking about Mamma Mia, of course. This tune puts you in an absolutely great mood but it was never ever intended to be released as a single: they offered it to the pop group Brotherhood Of Man but they turned it down. So Abba released it in Australia in August 1975, just to see how it would go... and it spent 10 weeks at No.1. Epic Records took notice of this and released it in the UK, where it also made it to No.1. It was the second single in Abba's run of 18 consecutive top-10 UK chart hits. **AD: Now that doesn't happen by accident – so people who are still saying they don't like Abba, delve deep into your soul.** I'm going to go and watch Mamma Mia again at the theatre.

Not all of ABBA came from Sweden. Anni-Frid Lyngstad was born in Norway.

2 TAKE A CHANCE ON ME

What a song! The thing about this is that, when it was recorded, to get that "take a chance, take a chance" repetition at the start they had to record it about 50 times – they couldn't just do it twice and drop it in with a computer like they do today. The song was released as a single in 1978 and was absolutely huge. It hit No.1 of course in England, plus Ireland, Mexico, Austria and Belgium, and No.3 in the US. It was their seventh No.1 in the UK. Again, don't doubt Abba. And this was their third consecutive No.1 in the UK. There have been several covers of it. Erasure did a version of it in 1992 and that got to No.1 as well... but my favourite cover of this song is by Alvin And The Chipmunks. You've got to listen to it. Genius. **AD: It's another song ruined by Alan Partridge but the original is the best.**

3 WATERLOO

This was their breakthrough song. The music was written by Benny and Bjorn but their manager at the time, Stig Anderson, had to add the words. The hook required a strong three-syllable word and, because it was written for Eurovision, it had to be something that could be understood without a translation. So Stig came up with... Honey Pie. It was going to be called Honey Pie, which really doesn't work. And he went through his wife's cookbooks to look for Honey Pie and it didn't exist. So he thought, well, that makes no sense, it doesn't mean anything. He then read a book of famous quotations and came up with Waterloo, and it was perfect. Within a couple of hours he'd written the lyrics using Napoleon's defeat at Waterloo as a metaphor for a young woman who eventually gives in to a suitor's persistent pleading with her. When they came to England for Eurovision they were put up in the Napoleon Suite in the Grand Hotel in Brighton – there's an omen – and they won the competition. And here is the amazing thing: the British judges gave them zero points for this song, which is an absolute disgrace. **DG: I'd love to know who that was, what numpties.** I felt ashamed when I read that. One of the best Eurovision songs ever and the British judges gave it nothing!

2 SOS

There's so much going on in this song. There's the classical baroque-style keyboard at the start and the flourishes from Benny are absolutely brilliant, and Agnetha singing like she's crying. Now this song brought Abba back to life. Waterloo got to No.1 and they won Eurovision; after that they had four flops and another song that barely scratched the Top 40. And then they had this. It hit the Top 10 and there was no looking back. It's acknowledged as Abba's first truly classic pop single. And here's a little fact about SOS as well: Pete Townshend of The Who once bumped into Benny in the States and told him SOS was the best pop song ever written! I defy anybody to say they don't like this song.

1 THE WINNER TAKES IT ALL

This was a No.1 hit but it's so much more than that. In Mamma Mia, the musical, there's a song that has me in floods of tears – it's called Our Last Summer. It's a beautiful song, written by Bjorn about a love affair he had in Paris when he was younger. And again, The Winner Takes It All has deeply personal lyrics written by Bjorn. The words are inspired by his break-up with Agnetha; and although he always said it was not exactly the story of their divorce because there were no winners in that situation, whenever she performed it she kept telling herself not to let her feelings take over while singing. After recording the vocals she cried buckets in the studio. Easily her best ever vocal performance. And she said it was a masterpiece, the best Abba song ever. But think about it, you've got the guy who wrote it about his divorce from the woman who's singing it. This song comes genuinely from the heart.

1 DANCING QUEEN

Wahey! This is their most well-known hit and my No.1. It came two years after Waterloo and it was originally called Boogaloo. **AD: I didn't know that.** It was typical Bjorn. He was always changing things, he was a perfectionist. It was released in Sweden in 1976, and in April 1977 Dancing Queen became Abba's first and only No.1 in the US. **AD: It's a great song.**

Look closely and you might spot Abba's mysterious fifth member

TOP FIVE @ 5 GERMAN SPORT STARS

We were talking about the Bundesliga the other day and it got us thinking... I am doing German footballers in my lifetime and Darren is chucking in some different sports. **DG: I've got two footballers. I played against one of them and kicked him up in the air so I've got to put him in.** Fair enough!

5 KLAUS FISCHER

This guy might not be too familiar to some of you of a certain age, but for me he was my favourite foreign player growing up. So this is a personal pick – it's Klaus Fischer. And this is where my O-Level German comes into play: he was known as Herr Fallrückzieher – that's Mr Bicycle Kick to you and me. He was the overhead kick specialist and scored one in a World Cup semi-final in 1982. There's even a video of him doing one in a photographic studio recently – at 69! **DG: Check it out online. He absolutely middled it, not off his shin like Rooney. He beat two keepers!** He scored 226 goals in 349 games for Schalke. Not too shabby! Arguably their greatest ever player. He got 32 goals in 45 games for West Germany as well. He was in a World Cup sticker album I had as a kid, and he was the first German player I got. I stuck him in there and he was the only one on that page for ages and I thought, "Right, he's my man."

5 BERNHARD LANGER

I'm starting off with someone from the world of golf: Bernhard Langer. He inspired the next generation of German golfers. He's a two-time Masters Champion and in 1986 he became the first official world number one. He turned pro in 1972. He's now over 60 and he's still dominant in the world of golf on the Senior Tour, having won 11 Senior Major Championships. It's ridiculous how he performs. When he was playing on the European Tour he had 42 wins, second of all time, and had three on the PGA. In terms of Ryder Cups, he played 10 as a player, with six wins; and he had one as a non-playing captain and, guess what, he won that as well!

4 LOTHAR MATTHÄUS

Do you remember that individual goal he scored against Yugoslavia in 1990? It was brilliant. He was captain of the German side that won the World Cup that year and European Footballer of the Year to boot! Then in 1991 he was the first ever FIFA World Player of the Year. He played for Borussia Mönchengladbach, Bayern Munich, Inter Milan, then back to Bayern. As well as winning the World Cup in 1990 he was a runner-up in '82 and '86. How about that for a CV? A total legend of German football... and I played against him at Upton Park and put a boot through him. Big-time. **AD: Jolly well done. That's the English way!** It was a proper tackle, halfway up his leg! He wasn't happy.

4 THOMAS MÜLLER

This is an interesting one because I'm not saying these are my Top Five best ever German players, they're just the ones I'm most intrigued by. Thomas Müller is always making and scoring goals but he looks awkward. He doesn't look like a footballer and his technique is severely lacking. But despite all that, he always seems to have a massive impact in creating and scoring goals. And you don't last at Bayern Munich if you're rubbish... but he is rubbish! He's the best 'rubbish' footballer there's ever been. And I love that about him. **DG: He is living the dream.** Yeah, absolutely. **DG: It looked like he was on his way out a couple of seasons ago but he's back in the groove now.** I'm not sure he'd agree but he really is the best 'rubbish' footballer there has ever been.

3 JÜRGEN KLINSMANN

He played in 108 matches for Germany and scored 47 goals. What about that for a record? Jürgen Klinsmann played in six major tournaments between Euro 88 and France 98 and he scored in every single one of them. He also won the UEFA Cup with Inter Milan. Played for Spurs twice, scoring 29 goals in 56 matches, and saved them relegation in 1998 before retiring. And of course, he won the World Cup and the Euros. What more do you want? He went on to manage Germany in 2004. He has also managed Bayern Munich and the US national team. **AD: Very impressive, you've got to say. He had such a massive impact on the Premier League when he was at Spurs.**

3 MESUT ÖZIL

Right, my number three is a bit controversial. **DG: How has he got in your top five?** It's not necessarily the best, it's not even about favourites really, it's all about the intrigue that surrounds Özil. And let's not forget how brilliant he used to be, because he really was one of the best players, one of the most talented players on the planet. And then he got 'Wengered' at Arsenal. One of the world's greatest when he joined Arsenal in 2013, but since then he's had only a handful of games where he's caught the eye... and even then, those were not against top-class opponents. Unai Emery saw through it, but Özil has outlasted him. He's turned into an enigma at best, although a more appropriate description is probably 'overpaid passenger'. He has given up international football but then he seems to have given up playing any football five years ago. And I'm being kind. It's such a shame because he was brilliant, wasn't he? **DG: Absolutely he was brilliant. Playing for Germany, everything went through him. He has had some good times at Arsenal but he's not been part of a great team.** He is in my Top Five for the enigma value. I just wonder what his legacy will be. He's almost in there for the comedy value.

Klinsmann gets caught in mid-dive

2 STEFFI GRAF

That match she played against Monica Seles in 1992 at Wimbledon, winning in two sets, was awesome considering Seles had beaten her on a few occasions. But the reason Steffi Graf is in my Top Five is that she set the standard for women's tennis moving into the future. She won 22 major titles in the Open era. She burst onto the scene at 17 years old and defeated Navratilova in the 1987 French Open final. She lost nine major finals too but she never complained. She was pure class. There were no excuses, no tantrums. As a teenager, in 1988, she swept the only calendar career Grand Slam – which included playing on hardcourt, clay and grass – and just to top it off she went and got the Olympic gold as well for good measure. What about that for a record? She was ranked number one in the world for 377 weeks! **AD: She was a secret crush of mine so I don't mind her being in your Top Five at all!**

2 GERD MüLLER

Are you all sitting down? Just listen carefully and try to stay calm as you listen to Gerd Müller's stats. He scored 68 goals in 62 games for Germany. He scored 565 goals in 607 games for Bayern Munich. He won four Bundesliga titles, three European Cups, a World Cup and the Euros. He scored three goals in those European Cup finals. He scored the winner in the World Cup final and two goals in the European Championship final. What is German for ridiculous? [*lächerlich, Ed*]. Thinking about it, he should be my number one...

1 MICHAEL SCHUMACHER

Seven-time World Champion and he didn't win these titles by simply having the fastest car. He did on two occasions, in 2002 and 2004 – there's no doubt whatsoever he had the fastest car for those – but the other victories came from the skill of the driver. Michael Schumacher enjoyed 91 race wins, 68 poll positions, 77 fastest laps, five consecutive titles between 2000 and 2004. He raced with the Jordan team, Benetton and Ferrari and then he made a comeback with Mercedes before Lewis Hamilton took that seat. That's why he's my number one. **AD: Can't argue with that, but here's mine...**

1 FRANZ BECKENBAUER

A Bayern Munich legend is my number one: Franz Beckenbauer. He won everything with them, then after helping boost North American soccer with the New York Cosmos he won the title with Hamburg back in Germany. As a player he led West Germany to World Cup and Euros wins in the 1970s. He won two Ballons d'Or! Not one but two! As a manager he won the World Cup with Germany, the Bundesliga with Bayern and a French title to throw in there at Marseille. You can't ignore him.

This guy's in love with Schu (not literally)

TOP FIVE @ 5 SCOTTISH FOOTBALLERS

Our lists were very similar here so, in order to make it a little bit quirkier and to avoid duplication, I've tweaked mine. My Top Five are Scottish players who have played most of their football this century, and Darren's are players he's seen play in the flesh and from a slightly earlier period. Got that? Good. I'll go first...

5 KENNY MILLER

I saw the goal he scored against England at Wembley in 2013; I was at the game. It was an absolute stunner and I was thinking I didn't know Kenny Miller had that in him. But actually, when you look back, he had a hell of a career. He was with Rangers and Celtic, he won titles with both. Won promotion with Wolves and scored a winner against Man United when Man United were good. He was not always a prolific goalscorer in that he didn't bang in double figures every season but he always gave 100% – and while he didn't quite establish himself in the Premier League he certainly was a top second-tier football player in terms of the English game. **DG: I think his best years were in Scotland but a fantastic player.**

3 JACKIE McNAMARA

In his Celtic heyday he was a joy to watch – he played with a culture and a grace possessed by very few. It was just the way he caressed the ball. But at the same time, Jackie McNamara could also defend and could play anywhere across the backline. He could attack, defend... and he could play. **DG: Another who played most of his football in Scotland, he came down here with Wolves but it didn't really work out. That said, I am surprised he didn't play for Scotland more than 33 times.** I agree, but the managers at the time often preferred English players who qualified [*to play for Scotland*] somehow. He won four titles with Celtic, and three Scottish Cups as well, and was a UEFA Cup runner-up. So he had to be in there.

4 STUART ARMSTRONG

Some people might be surprised he's in there... but not if you've watched him play on a regular basis. He scored a cracking header for Scotland against Lithuania in 2017. A super-talented footballer who made it in the Scottish top division and one of not many to come to the English Premier League who, without being spectacular, has held his own. Gordon Strachan always raves about Stuart Armstrong so I took the time to watch a lot of footage from his time in Scotland and down here, and he's right. What he needs to do now is put together consistent high-level performances for Southampton to showcase the talent he has clearly got. **DG: He's at a good club, but I think he needs to show what he can do for a top-six side before he can be talked about in the most glowing terms.**

2 BARRY FERGUSON

Leader, warrior and winner. Five titles with Rangers, five Scottish Cups, five Scottish League Cups and a League Cup with Birmingham City. I think we can say that he managed to establish himself as a quality Premier League player. **DG: I agree. He was also outstanding at Rangers and they saw the very best of him, so much so they signed him twice. I'm not surprised he's so high up.** The only surprise for some people, really, will be that he's not my number one...

1 ANDY ROBERTSON

There can't be any real argument about who is the best Scottish player to have played most of his football this century. Andy Robertson has won a league title with Liverpool and the Champions League – how many other Scottish players would get into that Liverpool side? Well, no other Scottish player would get anywhere near that side. **DG: It's true, but not only has he played in an unbelievable team, he's shone in an unbelievable team. He deserves all the plaudits.**

That's my Top Five, now here are Goughie's... and they are the best Scottish players he has actually seen play live. **DG: I saw three of my five play in the same match, on 19 January 1982 – Barnsley 1 Liverpool 3 in a League Cup quarter-final replay – so that gives you some idea of the era when most of these guys were playing...**

5 ALAN HANSEN

This is my first one from that game – and if you want to talk about a footballer who can play out from the back, you have to talk about Alan Hansen. He signed for Liverpool from Partick Thistle for just £100,000, played over 600 games for Liverpool and won too many trophies to list. As captain he led them to their first double in 1986; but in terms of how he played the game, he was solid in the tackle and read the game superbly. He was so skilful for a centre-half that I believe if were playing now he would be in the Premier League at the highest level. **AD: The amazing thing about that was that he and Mark Lawrenson sometimes played together at centre-half and both were so calm and serene – there was no John Terry type throwing himself at everything, and it kind of set the tone for just how brilliant that Liverpool team was.**

4 GORDON STRACHAN

My number four started at Dundee but had huge success with Aberdeen under Alex Ferguson. He won two League titles, three Scottish Cups and a European Cup-Winners' Cup. Then he went to Manchester United and played for a few seasons when they were in that rebuilding phase. I think he only won the 1985 FA Cup with them, but then he went to Leeds and as an older player there he was absolutely outstanding and was the Football Writers' Footballer of the Year in 1991, the first player to win it in both England and Scotland. The next year he was the heartbeat of the team that won the title. I used to love watching him play.

3 GARY McALLISTER

This guy, of course, used to play next to Strachan. I've got huge admiration for him and have spoken about him many times on talkSPORT. It's Gary McAllister and I think he's massively underrated. I bit like Strachan, he just got better with age. I know he had a successful time at Leicester, and of course Leeds, but he was getting on when he got to Liverpool and yet became such an important player for them. He got 57 Scotland caps but should have had lots more. He was such a set-piece threat and then there was his passing. He was the original satnav for me, what a footballing brain! He controlled matches and there are not many players able to do that. **AD: You're right. Again, such a cultured player and another who carried on playing at an incredible standard until late in his career.**

1 KENNY DALGLISH

This won't be a shock to anybody. Kenny Dalglish. I don't really have to say anything, do I? He won trophy after trophy after trophy. A record 102 caps for his country... Players' and Writers' Footballer of the Year awards, Ballon d'Or silver in 1983. Extraordinary skill, technique and football intelligence, and I used to love watching him play. Even when I was watching Liverpool against Barnsley as a kid I was admiring him on the other side. And he was brilliant at Celtic before he even got to Liverpool. **AD: I might have put Souness number one and Dalglish two but there's nothing in it.**

Dalglish: more popular than a deep-fried can of Irn-Bru

2 GRAEME SOUNESS

A proper hard boy and another player I saw against Barnsley in 1982, I think he'll have probably been captain. Graeme Souness started at Spurs but didn't play a full game with them. They sent him out on loan before he went to Middlesbrough. After that he went to Liverpool where he played 247 matches, winning three European Cups, five League titles and four League Cups. Incredible. And not to forget 54 Scotland caps. This was down to his passing, vision, strength, technical ability... and the tough tackling for which he was famous. More importantly, though, he was a leader. **AD: He had the lot, Graeme Souness. Let me tell you something else about him. I had a coffee with him a few months ago and we chatted about life, sport, politics, history and football. It was an engrossing few hours. He is a lovely bloke, very misunderstood.** I tell you what, though – I wouldn't like to get on the wrong side of him. I played golf with him a few years back, I was in the same four-ball, and boy did he take it seriously. The only reason he's not number one is because of this man...

TOP FIVE @ 5 COMEDY FILMS

The Top Five comedy films: what could possibly go wrong? **DG: I went for films that really make me laugh, but that doesn't mean it's a really great film.** It's all down to personal choice and the mood you're in. We might do this again tomorrow and choose five different ones...

5 AIRPLANE!

This 1980 spoof of the airborne disaster movies is my number five. **DG: This would have been in mine if we hadn't shared them out. I love it. I watched it four times in eight days once. It's the one-liners that make it for me.** So much of the humour is visual but Otto the inflatable pilot steals the show. **DG: And Leslie Nielsen. He's brilliant.** Yes, he is. A genuine talent.

5 ELF

Some people might think this is a strange one. I'm not a massive fan of Will Ferrell but he is absolutely superb in Elf. He plays Buddy, a human raised at the North Pole by Santa and his real elves. It's the first film on the Christmas film list for me – it's one the whole family can sit down and watch together. One of the funniest scenes is when he's on the mailroom table, and he's drunk but he doesn't realise he's drunk. He's still a little kid in an adult's body, really. It's just fantastic humour. **AD: Never seen it, mate.** Seriously?

4 THE MEANING OF LIFE

Monty Python wasn't always my favourite TV show but I liked the films: The Life Of Brian, The Holy Grail and this one. When I first watched The Meaning Of Life, it was on an old VHS and I'm not kidding you but when I first saw the Mr Creosote scene I would rewind it over and over again, watching it time after time, and I used to laugh so much I could barely breathe. It was so funny. **DG: I've not seen it.** There are other scenes that are probably inappropriate for this but that scene clinched it for me.

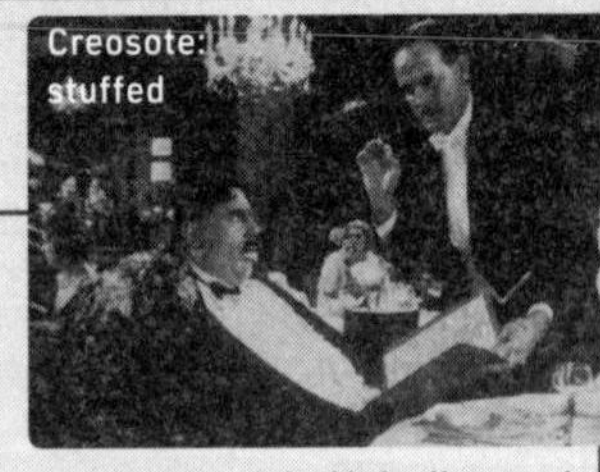

Creosote: stuffed

4 MRS DOUBTFIRE

The genius that was Robin Williams. He plays a struggling actor and a divorced dad in Mrs Doubtfire. It's quite sad and there is a serious message, but there's pure comedy all the way through it. He's divorced but he wants to stay in contact with his kids so he dresses up as an older Scottish woman and gets hired by his ex-wife as their nanny. It's barmy and it's silly. It made $440 million worldwide. A huge film and hilarious. **AD: I have seen that! All the ingredients for a funny movie are right in there.**

3 CLOCKWISE

John Cleese plays a headmaster obsessed with timekeeping. Things go spectacularly wrong when he finds himself abducting a pupil and robbing a petrol station. It's a really funny film. I went to the cinema on my own to see this as nobody wanted to see it , but it remains one of my favourite films of all time. Love it. **DG: I know loads of people love it but the Monty Python stuff is not really for me.** It's more Fawlty Towers than Python, to be fair.

3 TED

It's Christmas morning and John wishes his teddy bear could walk and talk. And it happens: Ted becomes his best friend for life. Even when he's in his 30s, working and smoking weed, Ted is still there. He gets in between John and his girlfriend and she puts him under pressure to leave the teddy bear. Mark Wahlberg is brilliant in this. **AD: I went to the cinema to see it and really wanted to enjoy it, but I found the best bits had already been used in the trailer so I was a bit underwhelmed.**

2 THE MASK

The special effects to turn Jim Carrey into a cartoon are brilliant. And he is brilliant. One of the funniest scenes is when he's surrounded by police with lights on him and he turns it into a theatre show. He starts dancing and the police join in. Jim Carrey – you either love him or hate him, and I am definitely in the love camp. Hilarious. **AD: I'm firmly in the other camp. I can't stand The Mask.**

2 TRADING PLACES

Let's get back to the comedy with my number two – it's Trading Places. I don't need to say much about this because at that particular time Eddie Murphy was at his peak and at his funniest. It's a sensational film, really. It is based on a Mark Twain book, The Prince And The Pauper, and it's great. **DG: I'm with you, love it.**

1 THE HANGOVER

The film is about four guys who go on a stag do to Vegas. And do they party? It all goes horribly wrong. They wake up in a hotel room wrecked. The groom is missing, there's a tiger in the bathroom and Mike Tyson even turns up, but they have no memory of what happened. Great humour throughout but, because of this film, everybody is scared to death to tell their other halves that they've been invited to a stag do in Vegas!

1 BEVERLY HILLS COP

This is just the funniest film: Eddie Murphy as Axel Foley, a fast-talking maverick Detroit cop at large in Beverly Hills. Total genius. Beverly Hills Cop is the film that made him an international superstar. I must have seen it about 20 or 30 times. Had to be my number one.

Foley: chuffed

TOP FIVE @ 5 BEACHES

We actually agonised over this for quite a long time and whether we should do it or not. Is it cruel? Or could it lift the spirits? OK, so we're just going to take people on a virtual holiday here. We're just trying to evoke some nice images in people's minds...

5 GODAHL BEACH (St Vincent And The Grenadines)

I was going to start with a beach in Australia. I'm not, but let me just give you this one example: Scarborough Beach. It's like an amphitheatre and we played beach cricket there, which was amazing – but that wouldn't have got a vote for the beach itself, it was just beach cricket, so I'm not going to go for that. Instead I'm going to go for somewhere I once went on holiday. In fact I went there twice – it was fantastic. It's called Godahl Beach and it's on Canouan Island, in St Vincent And The Grenadines. It's half a mile of white sand. It's heaven, and the reason I remember this is that my kids were a lot younger and it was the season when baby turtles were going into the water. Most of them don't make it, they don't survive because the birds come down and grab them, but all the families on the beach were picking up these little things and carrying them to the water and watching them swim off. It was absolutely amazing. It's only a small island, maybe five miles across, and it was hatching season and I'll never forget it. Some of Pirates Of The Caribbean was filmed there too so it gets lots of tourists.

The first World Surfing Championship was held at Manly Beach in 1964

5 MANLY BEACH (Australia)

You mentioned the beaches in Australia and my number five is one. I've only ever been to Sydney and Melbourne and never visited the Gold Coast, so this is Sydney-based. Coogee Beach is OK; I think Bondi is pretty terrible and can't see the attraction, unless you're a surf dude. **DG: I didn't like either of them.** The one that did it for me was Manly Beach, which is north of Sydney. It's where you can relax, you can have fun. And I've got a memory there with me and my boy – he must have been about 12 or 13. We went on a family holiday to Oz and we were playing football on Manly Beach. I've got a beautiful picture of him silhouetted with the sea behind him, Manly Beach there, sand being kicked up as he kicks the ball... it just brings back so many memories and it was just a lovely, lovely place. Everything was calm, just a really friendly, lovely place where you could relax and have yourself a load of fun. **DG: I've been there as well. There are a lot of good ones in Australia and I could have chosen a few of them, but I didn't go for any in Australia. I just couldn't do it.**

4 COPACABANA (Brazil)

Let's move on. Guess what I picked? It's called Copacabana. But the song isn't about the beach in Rio, it's about a bar in New York. And the clues are in the lyrics. Not a lot of people realise this, but if you look at the lyrics to the Barry Manilow song he talks about the hottest spot north of Havana. There's no way the Copacabana in Rio is north of Havana! So you do a bit of research on the song, and you find out that Barry was in Rio de Janeiro and he asked somebody if there had ever been a song about the Copacabana because he thought it was such a great word. And there hadn't. So he got together with his two other songwriters, Jack Feldman and Bruce Sussman, and they came up with a song called Copacabana... but it's really about a nightclub in New York City that Barry used to go to. So there you go – this is a real education, isn't it? But actually Copacabana, the beach in Rio, isn't that great. It's probably not the nicest beach in Rio. Ipanema is nicer... and there's also Leblon, just further up, which is almost certainly nicer. But it's the character of the Copacabana. It's iconic. It's where we spent most of our time in Rio during the World Cup in 2014. The waves! I love to do a bit of wave-jumping, but wow, the waves are ferocious on the Copacabana. The sand is golden, the sky when it's stormy can be absolutely dramatic. I've got a magnificent picture of the sky during a storm off the coast from the beach. I love it. The sky looks like it's so angry and about to explode on the earth.

4 WEST WITTERING (Sussex)

Yes, you might say where is that? It's in West Sussex and it's absolutely stunning. It's probably better to visit in the winter, when it's colder – you can take the dogs on there. It goes on forever. It's clean and it's safe but it does get really busy in the summer, and that's why I'm saying the winter is the perfect time to go. Photogenic from start to finish. I went there about four weeks ago and it was a stunning day, I fell in love with the place. That's a place I could live, somewhere near that beach.

3 GREAT BAY (Scilly Isles)

For number three I've gone for one on the Scilly Isles. Over there you've got so many to choose from. There's Samson, Tresco, St Agnes... but the best beach there is called Great Bay. I go out with my backpack, a packed lunch, a couple of bottles of champagne, the dog and my wife, and we walk for about two and a half hours along the coast, all through the sand dunes, then come back out, sit on the beach and have a picnic. The temperature of the sea is warmer than you'd think and the waters are really calm.

Godahl Beach: it's OK but it's not Norfolk

3 BAMBURGH (Northumberland)

This one is in Northumberland and I first went there for my 21st birthday. It was a beautiful day in the middle of May. Beautiful sand and Bamburgh Castle in the background absolutely makes it. It's unspoiled and untouched, and even on a brilliant summer's day it's never jam-packed. It's like stepping back in time.

2 HOLME BEACH (Norfolk)

It's a lovely little drive to get to this one, actually. And once you get there it's fantastic place to holiday. Not many people know about Holme Beach. There are bigger and more well-known beaches so it's pretty quiet all the time. To the left is the old white lighthouse of Hunstanton and the colourful cliffs. You've got the Nature Reserve right by you. It's very dog-friendly, in common with all the beaches I like. And I'll tell you why it's special: my wife actually proposed to me there a second time. **AD: Shut up! Really? I didn't know that. That's amazing.** I go on a yearly basis, I'd recommend it.

2 ROSSCARBERY (Ireland)

As you know, I absolutely love Ireland. I absolutely love every single part of it. And I'm told there are better beaches in Ireland but this is the one I know and I love it. It's at the far south-west tip, next stop America, and I love it. It's peaceful, it's beautiful. I'd describe it as a small slice of heaven.

1 DURDLE DOOR AND LULWORTH COVE (Dorset)

I'll go first with my top choice. The Jurassic Coast stretches from Exmouth in Devon to Studland Bay in Dorset. You'll recognise this bit from the picture: it's a big rocky archway, it's world-famous and it's something to behold, absolutely breathtaking. I had one of the best days of my life there, swimming in the sea with my daughter years ago. I've both swum through and kayaked through Durdle Door and not many people can say that. **DG: Is that where they got Dumbledore from?** Probably not.

1 BOULDERS BEACH (South Africa)

I was going to go large and say Maundays Bay in Anguilla but instead I'm going to go for something that's slightly off-centre: Boulders Beach in Cape Town. It's a penguin colony. Yeah, I mean, the penguins made it their home in 1982. I first went there in 1991. There weren't that many penguins there – the odd one would pop past, but now it's the opposite. It's a very protected area for penguins and you have to pay an entrance fee to get in. There are 3,000-plus penguins there now. You can swim in the sea and sometimes the penguins will go and swim with you but the scenery is incredible, as anybody who has been to Cape Town would tell you. You have to take a clothes peg for your nose but it's definitely worth the visit.

Durdle Door: not a wizard

TOP FIVE @ 5 SPORTING CELEBRATIONS

I'm loving this one. There are so many different sporting celebrations – funny ones, emotional ones, impromptu and well-choreographed ones – and they happen across all sports. This is another list that could be totally different on another day but, today, these are our Top Fives...

5 MONTY PANESAR

Do you remember this guy leaping around and high-fiving everybody in mid-air whenever he took a wicket? I absolutely loved it. It gave cricket a real energy, something different, a fresh enthusiasm that I thought was magnificent. He made wicket celebrations look like goal celebrations. It was his genuine excitement. And it also made people love Monty Panesar. **DG: Left-hand spin bowlers have always got a bit of a mad side to them. Fantastic.**

The Beard Liberation Front named Panesar as winner of "Beard of the Year" in 2006

4 THE SOUTH AFRICAN CROWD, 2010 WORLD CUP

We've talked about this goal before, but the celebration after Tshabalala scored the opening goal in the World Cup 2010 for South Africa was something else – and we were there. The whole stadium erupted as a local lad from Soweto scored their first ever World Cup goal. All the players ran towards the fans and did the Macarena in the corner. The noise in the stadium was electric. And it was a magic moment for everyone who was there, whether you were a South African fan or not. **AD: The whole thing was choreographed and wonderful.**

5 MIKE IACONELLI

I have put this American guy in but I'm sure nobody's ever heard of him. His name is Mike Iaconelli and he is absolutely bonkers. He is a professional fisherman and you can find this on YouTube. He is sitting on a boat and has been waiting and waiting for this one fish, and when he finally catches it he's an emotional wreck. He's lying on his back holding the fish in the air screaming, "Never give up, never give up, never give up!" It wasn't even a big fish! It was a tiddler. You've got to watch it!

4 JÜRGEN KLINSMANN

The Premier League was in its infancy when this guy turned up for the 1994-'95 season. There was a lot of criticism when Klinsmann signed for Tottenham, a lot of talk about how he was a diver and a cheat and how referees needed to be aware of this. And so when he buried a brilliant header against Sheffield Wednesday, he celebrated by launching into this massive dive onto the floor. Brilliant. Everybody was laughing, it was a superb celebration. **DG: That's right up there, a beauty that most people will remember.**

3 STJARNAN FC

This team have become sporting celebration legends. It's an Icelandic football team called Stjarnan and their routines almost always go viral. They did a human bike, a baby's birth and ballroom dancing, but the best one is the 'big catch photo' salmon celebration. It's been copied countless times but they were doing it back in 2010 when Halldor Orri Bjornsson dinked a brilliant little penalty over the keeper. All the Stjarnan players run after him, he casts his line out, catches one of these teammates who pretends to be a salmon and flip-flaps all the way towards him, and then the team all hold the 'fish' up and one of his teammates pretends to be the photographer to take the picture. It has been copied so many times but this is where it started! **AD: I remember it at the time, although I didn't realise it was that long ago. The guy on the ground who is the salmon gets it spot-on.** He's a genius at it, mate, he's a brilliant fish.

3 JIMMY BULLARD

My number three took place in November 2009 but you have to go back almost a year to Boxing Day 2008 for the full story. Hull were at Man City, losing 4-0 at half-time. They were being thrashed. So Phil Brown, the manager, kept them on the pitch and had the team-talk in the penalty area with the players sitting down in a circle while he's standing in the middle telling them off in front of their own fans. Fast-forward a few months and Bullard scores a late equaliser at Man City from the spot – he instructs all his teammates to sit down in the same circle as before and pretends to be Phil Brown, wagging his finger at the players one by one. Now, there's a couple of things here. First of all Jimmy Bullard wasn't even at Hull when Phil Brown did the infamous team-talk and wouldn't have stayed around to be mugged off like that; plus he claims the follow-up wasn't his idea – but it is exactly the kind of thing he would do. **DG: I know people who've played with him and they say you can't switch off for a minute when he's around, he's easily bored.**

2 EMMANUEL ADEBAYOR

This was also at Man City. The background to this celebration is that in the summer of 2009 Adebayor left Arsenal for City, blaming the bad relationship he had with the Arsenal fans for the move. A month into the season and Arsenal go to Man City. Adebayor has 25 on his back because he cost £25 million and he is booed by the away fans with every touch. He could have been sent off for a foul on Fabregas and should have been sent off for a foul on Van Persie. When he headed home a Shaun Wright-Phillips cross, he charged up the other end of the pitch to celebrate in front of the Gooners. He slid on his knees with his arms out, staring at them as if to say, "What have you got, then?" Those fans were chucking all sorts at him. If you watch it back, one of the fans looks like he's trying to get on the pitch and the stewards are holding him back. Those Arsenal fans are absolutely raging. **DG: The emotion got to him. It was a proper sprint from one end to the other. No one could catch him!**

2 ERIC CANTONA

If you missed it at the time, you might know this celebration from playing FIFA. My number two followed Eric Cantona's goal for Man United against Sunderland in 1996, in his comeback season after the ban for the kung-fu kick on a fan. The goal itself was magnificent. He started the move, sprinted 25 yards, got the one-two and then chipped the keeper. They call the celebration peacocking. He slowly rotated on the spot before raising his arms for the teammates to come and jump all over him. It is pure arrogance. But it's one of the best, most simple celebrations you'll see.

ic plays it cool

1 SHELDON COTTRELL

Every time I see this it makes me laugh. I could have chosen loads of different examples involving the West Indies cricket team because they are the best at these celebrations, proper show ponies. Sheldon Cottrell works for the Jamaican Defence Force. That's his job, it's relevant here. He plays a little bit of cricket and has got pretty good at it over the last few years with his performances in World Cups and the Indian Premier League. He's a left-hand fast bowler. So, when he gets someone out, he goes on a proper march down the wicket to the middle, stands to attention and then salutes to the side of his head, a proper salute, as a mark of respect to his colleagues in the forces. I love it on all fronts. **AD: That's a really good number one. Here's mine...**

1 MARCO TARDELLI

There are 69 minutes gone in the 1982 World Cup final. Star of the tournament Paolo Rossi has put Italy one up against the favourites, West Germany, when the ball falls to Marco Tardelli. He fires home that second goal, the killer goal. That seals it, surely. In that moment he realises the game is won – he's won the World Cup and he's scored in a Word Cup final. He sets off on his celebration running anywhere, no real direction, no real destiny. His fists are clenched, arms low and out wide, his face contorted with emotion and passion. It absolutely is the celebration of a man for whom the goal, the World Cup and his country mean absolutely everything in that one moment. Whenever people pretend that football doesn't matter, I have this image of Marco Tardelli in my head and I know that these people are wrong. Pure passion and emotion right there.

Marco Tardelli was the Republic of Ireland assistant coach between 2008-2013

Marco plays it a bit less cool

TOP FIVE @ 5 SONGS OF THE '90S

This one was much trickier than you might think. **DG: I had a couple of nailed-on certs until I double-checked and found that they came out in 1989 so that threw me.** I know, time flies and your mind plays tricks. Let's get on with it before we forget where we are...

5 LOSER (Beck)

It got to number 15 in the UK charts but is in here at five on my list. It's a personal favourite of mine. When I was at music radio they used to chuck the CDs they didn't expect to play in the bin, but I rescued this one and it's an absolute banger, one of the best freebies I've ever picked up. In the chorus he sings "soy un perdedor", which is "I am a loser" in Spanish. And he is saying he is sorry because he can't rap properly and he's a loser. It's the song Nirvana wished they'd done.

5 BITTER SWEET SYMPHONY (The Verve)

It might shock you that I've gone for this one because it's more the kind of music you like, but it's just a great song. There was controversy surrounding it for years because it was based on a sample from an orchestral cover of a Rolling Stones number, but I think it was resolved recently when Mick Jagger and Keith Richards let Richard Ashcroft, the lead singer of the Verve who wrote it, keep the future royalties. It was No.2 in the UK in June 1997. **AD: Did it not get to No.1?** No – it stayed in the charts for three months, though, and then they released it in the US and it got to No.12 so the royalties would have been a big deal. **AD: I remember the video where Ashcroft is bulldozing through everybody on the pavement. They used it on TV for England games, I think they still do... and although it's a great, great song, I got sick and tired of listening to it at one point.**

4 OCEAN DRIVE (The Lighthouse Family)

This is more my style, easy listening. **AD: You're not wrong. I almost dropped off.** The Lighthouse Family with Ocean Drive... I could have gone with High or Lifted by the same band, similar beat, similar tunes, but I went for this one. **AD: But they're all the same song!** You can just sit in your car with the top down and... **AD: Fall asleep?** ...blast it out. People think it's named for somewhere exotic but it's actually named after the drive from Roker Pier in Sunderland to Ocean Road in South Shields. **AD: Nice stretch of coast, but I'd have been thinking about an ocean drive in California.** That's what I'm saying. It's been released twice. The first time it got to No.34 in the UK charts. The second time they released it with slightly different vocals and it reached No.11. **AD: I am not saying it's a bad song, it's very '90s, but it doesn't challenge you. It's too easy listening for me.**

4 RETURN OF THE MACK (Mark Morrison)

This is a nightclub banger. My number four comes from a time I was clinging on to my nightclub days and this was a song that got you on the dancefloor. Mark Morrison with Return Of The Mack. **DG: Is this the one where one of the guy's bodyguards gave you a clip?** It is, but it didn't stop me loving it. I was at an event with Mark Morrison and he had two minders. I went up to him to thrust a microphone in his face and one of these minders just brushed me out the way with his forearm and sent me flying! **DG: You should have put a claim in, mate. It could have been life-changing!** It was No.1 for two weeks in 1996 but he didn't really follow it up. And do you know where he is from? He's from Leicester!

3 ALL TOGETHER NOW (The Farm)

This was 1990 so just sneaks in, timewise. It had to be in, All Together Now by the Farm. Great lyrics from Peter Hooton. Just study the words. We played it on the station for the anniversary of Hillsborough but this is a timeless classic, it'll stay fresh forever. Hooton's a massive Liverpool fan but I've got a feeling that Everton took this on for a cup final. The video is perfect and the album is brilliant as well – Groovy Train was on there.

3 BROKEN STONES (Paul Weller)

This going to be another surprise for you. What a tune. It was Mark Butcher who really got me into this song by Paul Weller. He played it all the time. I said to him, "Who sings this?" And he said, "Are you joking? It's Paul Weller." And I said, "Who's he?" **AD: You've got to be kidding me.** I was kidding! Mark would play it on his guitar and sing along and he was unbelievable. I listened to it all the time on tours, especially the Australian Tour. It only got to No.20 in the UK charts in the autumn of 1995. It has a simple message, really: whatever is broken in life is there for the fixing. **AD: Chillout songs for you here...** In the 1990s I needed to be chilled out and that kind of reflects the songs I was listening to. I was at my peak in professional sport then, and I used to get so wound up that I needed to listen to chilled-out stuff on my way to the ground. A lot of sportspeople listen to upbeat songs like the Rocky theme tune; I was the opposite. I needed songs that would calm me down because I was already there – the water was flowing out of the top of the bottle.

Weller: that's entertainment, sort of

2 **ANGELS (Robbie Williams)**

You wanted this for your Top Five but I bagged it. It's Robbie Williams and Angels, from 1997. It's become his signature song and it was the one that really put him on the map after he split from Take That. He went on his own and got to No.2 with a cover of George Michael's Freedom, and again with Old Before I Die... and then he started to fade. Angels was the fourth single off his first album and absolutely made him the biggest pop star in the late 1990s and early 2000s. In 2005 the Brit Awards voted this song the best song of the past 25 years – but it only reached No.4. **AD: What?** Even worse, in the US it only made No.53 **AD: What? I can't believe it didn't make No.1.**

Angels by Robbie Williams was kept off the No. 1 spot by three other releases including Teletubbies Say 'Eh-Oh', which went straight in at No. 1 on December 7th 1997. Angels entered the chart at No. 7.

2 **THE LIFE OF RILEY (The Lightning Seeds)**

This might be better-known as the music they used to play on Match Of The Day behind the Goal Of The Month montage, but it's actually Life Of Riley. Now this is from an album called Sense by The Lightning Seeds, who went on to do Three Lions with Baddiel and Skinner; it was on my turntable non-stop in the mid-1990s. The single only got to No.28 but I don't care if people didn't buy it because I love it – I didn't buy it because I had the album. This is one of those songs that everybody knows but they might not be aware who it's by. You can't not like that.

1 **IT'S LIKE THAT (Run-DMC vs Jason Nevins)**

In 1998 this was six weeks at No.1 and the third-biggest-selling single of the year. The video is a classic, a girls-v-boys breakdance-off in a multistorey car park in LA. Of course. Nevins is in the video at the start with the yellow-tinted glasses. It's my No.1 because it stopped the Spice Girls from extending their run at the top with Stop. It is one of the all- time great hip-hop songs. And you have to tap your feet at the very least, with the trainers with no laces. Everybody of a certain age knows what I'm talking about. You didn't see that coming, did you? **DG: No, not at all!**

Run-DMC: only did it to annoy the Spice Girls

1 **CHAMPAGNE SUPERNOVA (Oasis)**

Honourable mentions to Pulp's Common People, Puff Daddy's I'll Be Missing You and Blur's Parklife, but my number one is a belter. It's Champagne Supernova. This is also my number one Oasis song. Paul Weller is on guitar and he's a backing vocalist on this song. It was released in 1996 and it goes on forever; it's easy listening with a rock edge.

TOP FIVE @ 5 SPORTING DYNASTIES

We had a phenomenal response when we tweeted out that we were going to be discussing this. You and I weren't so sure when the producer first suggested it but it was a really good idea and I've enjoyed compiling it. **DG: Yep, it's a great topic, this one...**

5 CHICAGO BULLS (1991 to 1998)

Jordan: the Rory Delap of the NBA

How these guys dominated their sport. I had to have them in after watching The Last Dance. You can only say they were absolutely brilliant under coach Phil Jackson and the star player, of course, Michael Jordan, who led the Bulls in 1991 to 1994 and then 1995 to 1998. None of those finals went seven games [*it's best of seven*]; they only lost 25 games in those six years. Look at some of the players they had on there. Scottie Pippen was there throughout. Horace Grant was there for the first period, Dennis Rodman for that second run... and Steve Kerr, who kind of epitomises what Michael Jordan can do to a player. They say Steve Kerr is not the most talented, that he didn't stand out among these other pros, but Jordan turned him into an absolute beaut. **AD: I think for a documentary to come out more than 20 years later and go viral says it all about that particular dynasty. It's also worth noting that Steve Kerr has gone on to coach Golden State Warriors, who have been dominant in the NBA in recent years.**

5 WIGAN RUGBY LEAGUE FC (late 1980s to early 1990s)

Not my team but certainly my number five. In the Challenge Cup, Wigan were dominant from the late 1980s into the '90s. They were unstoppable. They won the cup at Wembley eight years running and the list of players who were part of that is a who's-who of rugby league: Ellery Hanley, Henderson Gill, Shaun Edwards who won them all, Joe Lydon, Denis Betts, Jason Robinson, Martin Offiah, Andy Farrell and many more. So from 1988 to 1995 they dominated one of the most prestigious and historic competitions in sport. John Monie won four of those cups but the players did it with different coaches. Imagine getting to all those finals and winning them all!

4 YORKSHIRE CCC (1959 to 1968)

I had to have this in. I had the success of Yorkshire from this period rammed down my throat from when I joined in 1988. But, looking back, they deserve the praise. They won seven County Championship titles in that period. They had Brian Close, Fred Trueman and Ray Illingworth, who we all know through their England performances. Six of the seven titles were won on the last day of the season. Talk about pressure and being able to get over the line! **AD: How can you top that?** I found it a bit intimidating when I went there – that sense of expectancy is not always a good thing. It was only when we moved some of the older photographs that we started to win things again.

4 WALES RUGBY UNION (1970s)

This Welsh team were utterly sensational in the 1970s: Gareth Edwards orchestrating everything, dictating the match, the tempo, the excitement and the entertainment from scrum-half. He was probably the greatest Welsh player ever. Then you had the finesse of Barry John and Phil Bennett and Gerald Davies on the wing with JPR Williams setting the standard at fullback. From 1969 to 1979 Wales either won outright or shared eight Six Nations, as it's known today, and that included three Grand Slams and six Triple Crowns. The Rugby World Cup only started in 1987, believe it or not – if it had started 20 years earlier Wales would have dominated it and England would be in their box. **DG: Can't argue with that.**

3 LEEDS UNITED (1968 to 1974)

Don Revie became Leeds boss in 1961. They were a nothing club in the second tier, doing nothing and going nowhere. But between 1968 and 1974 Leeds won the title twice, the Fairs Cup twice, the FA Cup and the League Cup. They dominated. They were unrivalled – others won titles in that time but none had come from where they came from or gone to where they got to in such a short space of time. And the thing about Leeds under Revie was that they were so full of character, quality and controversy, they still get talked about now. So I think they're one of the great football dynasties. **DG: Some fabulous footballers – and a manager who stood up to Brian Clough and made him think, "Hang on, I've got some serious competition here."** More Yorkshire glory for you!

3 FERRARI F1 (2000 to 2004)

Michael Schumacher was their main man, and between 2000 and 2004 he partnered Rubens Barrichello – who was the perfect partner for him because, while a good racer himself, he was never going to win the title. Schumacher went there in 1996 and it took a while for him to get going. But once he got going in that Ferrari, dear me! In those five years they won all 10 championships available. In 2002 Ferrari won 15 of the 17 races, and in 2004 they had 13 wins for Schumacher – 12 wins in the first 13 races. But other than that it was a real battle – they didn't always have the fastest car and it wasn't a cakewalk. **AD: I love this. You've gone from Chicago to Yorkshire to Italy. I wonder where you're going to take us next?**

Schumacher with Barrichello and Ferrari boss Jean Todt at the launch of his new cap

2 BARCELONA (2008 to 2012)

I'm taking you to Spain for my number two: I'm going for Barcelona under Pep Guardiola. From 2008 to 2012 he presided over amazing success at the Nou Camp. And let's bear in mind that they hadn't won anything for two years when he took over, even though a young Messi had been playing regularly. Pep won three titles, two Champions Leagues and two Copas del Rey. He imposed a style that got the best out of Messi and he got the best out of the other players as well. Arguably the greatest club side in this period. They were irresistible, a joy to watch: a standard was set, a blueprint for how Barcelona should play the game. And listen, they had sensational players but it was a special and successful time when Pep was there. **DG: Absolutely, and they still get talked about.**

1 LIVERPOOL (1970s and 1980s)

Bill Shankly started it, Bob Paisley continued it, and Liverpool dominated at home and abroad in that period. They were untouchable: nine titles in 12 years, four European Cups between 1977 and 1984. In the late 1980s they played the kind of football Barcelona later played and they were breathtaking. There was Barnes, Houghton, Beardsley, Hansen, Rush... and they could all play football. And it lasted a long time, that's the key. Nobody matched the sustained success or quality of Liverpool. **DG: I thought the Sir Alex team shaded it, but only because it was all done with one manager.** That Liverpool team is the one that resonates with me because they were solid and spectacular when I was growing up.

2 MANCHESTER UNITED (1990s to 2013)

I've picked football as my number two as well, but a bit closer to home. When Sir Alex Ferguson arrived at Manchester United he was under pressure at times in the beginning; but what he did there eventually, with the trophies he delivered over a sustained period, was absolutely ridiculous. The highlight was 1999, obviously, and the Treble – and Sir Alex got his knighthood too. They went on to be World Club Champions in 2008. He claimed four League Cups, five FA Cups, two Champions League titles and 13 Premier League titles. I almost lost count, there are that many honours! That's the dominance he had.

1 WEST INDIES (late 1970s to early 1990s)

From the late 1970s, throughout the '80s and into the early '90s, they were an unbelievable team. I watched the Fire In Babylon documentary about them recently. Wow. How powerful they were under Clive Lloyd, then Viv Richards. They had Greenidge, Haynes, Marshall, Roberts, Croft, Holding, Garner. They absolutely battered the opposition time and time again. It all started with an embarrassing tour of Australia; they turned up in England a year later and Tony Greig said he was going to "make them grovel". The West Indies just turned into a wrecking machine at that point, they really did. Those West Indies bowlers were my heroes, and that's why this is the number one sporting dynasty for me.

TOP FIVE @ 5 ENGLAND SHIRTS

There are so many to choose from but the current one looks like it's been designe[d] to wear on a night out. **JO: I don't think they're aiming it at footballers[,] it's like it's supposed to be worn with jeans.** Any problem with grown me[n] wearing football shirts, Jamie? **JO: No, I've got a couple of retro ones. I'[d] wear them down the shops.** You'd look awful, you shouldn't do that.

5 EURO 96 (GOALKEEPER)

I am going for a goalkeeper's kit because of David Seaman, probably the greatest ever England keeper. He wore this in Euro 96. It was made by Umbro and it was yellow with a mishmash of green and blue stripes across it. A crazy, crazy shirt. **AG: You know the thinking behind shirts like those was that they put strikers off their game, made the keepers look bigger?** He was wearing it when he saved Gary McAllister's penalty in the England v Scotland game but I wouldn't put it down to the shirt. My dad always used to get me goalkeeper shirts for my birthday. I don't know why, because I never played in goal. **AG: I don't mean to be rude, but you're quite short so there's no way you were going to be a goalkeeper.** I'm OK in goal! I'm like a cat. In a pre-season friendly I might throw myself in.

4 EURO 96 (HOME)

The badge in the middle, the number eight, all white, Umbro. It's Euro 96 and therefore Gazza. **AG: When I think of that shirt I think of Stuart Pearce scoring that penalty against Spain.** The Gazza moment for me, the goal and the dentist's chair. **AG: I found that the collar flicked up and never settled back down.** It was a bit baggy, but I used to wear it with the collar up.

4 1986 WORLD CUP (HOME)

This is a personal pick as it was the first England shirt I ever had. It was very plain, although it had white stripes within itself like you get on a mown lawn. It makes me think of Lineker scoring a hat-trick against Poland. **JO: That's a lovely shirt. I'd wear that down the pub.** As I've said, I find grown men wearing football shirts to venues other than stadiums quite weird, particularly if they've got their own name on the back.

Keegan: "I will love it if they let me keep this shirt, love it!"

5 1982 WORLD CUP (HOME)

I've got this one. It's a fantastic shirt. This is the one with the red, white and blue on the shoulders, which is obviously synonymous with the 1982 World Cup – and, for me, with Kevin Keegan missing a really simple header after coming off the bench against Spain, when all he had to do to take us into the last four was score.

3 **1998 WORLD CUP (HOME)**
The Michael Owen moment stands out as a memory, and so that England shirt from the World Cup in 1998 is my number three pick. It had red stripes down the side and red numbers on the front and the back, and was baggy. **AG: Do you like numbers on the shorts?** Yes, I don't mind that. **AG: Socks?** No, you can go too number-crazy.

3 **1990 WORLD CUP (HOME)**
Again it was plain, but just below the neckline it had a little V with lines in it and the Umbro logo all around the cuffs of the sleeve. And when I see that shirt I see Gary Lineker saying "Have a word with him" to Bobby Robson, about Gazza, who was filling up. That shirt was absolutely fantastic.

2 **2008 SHIRT (AWAY)**
This is personal to me. It's the England shirt I wore when I was playing for the Under-21s. It's red with the badge in the middle, the away one with the blue line across it. And I remember putting that shirt on and walking out and thinking, "I am representing my country." I was very lucky, I played for England from 16 right through to the U21s. **AG: What was it like pulling on an England jersey?** One of the proudest and most incredible moments of my life. It was the first time I was involved in a big tournament; we played Brazil and Germany, and I remember seeing my dad in the crowd and he was crying.

2 **1966 WORLD CUP (AWAY)**
This shirt has to be in, obviously. It's not my number one but it's still cool to wear now, the red one with the long sleeves – the Bobby Moore one with the number six on it. So cool. I once saw George Cohen's 1966 World Cup shirt framed on a wall in a rugby club, and just being that close to it sent chills down my spine.

Bobby Moore was supplied with two red England shirts for the World Cup final in 1966. One of them sold for £44,000 to a private collector in September 1999.

1 **2001 WORLD CUP QUALIFIER (HOME)**
My number one is the white shirt that David Beckham was wearing when he fired England into the World Cup of 2002 with a free kick against Greece. What a moment. The shirt had a red line straight down the front, with the Three Lions badge on the left where it belongs.

1 **1982 WORLD CUP (AWAY)**
I've gone back to 1982 again but this is the red kit, my absolute favourite, and the one Bryan Robson was wearing when he scored what was then the fastest ever World Cup goal. It was 27 seconds into the England v France game. I loved this shirt and it takes me right back.

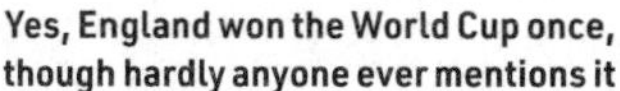

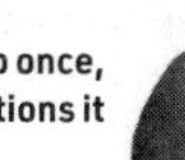

Yes, England won the World Cup once, though hardly anyone ever mentions it

TOP FIVE @ 5 BEATLES SONGS

I've been a massive Beatles fan since I was a boy. I never saw them live, obviously, but I went to see Paul McCartney, he did several Beatles songs and that was the best gig I've ever been to. We've got five each and it'll be interesting to see how many overlap, so let's start...

5 LET IT BE

This one was released in 1970. It only got to No.2 in the UK, which surprised me. **AD: What!?** But it was No.1 in the US obviously, as you would expect. But the reason it's not higher in my list is because, as fantastic a song as it is, the Beatles actually announced they were splitting just a month after it came out. I think the last album they recorded was Abbey Road and but Let It Be was released after that. Anyway, it's an all-time classic. **AD: Yes, absolutely. Love singing along to it.** Putting this list together has got me back into the Beatles. Sorry, talkSPORT, you'll have to take a back seat for a couple of days. Whenever I'm in my car, I will actually listen to the Beatles. **AD: In some ways I'm amazed it's your number five... but it's not even on my list, which amazes me even more. There are just too many incredible songs.**

5 CARRY THAT WEIGHT

This not a well-known song, actually. People might know the hook, or that riff, and not even realise it's the Beatles – but if you listen to Abbey Road, there's a medley of songs that are, like, 90 seconds to two minutes long on the B-side of the album. It's the most amazing journey of music you could get through and basically signals the end of the Beatles – that's how they sign off, with that medley of brilliant music. This is the one that stands out to me. It's called Carry That Weight and I have always loved it. It's more the medley than anything else, but I absolutely love this one. It just shows you how different their musical styles were throughout the years. That final album summed up the Beatles from start to finish.

4 I SHOULD HAVE KNOWN BETTER

Oh, what a song! **DG: I'm trying not to join in. It's my karaoke, mate!** Absolutely love this from A Hard Day's Night. It's from the film, from the soundtrack. It's kind of another one that goes under the radar a little bit when you think of all the Beatles classics. **DG: I absolutely adore this song! Beautiful.** I agree with you. I love singing along with it but I can't sing along with it. Can we ramp it up a little bit more please? Absolutely fantastic – that's my number four, I Should Have Known Better. So what's yours?

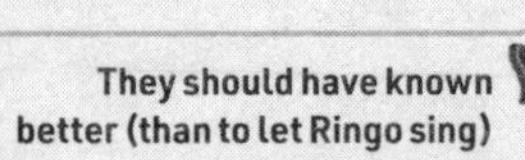

They should have known better (than to let Ringo sing)

4 YESTERDAY

Do you know why I picked this? **AD: Go on.** They didn't release it as a single in the UK. **AD: What?!** Yep, it began as a song that McCartney was going to call Scrambled Eggs. He dreamed of it and he wrote it all down, but they obviously changed it. They did release it as a single in the US and it became the most played song on American radio for eight years. **AD: Absolutely amazing. I know the scrambled eggs story. Do you know what the second line was? His next line was: "My darling, you've got lovely legs". Didn't quite hit the spot so he changed it. It's an absolute classic! You know you sometimes hear people saying, "I don't really like The Beatles"? I find that impossible. How can you not like something like this?** You listen to different music coming out all the time but I'm on a mission now to listen to all the Beatles songs. **AD: You could be there all weekend.** Somebody's just messaged me saying Golden Slumbers, also on Abbey Road. Magnificent.

3 SHE LOVES YOU

What an absolute tune. 1963. It was their breakthrough to international stardom, this song. People loved it but, and I know this sounds daft, it was a flop in the US. No.1 in the UK, obviously. But this is the interesting thing about this song: they released it again after I Want To Hold Your Hand reached No.1 in America, and this time this one went to No.1 as well. **AD: This is just a great three-minute pop song with a chorus that's almost like a football chant. Everybody can join in with it. A piece of genius.** When I look into the Beatles, I'm amazed how quickly they got it together. Very rarely did it take them longer than, like, five or six takes. They were so quick – once they got in front of each other, a few practice goes and then bang! That was the one.

3 HERE COMES THE SUN

What a great tune. George Harrison wrote this. Just a beautiful, beautiful song. Actually, do you know what I'm just thinking? It's appropriate for what the world has just been through because, when you see the light at the end of the tunnel, here comes the sun and it's going to be OK. Seriously, it's the right song to be playing. It's getting me all emotional, actually. It's just a joyous, beautiful tune, isn't it? So inoffensive and relaxing and wonderful, lovely. Another great track that was on Abbey Road.

2 AND YOUR BIRD CAN SING

"You don't get me!" **DG: Nobody gets you, Ade!** This is a John Lennon classic. This is from Revolver, probably my favourite album, and it's called And Your Bird Can Sing. It's almost impossible to get your head around how Harrison changes chords so quickly, and the riff just drew me in. How *do* you play that? **DG: I will be playing that on the guitar later. That's the task.** I love this song. The first time I put Revolver on and heard this, that was a wow moment. It has always been in any Beatles top five I've ever done.

2 I WANT TO HOLD YOUR HAND

That's a beauty, isn't it? Written by Lennon and McCartney in October 1963. This is the one that set off Beatlemania. **AD: The invasion of America started with this song.** I said to you earlier that they then re-released She Loves You in the US and that went to No.1 as well. Well, this actually knocked She Loves You off the No.1 spot in the UK and it was the first time an act had replaced itself with another song at the top. **AD: I didn't know that. Great little nugget of information. People are listening to this and dancing in their kitchens right now, love it.**

Sgt Pepper's includes some of the best Beatles songs of all – none of which are mentioned here

1/1 HEY JUDE

Well, I know this is my number one and I will be amazed if it's not yours as well, Darren Gough. **DG: It is. Can you believe that? We agree on something.** Incredible, and we haven't conspired on this at all. When you say 'classic', this actually takes it to another level. I love the meaning behind the song, which I'll get to in just a second, but it's just a fantastic tune. I love the way it climaxes, love that chorus at the end. Everybody loves a chorus they can join in with. It's the nah-nah-nahs at the end that everybody loves. Do you know the meaning behind this song? It's a beautiful thing. John Lennon's son Julian didn't really see his father that much and McCartney went round one day and was playing with Julian, just having a good time with him, and decided to write this for him. I'm thinking to myself, this is Paul McCartney, still in his 20s, world superstar, decides to write a beautiful song with a really beautiful message to Julian Lennon, who's a little boy. What an incredible story, and look how big the song became. That's a message to Julian, just a lovely message for a little boy whose parents had just got divorced. Such a beautiful thing for Paul McCartney to do. **DG: This did 8 million copies worldwide. UK No.1 for two weeks, US No.1 for nine weeks. What I like about it is, I've seen Paul McCartney live as well and he always does this as his last song. It gets everyone singing because they all know it. It's also massive at sporting events.** Are we coming up to the nah-nahs? I think we are... here we go... [*singing along to Hey Jude*] Come on all of you, join in!

Paul McCartney's handwritten lyrics to Hey Jude sold at auction for $910,000 in April 2020. The buyer was an anonymous American collector.

TOP FIVE @ 5 PREMIER LEAGUE BARGAINS

How difficult was this for you to work out your Top Five, Jamie O'Hara? **JO: There have certainly been quite a few incredible bargains in the history of the Premier League, including some frees, so it was actually quite hard. But I'm happy with my Top Five and they're better than yours.** Well, we'll see, won't we...

5 N'GOLO KANTE

Signed for £5.6m by Leicester and won the Premier League title in his first season! You cannot deny N'Golo Kante is an unbelievable player. He then went on to sign for Chelsea for around £32m. So judged as a bargain, what a player. **AG: I can't argue with that – one of the best players in the world in that position, he would be in every Premier League club's starting XI.** When you look at where Leicester came from, struggling in the relegation zone, then having that season where they signed him and going on to win the title, that's incredible recruitment. I think he's the best player of that type, the holding midfielder, to arrive in the Premier League since Claude Makelele.

4 ANDY ROBERTSON

First he moved from Dundee United to Hull City for £2.85m, and then he went to Liverpool for £8m. What a signing! We were talking about Ashley Cole being England's best left-back, but for me Andy Robertson is the best in the world right now. I can't see anyone better. I mean, he would be another £100m player now. He's won the Champions League, he's won the Club World Cup and the Premier League as well. **AG: Is it a bit too soon to rate him? Brilliant player, obviously, but when you compare him to Cole, who won over 100 caps, he's barely played 100 games for Liverpool. Is it too soon in his career to say whether he was a bargain?** £80m for Maguire. You can't tell me Robertson isn't a bargain.

5 ASHLEY COLE

My number five went from Arsenal to Chelsea in 2006 for £5m! Five million pounds for the best left-back this country's ever produced! That is just absolute peanuts. Ashley Cole won eight trophies in those eight years at Chelsea. Four FA cups with Chelsea to add to the three he won at Arsenal, plus the Champions League and the Europa League. Over 100 caps for England – incredible, and only five million pounds! That's a bargain, isn't it? **JO: It was a very sour move and that dampens it a little bit, plus he didn't come from nowhere – he was already achieving at Arsenal. But definitely a bargain. How much would he be worth now? It's over £100m for a player like that nowadays.**

4 SEAMUS COLEMAN

How much do you think this player cost when he moved to Everton in 2009? It was £60,000! £60,000 for Seamus Coleman. **JO: I've bought cars more expensive!** Well, yes. Darren Bent was talking about his Bentley that kept breaking down and that cost more than Seamus Coleman. A brilliant, consistent right-back. He's played over 250 games for Everton and over 50 games for Ireland. He is quick, skilful and hard-working, and he loves to get forward – he loves to attack and he's a great leader. I think he's the Ireland captain as well. See, I think it was 60 grand, but it rose to 300 grand based on appearances. If you are talking bargains then 60 grand for a regular, consistent leader in your team is a great one. **JO: Underrated, top player, and you don't stick around at a club like Everton for that long if you can't play. That's money well spent.**

Coleman: cheaper than a Bentley and much easier to clean

3 JÜRGEN KLINSMANN

He was signed for £2m by Spurs from Monaco. Player of the Year, 21 goals in his first season. A Spurs legend and he gave us the Klinsmann slide! When you think about a foreign player coming to play in the Premier League, who has left a legacy like he has, you don't look any further than Jürgen Klinsmann. He changed the way Spurs were as a football club, how we brought in foreign players... and all for £2m. **AG: All I'll say is that he was at the back end of his career, was only there for a season and played a handful of games. Is that still a bargain?** He came back again a bit later when we were fighting relegation, and helped to keep us up, but it's really about his legacy. You would normally pay a lot of money for a foreign player to come in and make a difference to the team like he did.

3 VINCENT KOMPANY

He signed for Manchester City from Hamburg for £6m in 2008. I look at Vincent Kompany and I think of a proper old-school centre-half in the Tony Adams or John Terry mould. A leader. An absolute rock. He was only 22 when he joined and was there for 11 years. He won four League titles and two FA cups. I think he is one of the best Premier League defenders of all time. And when you think they paid £6m for him – and in the same year they paid £18m for Jo and £32m for Robinho. Just £6m for one of their greatest ever players. That's a bargain, isn't it? **JO: Absolutely. An incredible captain. A great ambassador for Manchester City. I played against him and he had everything – he was good in the air and you'd never beat him one v one. He could score from corners, he could score from 30 yards. Ultimately, though, he was a leader of men – and probably one of the best investments the club has ever made.**

2 PHILIPPE COUTINHO

You might not put this guy down as a bargain in the traditional way but he is my number two for a reason. He cost £8.5m from Inter Milan to Liverpool and that in itself is a very cheap price for such a brilliant player; but the key here is that, off the back of his performances in a Liverpool shirt, they were able to sell him for £142m to Barcelona. With that money they signed Virgil van Dijk and Alisson Becker, which made Liverpool Champions League and Premier League title winners! That is a bargain for an initial £8.5m outlay. **AG: Yep, no doubt a good deal, but not as good as my number two...**

2 PETER SCHMEICHEL

A lot of people thought this player would be my number one but he isn't. I've got him at two... but it was a close call. He signed for Manchester United in 1991 for £505,000. The price was described by Ferguson as "bargain of the century". Peter Schmeichel was at United for eight years and played nearly 300 games. He absolutely bossed that backline – the reason that defence was so good was that he was behind them. Five League titles, three FA Cups, Champions League, Super Cup, did the Treble. A huge keeper yet light on his feet. I think the greatest goalkeeper ever... and United bought him for half a million pounds! **JO: Hard to disagree, but I'd add that he also had the best back four the Premier League has ever seen in front of him, in my opinion – and Edwin van der Sar came in later and did as good a job, just not for as long.** You're not having Van der Sar as the best goalkeeper of all time? **JO: Up there, but that's a tough call.**

1 PATRICK VIEIRA

Signed by Arsenal for £3.5m from AC Milan reserves. They plucked Vieira out of nowhere and he became one of the best footballers in the world. A titan, an 'Invincible', a one-man midfield. You can't name a more influential midfielder in the Premier League era. I honestly believe that Arsenal would have won hardly anything without him. **AG: Is Roy Keane in that category?** Yes, but Vieira also became a World Cup winner. For £3.5m. I don't like to say it as a Spurs fan but he is definitely my number one bargain.

1 ERIC CANTONA

That might be a bargain but it's more than twice as much as what my club paid for my number one. Howard Wilkinson, Leeds manager, wasn't a fan of Eric Cantona so he let him go to United in 1992 for £1.2m. We were eighth in the Premier League when he joined. He helped United to their first titles in 25 years. He helped win four League titles and two FA Cups (including the Double twice), and was without a doubt the missing piece of the jigsaw. He was the greatest bargain in Premier League history. **JO: His legacy is incredible. I can't say he wasn't a huge bargain.**

Cantona began his career at S.O. Caillolais and played most of his games in goal

TOP FIVE @ 5 NUMBER 9s

It's number 9s and it's Darren Bent's call. **DB: This is not just players who played in the position, but those who wore the number 9 on their back, so there will be a couple here who didn't play centre-forward but will have worn the number 9.** We've got completely different lists, so what do you think the main difference is between the two? **DB: I've gone for players I've seen with my own eyes and, on a few occasions, have actually played against.** OK, let's go, number 9s from any era who played with that number on their back...

5 ZLATAN IBRAHIMOVIC

I was lucky enough to see him play quite a few times in the United shirt, but the reason I've gone for Zlatan is that he's played for Ajax, Juventus, Inter, Barcelona, Milan, PSG, United, and of course the mighty LA Galaxy. When you were a kid playing in your back garden and you were pretending to be a player, you would obviously look at being someone with those clubs on his CV. And he played over 100 times for Sweden. Incredibly, I don't think he's won the Champions League. **DB: No, he hasn't, but I still thought about picking him... and then realised he played number 10 for PSG.** Yes, but he still played like a proper number 9: brilliant in the air, great hold-up play, powerful and skilful. **DB: No doubting his ability and the incredible goals he scores, but he just misses out for me.**

5 FILIPPO INZAGHI

When you think of a number 9 and someone who scores scruffy goals, but every goal they score means the most to them, like they've just won the World Cup or Champions League final, I think of Filippo Inzaghi. He is what you call the absolute number 9: he's in the right place at the right time. By that I mean someone will have a shot, it will take four ricochets and fall to him and he'll put it in the back of the net. **AG: Is there anything you wish you could add to your own game when you look at Inzaghi?** Yes, offside. I think Fergie said that Inzaghi was born offside! To be fair, I was the same, always making runs behind the last man but the linesman would stick his flag up. Same with Inzaghi, he'd be offside all the time... but you just knew that the one time he was not offside he would put it away. He just had that knack – because he wasn't really blessed with pace, he wasn't the strongest or most dynamic in the air, but if you look at the number of goals he scored and the positions he would take up, he was unbelievable.

Lewandowski: knocking on, and still knocking them in

4 HERNAN CRESPO

Before you try to steal him, this is my number four. What a centre-forward. His movement was scary. I played against him a few times when he was at Chelsea, and the defenders just didn't know where he was. Again, he wasn't the biggest but he was unbelievable in the air and his movement was so clever. He'd take up really intelligent positions so every time he got the ball to his feet he was in five yards of space, and whenever that ball was in the box he could finish it off. **AG: I'm thinking about him at Chelsea, not at the height of his powers perhaps, but was he a quick player?** He would practically hang offside the whole time, but the moment his team were ready to slide the ball through to him he would get back onside by a yard. The biggest thing about Crespo was his movement.

4 ROBERT LEWANDOWSKI

This player is the best number 9 on the planet at the moment: Lewandowski. He seems to be getting better with age. He has won seven league titles in Germany and, get this, over the last six seasons he's scored 40 goals or more in each one. He's got one in two for Poland and has over 100 caps. He's a wonderful finisher. He seems to be able to do it effortlessly with both feet and he's fantastic with his head. He's got the height, strength, pace and balance. I just can't fathom how he seems to be getting better. **DB: I agree, but what I hate is when people say it's easy in the Bundesliga. OK, he's playing for Bayern Munich and that's half the battle because they have the possession; but like Cristiano Ronaldo and Zlatan, he keeps himself in top condition. That's down to him.**

3 ALAN SHEARER

He has to be in this list. Forget everything else, 260 Premier League goals is just outrageous. You look at some of the great strikers we've had in this country and he is 50 ahead of Rooney. People talk about the Premier League being the hardest, toughest league in the world so that kind of return is incredible. **AG: I was watching the England-Holland game from Euro 96 recently and you almost forget how good he was at his peak.** People also forget the number of goals he scored at Southampton and Blackburn before he even got to Newcastle. And didn't he miss almost two seasons because of knee injuries? Incredible.

3 MARCO VAN BASTEN

There aren't many players you can instantly identify by the term '*that* goal' but this guy is one of them. If you say '*that* goal' for Holland in the 1988 Euros you know we're talking about Van Basten. I think it's fair to say this guy was a genius. He played for Ajax and Milan; out of 280 games he scored 218 goals. He won the Ballon d'Or three times, he won two Champions Leagues, he won the league seven times and he was part of the Dutch team that won that '88 European Championship. He was phenomenal. **DB: He was a bit before my time, but when I was a kid my dad bought me a pair of Marco van Basten Diadoras and I loved them.**

2 GABRIEL BATISTUTA

One of my all-time favourites. The long hair, the finishing – his goalscoring record is insane! It's got to be Gabriel Batistuta, or Batigol as they called him. The goals he scored, big goals in the Champions League... **AG: Scoring big goals, goals on important occasions – is that the difference between good strikers and great strikers?** Yes, the big world-class centre-forwards will always step up when their team needs a goal. Didier Drogba was probably the best at it but I'd put Batistuta alongside him – he was able to pull out a goal from somewhere. And the power he used to get on those shots. It was a real shame he never played in the Premier League.

2 SIR BOBBY CHARLTON

My number two is Bobby Charlton. I never saw him play. He was a big part of that England team that won the World Cup in 1966, obviously, and he won the Ballon d'Or. In 1968 he captained United to the European Cup, scoring two goals in the final. He was United's and England's leading goalscorer until Wayne Rooney took both those records, and he got over 100 caps. I just think he was the all-round complete number 9. **DB: There will be older people screaming that he should be number one and I get that.**

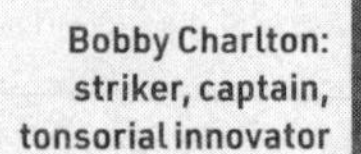

Bobby Charlton: striker, captain, tonsorial innovator

1 RONALDO

I think this guy was the greatest centre-forward of all time and I can't believe he's not even in your Top Five. **AG: I would have had both him and Shearer but left them out because you went for them.** He was unbelievable. He could do everything. He could dribble, he was powerful and quick. He came back from some major injuries to play for some of the biggest clubs in the world: Barcelona, Real Madrid, AC and Inter Milan. He won the World Cup with Brazil and two Ballons d'Or. For me he is the best number 9 to ever play. **AG: Fantastic choice but not as good as mine...**

1 JOHAN CRUYFF

I know traditionally he wore the number 14... **DB: I'm glad you realise that.** But he did wear the number 9 quite often for Barcelona and Ajax, and for Holland. My number one is Johan Cruyff. He won the Ballon d'Or three times. He won three European Cups with Ajax, led Holland to the World Cup final in 1974. And any player who comes up with some kind of movement or turn and has it named after them, you know they are special. In 1999 he was voted as the best European player of the century. Not even taking his managerial and football philosophy into account, I think he has to be the greatest player ever to have a number 9 on his back. **DB: One of the all-time top five players, definitely, but I don't think number 9 when I think of Cruyff. I think of number 14, and as a number 9 there is no way he is ahead of Ronaldo.**

TOP FIVE @ 5 SUPERHEROES

A lot of people tweeted in about the NHS when we said we were going to do this as a Top Five, and of course they are the real superheroes, but we are talking about the fictitious ones here. **DG: I'm not really a comic-book reader but I do have favourite superheroes from films.** Yes, me too. Off we go...

5 IRON MAN

He's an inventor, a genius, a billionaire and a playboy. I mean, what more do you want from a superhero? Tony Stark is Iron Man. His father was a genius before him, he had a weaponry business, and Tony Stark carries that on. But he gets some shrapnel in his chest, near his heart, and has an electro-magnet in a chest-plate to keep him alive... and that's all part of the suit that we'd all love to have a go in for half an hour. **AD: I actually went to the cinema to see an Iron Man film, believe it or not, and it was on the money. A really good movie. Robert Downey Jnr was excellent.**

5 CAPTAIN CAVEMAN

Don't hate me, but this has to be the world's first superhero – it even says so in the credits. **DG: I used to watch this non-stop. I love what he does.** His superhero features include pulling various objects from his long bodyhair, and he eats anything (sometimes the wrong thing). He speaks caveman-talk. 'Unga bunga' is his catchphrase. And he can fly as well. And, of course, he has three Teen Angels who go around with him everywhere – just sit back and admire the magnetism of the guy! Come on, what's not to love about the world's first superhero?

4 BLACK PANTHER

I never knew about this character until the film. In 2018, Black Panther became the highest-grossing solo superhero film ever... and it's terrific. If you haven't watched it, you should. It's an important film in terms of African culture, how the West views Africa, and the significance of having a black superhero. Plus there's some brilliant one-liners in it! Martin Freeman plays an American CIA agent, which took me by surprise, but he's really good. And when he's taken to the African nation of Wakanda he's blown away by how great it is. The moment of the film is when Zuri steps into a fight between the Black Panther and Killmonger – and the sequence of events is gripping, gripping cinema. And actually, Black Panther is the superhero who's number four on my list, but the Killmonger character, the tormented baddie, played by Michael B Jordan, is the product of his environment, the very characterisation of black pain. He's as complex a character as cinema has seen. The Black Panther calls him a monster of our own making. Don't just watch the film, understand it.

Iron Man: really good at ironing

4 SUPERMAN

Everybody will know this one. It was the first film I went to see at the cinema, in Barnsley with my dad in 1978. Afterwards I tried to fly because I thought I actually was Superman! It started way back in 1938 in the comic-books. There's a dark element here because Clark Kent is a guy who basically hides behind spectacles and a dark suit – he's mild-mannered and shy with an awkward personality, but he's also somebody completely different – somebody who is faster than a speeding bullet, as strong as you could ever wish to be. And despite his being alien, his adoptive parents bring him up to represent the very best of humanity. That's what I would say Superman is – the very best of humanity. **AD: A great film series, and again I've not read the comic-books but an iconic superhero. You said you came out of the cinema wanting to be Superman, when was this? A couple of weeks ago?** No, when I was 8, and it was a huge treat because we didn't go to the cinema very often. **AD: That 1978 film – what a cast! Christopher Reeve, Marlon Brando, Gene Hackman, Terence Stamp, Margot Kidder and more. An amazing line-up and a brilliant film worth revisiting.**

3 GREEN ARROW

I got this one from a TV series on Sky. I've watched every episode and the Arrow is Oliver Queen. He's from a very rich background and he gets stranded on a desert island after falling off his yacht, and he has to learn to shoot a bow and arrow to survive. **AD: Are you making this one up? I've never heard of this guy.** Not many have but he's absolutely brilliant, trust me. Crooks keep coming to the island because they use it as a hideout. So he uses his new skills to fight them and eventually gets off the island and fights crime back home – although he hides behind this persona of being a rich businessman. It first appeared in comics in 1941. **AD: Blimey.** And because he's so rich he's like this celebrity playboy in Star City. He has a sidekick called Speedy, he rides a cool motorbike and he shoots a bow and arrow like you've never seen. He never misses. Check him out.

3 BATMAN

Another billionaire good guy. This one is slightly more famous, though: Batman. I've got all the films and the quality thing about them is that I can rewatch them all – and I've not yet seen Joker, which came out in 2019. I'm going to go back through the whole set and finish off with that at some point. Like Iron Man, he's incredibly rich, with a great car and even his own cave. Who wouldn't want to be Batman? The only question I've got is, does Batman actually have any superpowers? **DG: He's got super-strength!** Has he? **DG: I would say so. You've seen him fight. POW! BAM! KAPOW! He never gets beaten in a fight.** OK, I suppose so.

Batman: really good at batting (unlike Darren)

2 ELASTIGIRL

Behind every great man is a woman who's even greater. So, Mr Incredible is a bumbling oaf. His wife, Mrs Incredible – aka Helen Parr, aka Elastigirl – is the true hero of the Incredibles. She saves him when they first meet. She saves the kids when their plane is bombed. And she keeps the family together while he's having a midlife crisis. Her superpower is that she can stretch into all sorts of positions. Think that through! I'm surprised she's not my number one. **DG: Hang on, there's a copycat thing going on here. Can't one of the Fantastic Four do that?** No idea, never seen it.

2 THOR

The master of thunder and lightning: he's got superhuman strength, speed, endurance and resistance to injury. One of the key members of the Avengers, the mighty Thor is my number two superhero. His first appearance was in 1962. He's great with all things with his hands: a warhammer, a sword, an axe and a mace. He can fly at supersonic speeds in the Earth's atmosphere but, listen to this, when he's in space he's faster than light! What more do you want than Thor?

1 CAPTAIN AMERICA

I just like the look, it's to die for. If I were going to go to a fancy-dress party I'd want to go as Captain America. He's got that shield and the mask. Steve Rogers is his real name and he's injected with a super-serum that turns him into a super-soldier, with all his bodily functions running at peak efficiency. He's an expert in martial arts but also has bulletproof armour and, most famously, the shield. Captain America is the only one who can lift Thor's hammer, and Thor once said he wanted to pass on the hammer to Captain America – so my one and two are very much a team.

1 JOHN HANCOCK

This is from the film Hancock, from 2008. Will Smith plays the troubled John Hancock, an alcoholic with superpowers who routinely tries to do good things but messes up. For example, he throws a beached whale back into the sea but sinks a ship at the same time. Then a guy he rescues takes him under his wing and starts to turn him into a positive force. He's a superhero, but a flawed superhero and that's why I love him. The way Will Smith plays him is also very funny. **DG: Yep, loved it. Hilarious.**

TOP FIVE @ 5 FA CUP FINALS

I love FA Cup finals, I love talking about FA Cup finals, I love FA Cup final stats, I love everything about FA Cup finals. What was the first FA Cup final you remember seeing as a kid, Goughie? **DG: I'm going to talk about it later, Man City v Spurs. I was 11.** I used to be able to go from 1973 all the way through, teams, goalscorers, the lot. Shall I start us off, then?

5 LIVERPOOL v MANCHESTER UNITED [1996]

There was a real buzz around the build-up to this one. It was all about the Spice Boys. I did a bit of training with Liverpool that year, believe it or not: I did a swap with John Barnes. He did some cricket training and I did some football. **AG: Why?** We had the same sponsors. So I had a day at Liverpool training with them and then he came to train with us. And he can play! Not a bad cricketer, John Barnes. Anyway, everyone thought it was going to be a thriller of a final because Liverpool were playing some fantastic football that season... but it became all about the Spice Boys and those white/cream suits. David James gets the blame for it because he was the Armani model and helped sort them out. Apparently none of the players knew until a few days before. The game was so boring the suits became the talking point. **AG: I think I'm right in saying that Helen Chamberlain from Soccer AM has Jason McAteer's suit from the day and wore it to Ascot once.**

5 LIVERPOOL v WIMBLEDON [1988]

I love history being made in any sport but none more so than in an FA Cup final. John Aldridge won a penalty and he did a little shuffle and stopped and then hit the ball, and it was saved by Dave Beasant for Wimbledon. It was the first time a keeper had saved a penalty in an FA Cup final. Wimbledon won 1-0, and it was a huge upset as Liverpool were giants at the time and Wimbledon were mid-table under Bobby Gould... but they were not overawed, in fact Vinnie Jones let Steve McMahon know he was there very early in the game. He would have been sent off today. For the upset, for Liverpool being beaten, that is one of my very favourite cup finals.

4 MANCHESTER UNITED v CRYSTAL PALACE [1990]

What a game this was. Ian Wright came off the bench to score two goals and it ended 3-3. He had suffered a broken leg earlier in the season and was desperate to be fit for the final, particularly because it was against United, and had to prove himself in a couple of practice matches. He just made the bench and when he came on he got two goals. Unfortunately it wasn't enough: it went to a replay and Crystal Palace lost 1-0, but for Wrighty's two goals that afternoon the game sticks in my memory.

4 BLACKPOOL v BOLTON [1953]

I told you I love the history of the FA Cup final and that's why I've picked this one. It was called 'the Matthews final' because Stanley Matthews had a blinder. He was responsible for supplying the bullets to Stan Mortensen, who scored a hat-trick that day. It's the only time a hat-trick has been scored in an FA Cup final. Blackpool were losing 3-1 and it came back to 3-3 on 89 minutes. And they won it 4-3 with a goal scored at 90 minutes plus two. Nat Lofthouse was on the other side. **DG: I don't think many people will remember this one.** But it's a bit of history. How old do you think Stanley Matthews was then? **DG: 51?** No, he was 38. And his cup final medal got sold a few years ago for £220,000. That's amazing, isn't it?

When Mortensen died it was said, "They'll probably call it the Matthews funeral"

3 EVERTON v MANCHESTER UNITED [1985]

This is the one where Kevin Moran gets sent off for a desperate tackle on Peter Reid. The supporters are chanting "Off! Off! Off!", and that cheer when he gets the red card... it was a terrible challenge. **AG: It wasn't that bad.** It was! Everton were going for the treble. They'd won the First Division title and the Cup-Winners' Cup. United had finished fourth that season. It was goalless after 90 minutes but Norman Whiteside scored the winner in extra time for United. But the thing back then was that if you got sent off you couldn't go and get your medal. **AG: I asked Ron Atkinson about this once and he told me that nobody knew where Kevin Moran's medal was after the game, but someone found it in the Royal Box later on and it eventually made its way to him.**

3 SUNDERLAND v LEEDS UNITED [1973]

If you don't know anything about FA Cup final history this is massive, because Sunderland were the first second-tier side to win the FA Cup since West Brom did it in 1931. And they beat Leeds United, who were the team of the 1970s. I've picked it because of the moment when Jimmy Montgomery made the save against Peter Lorimer. When I was a kid we used to have a VHS of great FA Cup final moments and that one was on it, and I watched it over and over again. Have you seen the save? **DG: Yes.** Trevor Cherry has a header, Jim Montgomery saves it and it's a good save. And then it comes back out to Lorimer, and as he makes contact it's definitely going in the goal but somehow Montgomery flicks his hand and the ball hits the crossbar. That is one of the greatest saves in FA Cup final history. And this is probably my favourite FA Cup statistic: that Sunderland side was the last team to win the FA Cup without one full international in the team.

This, Sunderland fans, is a trophy

2 LIVERPOOL v WEST HAM [2006]

I was at this one at the Millennium in Cardiff; I think it was the last one they held there. They call it 'the Gerrard final' for a reason. West Ham were 2-1 up and Gerrard scored to make it 2-2. Then West Ham went ahead again before Gerrard scored another from 30 yards out. What a strike. Bang! Into the bottom corner. It was an amazing goal, the crowd went absolutely mental and Liverpool went on to win on penalties. But West Ham were excellent that day.

2 MANCHESTER CITY v WIGAN (2013)

I love an upset in the cup and this is up there. Roberto Mancini was the manager and Pablo Zabaleta got sent off. Ben Watson, who had been out for a whole season after breaking his leg, came off the bench and glanced a header into the net. He'd only been on the field for ten minutes. A great moment for him. That Manchester City team was incredible but they'd downed tools before the game. And Wigan were relegated that season.

1 EVERTON v MANCHESTER UNITED (1985)

Your number three, the 1985 final between Manchester United and Everton, is a personal one for me. My old man was the photographer for Manchester United when they came down to London, so in 1983 when we played Brighton and drew with them in the first game I went to the banquet afterwards – but there was no FA Cup as the match was a draw. I was devastated. And of course, the replay was on a Thursday back then and I had school so I couldn't go. I was desperate to see the FA Cup and I knew I was going to the banquet in 1985 – so when Norman Whiteside scored that goal I ran into the garden and my dad followed me, like we'd scored the goal, and we were jumping on each other. I've got a replica shirt of the one Whiteside wore in that final and he very kindly signed it for me, it's on my wall at home. In fact, the picture I have of me meeting Sir Matt Busby on my Twitter and Instagram was taken at the banquet later that day.

1 TOTTENHAM HOTSPUR v MANCHESTER CITY (1982 REPLAY)

This is the first Cup final I remember. I had an affection for Spurs from the moment Ricardo Villa scored that goal – the most iconic in the history of the competition, in my opinion. He collected it about 35 yards out from Tony Galvin and nobody expected him to go on that run. It was almost like he dribbled past every player in the Man City side. Well, he didn't. He went past the same two players, Tommy Caton and Ray Ranson, twice. **AG: Villa was subbed in the first game – this was the replay.** He had a howler in that first game and they weren't going to pick him to begin with.

"Rickeeeee!"

TOP FIVE @ 5 AMERICAN TV COMEDIES

I'm very excited about doing this because I adore comedies and particularly American TV comedies. I've got five and you've got five and they're all different, is that right? **PG: They are, but there was one where you pulled rank and nicked one of mine so I had to juggle.** Let's start with one of yours then, Perry...

5 THE PHIL SILVERS SHOW (SERGEANT BILKO)

This is one for the teenagers! Sergeant Bilko is my number five. It was Sergeant Bilko in this country and for the re-runs, or sometimes just Bilko, but it was originally known as The Phil Silvers Show in America. That was in the late 1950s, and it later came over to our shores. It was always on in the school holidays. Bilko is a ducker and a diver and is in charge of a platoon in the American army. He uses his platoon to make money and set up gambling schemes, and he has this character Doberman as his kicking block. Even as a kid, you know when someone is naturally funny. He had the comic timing and quick wit. Phil Silvers was unknown before this series, and he became one of the major stars on American TV. So there's a bit of nostalgia because it reminds me of school holidays. I might not even have got some of the gags at the time but he just made me laugh. **AG: My old man used to watch this all the time.** You've hung me out to dry there. His dad used to like it...

The world's only Phil Silvers museum opened in Coventry in 2015 at the back of a TV memorabilia shop called Sgt Bilko's Vintage Emporium

5 IT'S GARRY SHANDLING'S SHOW

It was on for four years from 1986. It's genius for a lot of reasons. But the main reason is because it was one of the first comedies to break down the fourth wall, that barrier between the audience at home and the TV star on the telly. I can't believe I'm linking the two, but... a little bit like Miranda does. Also, the theme tune – it just did exactly what it said on the tin ("This is Garry's theme tune..."). I'm a massive Shandling fan. There's a documentary called The Zen Diaries Of Garry Shandling and it was directed and produced by his good friend Judd Apatow after Garry died a few years back; and I don't get emotional when I watch anything, I have never cried during a film, but when I watched this doc – it's something like four hours long over two parts – I don't mind telling you I actually cried. It's a phenomenal story about his life. I was only about 12 or 13 when I watched the show and it was one of my first introductions to comedy.

4 HAPPY DAYS

It was always on a Friday, about quarter past five just as the weekend was about to start. The theme tune gets you going straight away. And it's about Arthur Fonzarelli, aka the Fonz, who was officially the coolest man in the world for about three or four years. It was a little bit weird that Henry Winkler played the Fonz as he was probably about 45 at the time and he was playing someone in his twenties! It's based around an American diner with a jukebox called Arnold's Drive-In and among the characters were a couple of gingers, Richie and Ralph. But the Fonz could sort anything out – he was the smartest, the toughest, the most street-wise, with his leathers and his massive motorbike. I loved it.

4 FAMILY GUY

This came from the incredible mind of Seth MacFarlane. It focuses on a family called the Griffins, Peter and Lois and their kids. They've got a talking baby, a talking dog, and the gags are mindblowing – they go really close to that line you're not really meant to step over, and then they long-jump over it! Family Guy began in 1999 and there've been over 350 episodes, and every single one is as original as the very first one. The reason it's here and not The Simpsons is because I've seen more episodes. **PG: Brian the dog is one of the best cartoon characters of all time.**

3 MORK & MINDY

A spin-off from Happy Days. The legendary Robin Williams played Mork and this was his first big role. It's about an alien who comes from the planet Ork to look at human behaviour, and his relationship with a human called Mindy. It's like listening to one of Robin Williams' stand-up shows. They said they gave him the script but he was so brilliant at improvisation that they left spaces because he was better than the script. He was so naturally funny and quick. At the end of each episode he had to report back to Ork and relay what he'd found out about humans that day, and there was always a message in there. **AG: A little bit before my time. My grandad used to watch it!** Thought it was your great grandad. **AG: That's right, it was.**

3 FRIENDS

I had to put this in because it was on for 10 years, there were 236 episodes and 10 series. As a young adult, Friends was amazing and you sort of grew up with the characters. They all set trends: all the women wanted the Rachel haircut, all the blokes wanted to be like Chandler. They had a massive team of writers on that show, like 12 or 15 people sat around the table, which is why every punchline is perfect for the gag. It's just perfection and everyone I know loves Friends – and every time I come across it when I'm channel-hopping I always think "I've not seen this one" but then halfway through realise that I have. All the episodes stand the test of time. Everyone loves Friends, don't they? **PG: My wife doesn't, she can't stand it. Too mainstream.**

2 CHEERS

Set in a bar in Boston, and you want to go to that bar. You have so many great different characters. You've got Sam Malone, the handsome bartender all the girls fall for, played by Ted Danson, but my favourite was Norm, the big fat geezer who sat at the end of the bar and would just say the odd line. Woody Harrelson played Woody – that was his big break – and Frasier was a spin-off from this show. It was on a Friday night on Channel Four at about 10pm, and if we were playing away and staying in a hotel, Paul Merson and I would watch it and then The Golden Girls, which came afterwards. It never failed to hit the spot.

2 THE LARRY SANDERS SHOW

It's Garry Shandling again but this time he's playing Larry Sanders. He created this show with a guy called Dennis Klein; he's a late-night talk show host while Rip Torn plays the show's exec producer, Artie. The guests play exaggerated versions of themselves. There's three or four minutes of the 30 when he's on air and the rest is behind the scenes – it's like a mockumentary if you like, but he never acknowledges the camera. It must have been a big influence for Ricky Gervais when he was creating The Office.

1 EVERYBODY LOVES RAYMOND

Ray Romano writes this and he's obviously the star in it. My number one is Everybody Loves Raymond and nobody loves it more than me. It's about Ray Barone and his family. His mum and dad, Frank and Marie, live opposite him and are always interfering; he's got a downtrodden brother Robert, who is 6ft 8. It's about a dysfunctional family who love each other but don't get on. And the thing about Ray Romano is that he gives everybody else fantastic lines, killer lines. And that's very rare but he sort of spreads it around.

"Perry Groves loves me? *The* Perry Groves?"

1 CURB YOUR ENTHUSIASM

Not just the best American TV comedy but I think the greatest TV comedy ever written. There have been 10 seasons and 100 episodes, written by Larry David – who plays himself and who, in real life, is the writer of Seinfeld which, bizarrely – and I've tried many times – I just can't get into. Apparently all the scenes are ad-libbed. There's a beginning and an end and then they've just got to get there themselves. When it first began in 1999 there was a one-hour special filmed in a mockumentary style and it really grew from there. It has been nominated for 38 Emmys. It's all filmed on a single camera shot and I just think it's the greatest comedy of all time. **PG: I agree. This was the one you pulled rank on, it was going to be my number one. It's the observational stuff. Quite obviously genius.**

TOP FIVE @ 5 ELTON JOHN SONGS

We're doing all the top songs from the biggest acts in the world and so we can't really miss out Elton John, a guy who was the number one global recording artist at one point in the 1970s and who, through his love and support for Watford FC, also has a very strong connection with football. Let's step into our Top Fives...

5 STEP INTO CHRISTMAS

Did you see what I did there? This Elton John number had to be in the Top Five. Step Into Christmas. **DG: Are you joking me? It's not even Christmas.** I just love this tune. It's the one tune I want to hear on Christmas Day. When you first mentioned Elton John songs this was the first tune I thought of.

4 CANDLE IN THE WIND

I don't particularly like my number four. I liked the tribute to Marilyn Monroe, and then when he reshaped the lyrics as a tribute to Diana it became a really iconic song and that's why I picked it. I think it's lacking in some ways, but I was in news journalism at that time and covering the death of Diana and her funeral, so it's a song that resonates with me.

5 NIKITA

I was 15 when this was released. Elton is sitting in a Rolls-Royce, in front of the Berlin Wall, dressed in Watford colours for the video. It's a Cold War ballad about a Westerner who falls in love with an extremely good-looking girl called Nikita. Did you know George Michael sings backing vocals? **AD: Is that true? I didn't know that.** And Nik Kershaw too. **AD: It's like homeschooling being with you, Goughie.** It only got to No. 3. **AD: It's not quite Step Into Christmas but it's not bad.**

3 YOUR SONG

This is a song you can dedicate to anyone – it's a sensational love song. It only got to No. 7 in 1971, which makes you wonder what was going on at the time, but there you go. I love this song. It gets mixed reviews among the Elton fraternity – some love it and some think it's just trashy chart fodder. But when you break it down, musically and lyrically, it's a terrific tune. So that's Your Song. What's 'your song' at number three?

4 SATURDAY NIGHT'S ALRIGHT FOR FIGHTING

How's this for a change of tempo? This was on Elton John's best-selling album Goodbye Yellow Brick Road and released in 1973. It only got to No. 7 in the UK because it was banned on many radio stations due to the fact that they thought it would incite violence. **AD: Do you know the background of this song lyrically? He used to play the piano in a pub for money when he was a teenager and it always ended up with a fight, and that was the inspiration.**

3 CIRCLE OF LIFE

Very good. You either love this or hate it and I will get criticised in some quarters for picking it. It's Circle Of Life from The Lion King soundtrack. I'm a massive wildlife fan from my time spent in South Africa, and you kind of get to understand the circle of life there. The way Elton John puts Tim Rice's words to music here is absolutely brilliant. He was nominated for an Oscar for this song but lost out... to Can You Feel The Love Tonight, from the same movie. Which is another Elton belter.

2 ROCKET MAN

This is from Elton's 1972 album Honky Chateau. It reached No. 2 in the UK and No. 6 in the US. It's a fantastic song and I do love the story behind it. It's an astronaut who misses his family while he's away on a long mission. The guy who wrote the words was Bernie Taupin. He was driving to his parents' house, which was two hours away. He had no tape recorder, no pen or paper, and the first verse came into his head fully formed. He had to repeat it for two hours non-stop until he got there so he could run out of the car and write it all down. **AD: That's a great story. Thank goodness he remembered it!**

1 TINY DANCER

This beauty is over six minutes long and it's Tiny Dancer. It's got an intro before the chorus of about two and a half minutes and yet it's still one of the greatest songs ever written and performed. I defy anyone to dislike this song. Beautiful, isn't it? **DG: A beautiful song.** Bernie Taupin said it was about his wife at the time, Maxine Feibelman. And she said, only recently, "I knew the song was about me. I'd been into ballet as a little girl." It only reached 70 in the UK singles charts when it was released in 1972 due to the sheer length of it. Re-release right now!

1 I'M STILL STANDING

This was released in 1983 and is from the album Too Low For Zero. It was No. 4 in the UK charts, No. 12 in the US – all his songs do well over there. The song is directed at a former lover and it's not complimentary, with lyrics like "You'll wind up like the wreck you hide behind that mask you use". It's about how he recovers in a better place. And the best thing about this song is that Bruno Tonioli, the Strictly Come Dancing judge, is a dancer in the video. He always brings it up!

2 I GUESS THAT'S WHY THEY CALL IT THE BLUES

I first loved it as a kid because of 'the Blues' and my team, Peterborough, and then I realised it's a great song in its own right and features Stevie Wonder on harmonica, no less. It got to number five in the charts and is such a good singalong song. I know all the words to this and, to let you in on a secret, this is my karaoke song! I can listen to it all day and all night on repeat.

"Flamboyant, moi?"

TOP FIVE @ 5 SPORTING ICONS WE IDOLISED AS KIDS

So, what period are we talking about with your icons, Deano? **DA: Early to late 1990s, mostly.** I found it quite difficult, what about you? **DA: It wasn't easy getting them in order because at different times in my life I was a little bit obsessed with these people.** Let's start with your number five...

5 PETE SAMPRAS

The man with the hairiest arms I'd ever seen in sport. I used to watch loads of tennis when I was younger. I didn't play it but I loved watching and Sampras for me was the man. We talk about Federer now and he's basically like an upgraded prototype of Pete Sampras. The serve was just unerring at times. When he really needed a point Sampras would come up with the serve. Federer even serves like Sampras... and, like Federer, he had his rivals at the time: Andre Agassi, Boris Becker, and then some of the young guns. Sampras never seemed to show emotion and I loved that because the others would get riled up, but not Pistol Pete. **AG: What would happen if you ever met Pete Sampras?** I'd go all childish and tell him about when I was sitting there watching him win Wimbledon.

5 BRUCE LEE

This might surprise some people. It quite surprised me when it popped into my head. I was fascinated with karate when I was young, went to one class when I was nine, got kicked in the stomach, cried and came home. But I still wanted to be Bruce Lee. **DA: Is this not meant to be about sport stars, though?** Karate is a sport. **DA: But did he compete? Wasn't he just a film star?** He was probably too dangerous as an opponent. Have you seen Enter The Dragon? **DA: No, never watched it.** Do you know who Chuck Norris is? **DA: Is he ginger?** I wouldn't say that to his face. Bruce Lee fights Chuck Norris in Way Of The Dragon. And get this, I actually had a pair of foam-covered nunchucks. I was obsessed.

4 SEVE BALLESTEROS

A genius, an absolute genius. **AG: Great choice.** I love my golf. That win in the 1988 Open – wow! It was the fact that he wasn't like anyone else. He would hit it wildly, then hit these ridiculous shots from anywhere on the course – people will have seen the one where he's on his knees and he uses a three wood underneath the trees and it ends up on the green! But he had the personality as well. He could turn around and have a laugh with the crowd and with the TV cameras. For me he encapsulated what a superstar should be. He looked so cool and calm yet was still the best and let everyone in at the same time – he let the fans be part of it. Class.

Bruce Lee: not a real dragon

4 JIMMY CONNORS

We've both got a tennis player. I first saw Jimmy Connors on TV in 1982 in the Wimbledon final where he beat McEnroe. I loved absolutely everything about him. I loved his hair, his technique, his mannerisms, his confidence, his personality, the fact that he joked with the crowd. I bought the same Wilson racket he had with the steel shaft and the steel head, and I bought the Cerruti 1881 top that he wore. Do you remember that? **DA: Of course not, I wasn't born.** This is like doing a show with your grandson.

3 GARY LINEKER

I have chosen your friend as my number three. **AG: Gary Lineker? He is, we're mates again now!** In 1987 when he scored those four goals against Spain... but Italia 90 for me, that was the memory that got me into football. It made me want to be a footballer, it made me dream of playing for England. His performances, his goals, the goal against Germany: the knee, the swivel, the left foot. I loved the fact that all he wanted to do was score goals. It wasn't about anything else. And that's how I approached my whole career – I just cared about scoring goals. **AG: Do you think he shaped your future? Did he make you want to be a striker?** Without a shadow of a doubt. I was pretty good at most sports so I think I would have taken up whichever one really inspired me at that time. And I was watching Italia 90, watching him and the goals that he scored and the elation on his face. From that exact moment that became my dream, to play for England and score for England in a World Cup.

3 GLENN HODDLE

This may surprise a few people because it's no secret that I'm a Manchester United fan, but the first time I ever saw live football was Spurs v United in a League Cup game at White Hart Lane... and my dad was desperate for me to be a Spurs fan but I went United. Glenn Hoddle played that day. He had a perm and I thought, wow, this bloke looks really cool. And after that I wanted a perm! He was a genius of a player. I was lucky enough to see him playing in the flesh a few times. He wore the bagged-out shirt and looked just right. He was much too good for Spurs and should have been capped 100 times. I also loved the way he ran so I used to copy his run. My dad used to be a photographer and he got the job to do Ossie Ardiles' wedding, and I went along and met Glenn Hoddle there. There's a picture of me standing next to Hoddle. I must be about seven and Hoddle looks like a giant compared to me.

2 MICHAEL JOHNSON

For younger generations it would be Usain Bolt, watching him just streak away from the other athletes... but I was 13 in 1996 and to watch Michael Johnson and the way he ran – he had a really unique style, that sort of upright style – just to blitz that field in the 200m at the Atlanta Olympic Games and break the world record with 19:32 – and poor old Frankie Fredericks, his great rival, beats the old record but finishes second and ten metres behind him! I was just speechless after watching that. Plus I was really slow so that was awe-inspiring.

2 JIMMY WHITE

I first saw him in 1984 when he was in the World Championship final and lost to Steve Davis 18-16. And he was 12-4 down at one point. He was unbelievable in that final. I watched the whole final and cried at the end, and that was the reason why I love snooker. I fell in love with it because of him. I then went out and got the same cue as him and had the same cue action. Whenever I played with my mates I was always Jimmy White. He's still my idol but he's also a really close pal since we worked together at Eurosport. But the first time I met him professionally was when I was presenting the Premier League snooker for Sky, and I walked into a changing room and he was standing there just in his pants! Meeting your idol in his underpants!!! Very bizarre.

Jimmy White, in trousers

1 MARCO VAN BASTEN

My ultimate hero. And there's a few reasons why. One, the first memory I have of any football whatsoever is 1988 when he scored *that* goal in the Euros, and it still remains my favourite goal of all time. Two, Marco van Basten is Dutch and was born in Utrecht, which is where my nan is from, and she used to talk about him constantly when I was really young. She used to say, "Marco van Basten is the best player in the world. You've got to watch Marco van Basten!" She used to talk about Gullit and Rijkaard as well, but she would rave on and on about Van Basten. And three, I had the same surgeon as him for my ankle injury! He scored 200 goals – which, considering he was still in his 20s when he had to retire through injury, is pretty remarkable. **AG: Would you ever think about trying to replicate that goal during a match?** Every time the ball came over and I was in that sort of position. I only came close once, into small goals in a sports hall when I was about 15.

1 BRYAN ROBSON

Number one for so many reasons. Captain Marvel, leader of Man United, Bryan Robson. I loved his perm, he wore the number seven, he was fearless. He was effortlessly cool and I had pictures of him on my wall. He used to have his shirt bagged out at the front into a semi-circle and tucked in at the back. I don't know how he did it. So I got my mum to cut the bottom of my white school shirt in that shape and then properly sew it so it didn't fray and I could be Bryan Robson when I was playing football in the playground. I met him when I was doing stuff for MUTV and I was like an eight-year-old again and I loved that. Couldn't call him Robbo, though – still can't.

TOP FIVE @ 5 CLINT EASTWOOD FILMS

This legend turned 90 years of age recently and it got me thinking about how talented he is and how many decades he has spent at the very top as an actor, director, writer and producer. So, in tribute, it's our Top Five Clint Eastwood films. Let us make your day...

5 EVERY WHICH WAY BUT LOOSE

I've got a question for you, Darren Gough – because when I messaged you to say this was in my Top Five, you sent a laughing emoji back. Why? **DG: Because it's an absolutely hilarious film. And I love animals in films.** Having an orangutan in this movie makes it. The action is what's funny, rather than one-liners, and you've got to respect Clint for doing this film. It's 1978 – he's done the spaghetti westerns, he's done the crazy American cop bit and he decides to have a crack at comedy. Well, I admire him for giving it a go. Maybe a better script would have helped but he was desperate to break out from being typecast and he wanted to try different things. In the end he had to direct his own stuff to make that happen but he could have just carried on picking up the money, sitting on a horse or holding a Magnum. **DG: I like it, I think it's a funny film. "Right turn, Clyde."**

4 HEARTBREAK RIDGE

This is only a year after Pale Rider but his voice sounds completely different, like he might have spent a year on the sauce. Clint Eastwood plays Gunnery Sergeant Thomas Highway; he's coming towards the end of the road in terms of his career, he's lost his wife who works in a bar and is now seeing the bar manager, but he's desperate to get her back. He takes charge of a group of undisciplined Marines who've failed before and knocks them back into shape. It's all about his journey and how it changes him. A fantastic film! And, of course, he's got the usual cigar. **AD: I've never seen it.** When I think of Clint Eastwood I instinctively see him playing a cowboy even now, but when you watch a film where he is a war hero or a Marine I just think he fits those parts too. **AD: I agree. But no matter how many different roles he's played, you do tend to think of him sitting on a horse.**

5 PALE RIDER

This is a western that came out in 1985. I loved a western when I was a kid and I loved Clint Eastwood. He produced and directed this one and also plays the lead role, of course. It became the highest-grossing western of the 1980s. He's defending a group of goldminers because they've been terrorised by a band of cowboys who are doing everything to get their land. He plays a character called the Preacher who comes to their aid. **AD: My wife loves this film and I totally get why it's in your Top Five.**

4 DIRTY HARRY

This was the first film for the character of Harry Callahan. I was shocked that Dirty Harry was made in 1971. I couldn't believe it was that long ago. He plays an obnoxious, unorthodox but brilliant cop in San Francisco. There were loads of protests about this film regarding the treatment of women and police brutality but, when you look back, he was brilliant in it. And guess what? He didn't have any bullets left and the punk got it wrong. What a great scene, and the reaction of the guy on the floor at the end is fantastic. Of course, it led to a terrific series of films for the character: Magnum Force, The Enforcer, Sudden Impact and, in 1988, The Dead Pool. **DG: No surprise it's in there.** Except that it's only number four, probably.

3 MILLION DOLLAR BABY

A great film from 2004, so over 30 years after Dirty Harry. Clint Eastwood stars in Million Dollar Baby, he co-produced and directed it, and even did the music for it as well. I mean, is there no end to this man's talents? Incredible. He plays Frankie Dunn, a wizened, moody old boxing trainer, and Hilary Swank wants to be the boxer. Morgan Freeman's also in it and it's an incredibly painful and sad film. I certainly shed a few tears. **DG: I'm man enough to admit I've had a few tears over a film or two. When no one's watching!** There's nothing wrong with that. You get into a movie and the actors are so good that you're lost in that moment, and I think Million Dollar Baby is definitely one of those films. It had seven Oscar nominations and won four.

3 UNFORGIVEN

Here's another western. This was supposed to be his goodbye to cowboy films and so, rather than playing the bounty hunter who goes looking for his man, he plays an old and regretful gunslinger who's now a hog farmer looking after two kids after his wife passed away. He gets an offer from a young kid who can't shoot properly, one last job kind of thing, but he tells him he doesn't want to do it any more. He can't shoot because most of his shooting days were when he was full of whiskey. But a prostitute has been disfigured by this pair of cowboys, that gets to him and in the end he says he'll do it and sets off with his old partner, played by Morgan Freeman. I won't tell you the rest of the story in case you haven't seen it but it's about two men who used to be guns for hire and how that has affected their lives. There's a lot to unpack in this film and it won a host of awards, including the Best Director Oscar for Clint. **AD: I went to the cinema to see it and I remember thinking it was terrific.** It could easily have been my number one.

Dirty Harry: actually quite scrupulous about hygiene

2 WHERE EAGLES DARE

This one is a World War Two action film from 1968. Clint Eastwood is US Army Ranger Lieutenant Morris Schaffer who, alongside British Major John Smith – played by Richard Burton – has to take a team of elite Commandos into Nazi Germany to rescue a General. Where Eagles Dare is a fantastic war film. It's one of those films my dad forced on me as a kid. He was obsessed with Clint Eastwood and war films and westerns, so I was never going to miss this one. There's a nice twist in it.

2 PLAY MISTY FOR ME

Oh my goodness. This is from the early 1970s. Clint plays late-night radio host Dave Garver. He takes calls and dedicates the records to those who ring in. And a listener, Evelyn Draper, keeps asking for one song, Misty – as in "play Misty for me". She finds the bar where he hangs out after work, gets him into bed, and then she goes psycho and won't leave him alone. The end is absolutely petrifying. He is seriously brilliant in it and directs it as well. And I must admit, when I was much younger, it gave me second thoughts about getting into radio... and I've had a couple of little moments that weren't dissimilar. It's scary but tasteful and really well done. **DG: I have seen it but I think I'll have to watch it again.**

1 GRAN TORINO

Is it possible to be appalled by a character and admire him at the same time? Because that is exactly what happened for me with this one. Clint Eastwood plays the part of the veteran with such venom and anger in Gran Torino. He's absolutely believable. The ending of the film is superb – although, without giving too much away, I suspect a lawyer would probably get him off on a technicality. He produced, directed and starred in it. It is just brilliant. **DG: I knew it would be your number one because you never stop talking about it.**

1 ESCAPE FROM ALCATRAZ

In real life no one is supposed to have ever escaped, but they shut it down in the end, didn't they? Escape From Alcatraz came out in 1979 and it's the sort of film that does exactly what it says on the tin. It's about a prisoner who attempts to escape from a maximum-security prison on an island, which is Alcatraz, in 1962. He plays the character of Frank Morris, who has an exceptional IQ and has escaped from so many prisons in the past that they put him into Alcatraz to put a stop to his little game. Does he escape? That would be telling, but it's not as cut-and-dried as you think in the end. **AD: Doesn't this list just show how many brilliant films Clint Eastwood has made?**

TOP FIVE @ 5 DERBY GAMES

It's the five greatest derbies but with quite strict criteria. It's such a hot topic that we've restricted the choice to derbies we've been involved in – either myself commentating on the game or Darren actually playing in it. **DB: My five are derbies I've actually scored in.** OK, wow. But then, you have played for every team in the country. I'll go first...

5 NEWCASTLE UNITED v SUNDERLAND (2010)

The Tyne-Wear derby. The tactic that day was very much get it wide and toss it in the box to Andy Carroll and Shola Ameobi, and it worked an absolute treat. Kevin Nolan got a hat-trick that day and did the chicken dance. Do you remember that one? **DB: Yes, of course I do. Sunderland started off really well but when that first one went in they just capitulated. And when I say 'they', I mean 'we'.**

"Hooray for our glorious leader Mike Ashley!"

5 NEWCASTLE UNITED v SUNDERLAND (2010)

Yes, this is the same game – and I got a consolation goal at the end. I know we lost 5-1 but the reason it's got to be in here is that I have never experienced an atmosphere like it. Getting onto the coach and having to drive miles around the city to get to the ground under police escort, with fans attacking the coach... Before the game, the lads said that at St James' Park you cannot hear each other even if you're a metre apart. I thought they were winding me up, but when I walked out for the warm-up the fans were in there singing and we tried to shout to each other but could not hear a thing. It was an eye-opener. **SM: You grabbed the ball out of the net and ran back to the centre. Did you think the comeback was on?** I remember looking up at the away fans and there was hardly anyone left. And in Sunderland the following week hardly anyone spoke to me because we'd lost so badly.

4 SWANSEA CITY v CARDIFF CITY (2014)

The South Wales derby. Swansea won 3-0. What a fantastic atmosphere – it was naughty, though. There are always travel bans and they have to meet at a certain service station and be escorted in order for it to be safe under police guidance. The Swans were flying so high at this point – they were in the Europa League. It was brilliant. **DB: It's not just what happens on the pitch, is it? It's everything.** For me, it's about the experience. It wasn't the best derby or the fiercest rivalry but, ultimately, Swansea stayed up that season and Cardiff got relegated and a big part of it was that Swansea had beaten them. Cardiff had gone through a great period of not losing to Swansea up until this point so it felt like Swansea were on the up and Cardiff were struggling.

4 ASTON VILLA v WEST BROMWICH ALBION (2012)

Paul Lambert was the Villa manager. He hadn't played me the week before against Manchester City but had told me to get ready for the West Brom game. On the Saturday before the match he walked into the dressing room and stuck the teamsheet on the board and walked out. I went over to look and I was on the bench. My head instantly fell off. I was so angry and the lads asked me if he had told me. He hadn't. Anyway, the game started and the team were playing OK then Lambert told me to start warming up. I came on and scored after five minutes. It was a good goal, left-footed into the back of the net. But I was still so angry I started running in the direction of the bench. The lads were telling me not to go there and Barry Bannan jumped on my back. I carried him for about ten yards! I never got to play against Birmingham, which was frustrating as the lads said it was a great derby to be involved in.

3 CHELSEA v TOTTENHAM HOTSPUR (2008)

My number three is a London derby. We were getting battered. Juliano Belletti put Chelsea ahead 1-0 and I thought, here we go... **SM: Did you win this one?** No, it finished 1-1. There was a mix-up, the ball came through to me, Petr Cech came rushing out and I rolled it underneath him – in front of the Spurs fans as well. Great finish. Some Spurs fans will say the big derby is Arsenal but I always felt the Chelsea game was something else. I enjoyed that one, and my dad is a season-ticket holder at Chelsea so it was extra-special.

A Pompey fan wishing Harry all the best

3 PORTSMOUTH v SOUTHAMPTON (2005)

I was commentating for a local radio station. Not only is Portsmouth versus Southampton an intense derby, it's next level – especially when it's at Fratton Park. The atmosphere is always unbelievable but this was the best South Coast derby ever. Harry Redknapp had walked out on Portsmouth to manage Southampton less than six months before. You can't do that! It was a midday kick-off on a Sunday because they just couldn't take any risks. Harry had to have a police escort to get in. Portsmouth got a penalty after four minutes and they were 4-1 up after 27 minutes. **DB: Wow.** The whole place was going absolutely mad, off-the-scale crazy. Lomana LuaLua scores two goals and celebrates the fourth goal in front of the Saints fans at the Milton End by doing a somersault, pulls his hamstring and has to come off... and we didn't see him for the rest of the season. This game had everything. Also, it's worth pointing out that Portsmouth stayed up at the end of that season and Southampton went down. So again, it had a major impact.

2 EVERTON v LIVERPOOL (2020)

I've been lucky enough to do so many Merseyside derbies, because they're always at lunchtime on a Sunday or a Saturday and talkSPORT has had that fixture for years. The first time I did it, our batteries ran out because the producer forgot to plug in the kit and we went off air! But this particular match, the 2-2, had it all. Merseyside derbies always have something special and the best ones usually have a sending-off – Richarlison on this occasion – but it didn't stop there. There was a VAR controversy and a disallowed Jordan Henderson goal and then the coming-together between Jordan Pickford and Virgil van Dijk that unfortunately resulted in 'the injury'. It was behind closed doors so it didn't have the crowd element but it was a brilliant match.

2 ARSENAL v TOTTENHAM HOTSPUR (2008)

Arsenal 4 Spurs 4. **SM: Did you ever win any derbies?** Yeah, a few! This was one of Harry Redknapp's first games in charge. I came on and we were 3-1 down. Then Manuel Almunia dropped it and I tapped it in, so 3-2. Then they go 4-2 up and we think the game is over but we're still working hard. Jermaine Jenas scores a worldie and you're thinking, "We might get one more chance..." and then Luka Modric hits the post and Aaron Lennon, following in, taps the rebound into the empty net.

1 MANCHESTER UNITED v MANCHESTER CITY (2012)

My number one is the 164th Manchester derby. It was one of my favourite ever moments working. I had just said that Manchester City were interested in buying Robin van Persie and as soon as I said it he scored and I said, "I bet they wish they'd bought him now!" **DB: What a game! What a goal!** There were loads of things about this game: the narrative at the time was that City are coming but they haven't established themselves yet – Manchester United are still the big boys in town, they're still top dogs. But the characters involved in this match – Rooney, Fergie, Yaya Toure, Ferdinand, Kompany, Balotelli... United go 2-0 up in this game, two goals from Wayne Rooney, then City fight back and then Van Persie scores in the last minute. They bought him to score goals and win them the title and it worked! I also covered the 'Why always me?' 6-1 derby. And that was off the charts. I just love doing the Manchester derby, especially now the narrative has switched.

1 NORWICH CITY v IPSWICH TOWN (2003)

Listen, that's not as good as my number one: Ipswich 2 Norwich 0. **SM: You're kidding me?** No, my first derby. I scored the second goal. I was only 18 at the time. **SM: Was that the only one you won?** No, but it is the one that always sticks in my mind because it was my first one and I scored the winner. I took my shirt off, jumped into the crowd and got booked. So it had it all!

Darren Bent in action against Norwich in the Old Farm derby

TOP FIVE @ 5 GOLDEN OLDIES

What we thought we'd do for this one is look at players who have thrived after the age of 36. I've gone exclusively for players who appeared in the Premier League and done very well after their 36th birthday, while Darren has gone a bit further afield. I've also gone for impact and trophies won. **DB: Mine have also won trophies but were top-level right to the very end.** OK, let's find out...

5 JAVIER ZANETTI (Inter Milan)
The right-back for Inter Milan. He was there for 19 years and accumulated 143 Argentinian caps. That is crazy. He officially played 1,114 games; he was 40 when he retired and still in unbelievable nick. Javier Zanetti won everything and for me was one of the greatest right-backs to ever play the game. **SM: I went to his restaurant in Milan, it was amazing. Loads of memorabilia on the walls and, of course, he is vice president of Inter as well.** Captain of Inter and could play in the centre of midfield as well.

4 PAOLO MALDINI (AC Milan)
He spent 25 years at one club, AC Milan – 25 years at one club is insane and he was 41 when he retired but looked like he could have carried on even longer. **SM: These Italians go on for a long time, don't they?** He was arguably the greatest left-back ever, a serial winner. **SM: What a family legacy: his dad was there as a player and now I think his own son is on the books. It's like the Maldinis are woven into the fabric of AC Milan.** You know what, they probably reckon, seeing as it's worked once, let's keep recycling them.

5 DIDIER DROGBA (Chelsea)
He obviously did very well for Chelsea in the first period that he was there: won the Champions League and scored the winning penalty. **DB: And he scored the header that got them back into the game.** From that Juan Mata cross, the first corner of the game in the 88th minute! They didn't play very well that night. But he came back when he was 36. I did an event for Soccer Aid in the summer of 2014 and Jose Mourinho was the manager of the Rest of the World team at the time. We were sitting in the bar at the Lowry Hotel in Manchester and he said, "I'm gonna bring back Didier Drogba this summer." And I was like, "Why?" And he said, "I need it in the dressing room. I need winners in the dressing room. I need the mentality to get this group over the line next year." They won the League that year with Drogba in the dressing room. He was more of an influence off the field than he was on it that season, but he did score a really important goal at Old Trafford when Chelsea had a problem with their strikers and he was the only one who was fit. **DB: Would he make your all-time Chelsea XI?** I dunno. **DB: Simple question.** No it isn't, I haven't thought about it... maybe, yes.

He only came back for the Drog/dog headline puns

4 **TEDDY SHERINGHAM (Portsmouth)**

I met this guy during the Portsmouth period of his life. Teddy Sheringham was 37 and he joined up with Portsmouth after they got promoted to the Premier League in 2003. From the minute he came in he was an absolute star for the club. He scored on his debut and got their first goal of the season in a 2-1 win against Aston Villa. In the second home game of the season he scored a hat-trick against Bolton – it was their third game and they were top of the Premier League on a Tuesday night in the middle of September! He scored 10 goals that season. He was 38 by the time the season was out and made 38 appearances in his one spell at Fratton Park. He was brilliant as a leader in the dressing room, and he was brilliant on the field. A perfect foil for Yakubu. **DB: I don't agree with that. He's not world-class, an icon like Maldini or Zanetti.** He was a treble-winner, scored an iconic goal and has a world-class footballing brain.

3 **GIANLUIGI BUFFON (Juventus)**

Number three for me is this guy. **SM: Goalkeepers are banned.** Who banned goalkeepers? **SM: We all did. There was a meeting and we banned goalkeepers. If we include goalkeepers we'll be here all night; they go on forever because they don't do anything.** I wasn't made aware of this but now I am. Buffon. Juventus. He's 43 and still going. **SM: So Maldini was 41 when he retired, that's more of an achievement than a goalkeeper still playing at 43. He's got more miles on the clock.** Yes but Buffon is older and he's still going, at the highest level. He's still got to be agile.

Gianluigi Buffon and on and on and on ...

3 **LEE DIXON (Arsenal)**

Now this is a big hitter. It's Lee Dixon. **DB: Acceptable.** He was playing until he was 38 years of age. At 38 Lee Dixon was part of a squad in which he made 13 league appearances and 19 overall appearances in a double-winning team in 2002. The year before, he started the FA Cup final against Liverpool at 37. At that time Arsenal were one of the fittest teams, they were top of the league in sports science and nutrition, they were behaving correctly and Lee Dixon was still in the dressing room in his late 30s. You didn't get many then playing until they were nearly 40. **DB: No complaints here. He's an absolute club legend and he looked after himself.** He still does.

2 ZLATAN IBRAHIMOVIC (Sweden)

He's 39 years old and he's not slowing down. **SM: I used to find him really irritating but when he scored that goal for Sweden against England... it was the most remarkable goal I have seen from outside the penalty area.** That goal doesn't get spoken about enough, or that back-flick against Italy in the 2004 Euros – that was when he first appeared on my radar. And he's playing really well for AC Milan this season. **SM: Have you read his book?** No. **SM: It's a brilliant tale. He doesn't drink, does martial arts, yoga.** He calls himself a lion. For someone who has played for so many top teams it's hard to believe he has never won the Champions League.

2 GARY McALLISTER (Liverpool)

He had a terrific career. He played for Leeds United, played for Coventry City. He'd been fantastic for Scotland. At the age of 35 and a half, he joined Liverpool and was integral to the team that went on to win the League Cup, FA Cup and UEFA Cup in that season. And if you're sitting there thinking, well, Gary McAllister didn't play a part in that... oh yes he did. Because he scored a 44-yard free kick against Everton in the FA Cup run and he also took the free kick, which was the Golden Goal, after 117 minutes in the UEFA Cup final against Alaves to win the whole thing. What an inspiration. The great Gerard Houllier said McAllister was the most inspirational signing that he made at Liverpool. **DB: Funny you should say that, because I've worked under Gary and he had this annoying habit in a training session of showing us how it should be done any time somebody messed up. And he could do it with both feet.** And if you're going to argue that he was 35 and a half and not 36, his birthday was on Christmas Day so he was 36 when he won all those trophies.

Premier League legend Eric Cantona considers former Leeds teammate Gary McAllister to be the best player he ever played alongside

1 CRISTIANO RONALDO (Juventus)

Game over. Arguably one of the greatest players of all time. **SM: He's only just turned 36! He hasn't done anything since.** It's coming. He will achieve something. **SM: I respect his dedication. He sets the standard.**

1 RYAN GIGGS (Manchester United)

Well, when we talk about Premier League stars of a certain vintage I don't think you can exclude the one and only Ryan Giggs. He's my number one. He turned 36 in 2009, just months after he'd been part of a Champions League-winning team and was subsequently part of the squad that got to another final. He then won three Premier Leagues, a League Cup, two Community Shields and the BBC Sports Personality of the Year, scored in the Olympics in 2012 on home soil and played another 150 games for Manchester United. All after his 36th birthday. He could probably have picked up his pension while he was still fashioning goals for United. **DB: You've got no arguments from me on that one.**

TOP FIVE @ 5 WEMBLEY MOMENTS

It's over 20 years since the old Wembley closed its doors. So many memories. DG: I went to see England and Wales U16s when I was 10. You never know, Ryan Giggs might have been playing. I doubt it, he's younger than you... anyway, I'm doing the 'Old Wembley' and Darren the 'New Wembley'.

5 ENGLAND v SCOTLAND (1977)

A Scotland win at Wembley against England in the Home Championships in 1977: Scotland won 2-1. Gordon McQueen with a terrific header, 1-0. Kenny Dalglish, scruffy goal, 2-0. And Mick Channon with a penalty, 2-1. There were no fences at this time and all the Scotland fans came onto the pitch. I'm pretty sure a lot of people of a certain age will remember this so clearly – back then we only had three TV channels so millions will have seen it. The fans just poured onto the pitch, climbed onto the crossbar and snapped the thing. I was about eight at the time and that just stayed in my mind forever. There was no fighting, it was meant to be celebratory, but it wasn't right that they snapped the bar! **DG: Have Scotland won at Wembley since?** Yeah, Don Hutchison scored for them. An Englishman.

4 MANCHESTER UNITED v BENFICA (1968)

The European Cup final. It finished 4-1 to United but it was 1-1 going into extra time. Eusebio was playing, he hit the bar. Bobby Charlton scored two and was magnificent. Brian Kidd scored as well but the goal that everybody remembers is George Best's, where he rounds the keeper and slots it into the net and the keeper goes diving into the goal to try and save it. Something people might not remember from that final because the footage is in black and white was that United wore a blue kit. Can you believe that? **DG: It was a decent kit.** United can't wear blue, I'm not having that. But they were the first English club to win the European Cup. It was 10 years after the Munich disaster and we didn't have ABUs (Anybody But United) at that time and, believe it or not, the whole nation rejoiced.

5 ARSENAL v HULL CITY (2014)

The 2014 FA Cup final. I've got this one because it came the year after the upset when Wigan beat Man City. Can you believe this: Hull were 2-0 up after eight minutes thanks to goals from two centre-halves and everyone was laughing, thinking here we go again, this is brilliant. But an amazing Santi Cazorla free kick brought them back into it. At 71 minutes Laurent Koscielny scrambled it over the line and then in extra time, with 11 minutes left, Aaron Ramsey popped up and scored the winner. It was a great final. **AD: I think with Hull 2-0 up Arsenal had to clear one off the line.** Hull were amazing but what a comeback from Arsenal and a big goal from Ramsey after coming back from injury. **AD: We had him on the show the week after and he was still so excited to have scored that winner.**

4 HULL FC v WIGAN WARRIORS (2017)

This is one for you, Ade. It's Hull FC as the holders beating Wigan 18-14 in the Challenge Cup final to retain the trophy. **AD: Love it!** What a game. Marc Sneyd kicked so well for Hull and, although there was a controversial disallowed try for Wigan, Hull definitely earned it that day. Wigan are a club used to winning finals but this was their first defeat at the new Wembley and it was back-to-back Wembley wins for Hull FC, who had never won there until 2016.

3 HENRY COOPER v CASSIUS CLAY (1963)

When you go back and watch this again it just reminds you just how good a fight this was. The build-up was sensational. Clay called Cooper a bum and a cripple and the crowd hated Clay, they hated him. Henry got cut, that was his big problem throughout his career – and his corner wanted to stop it at the end of the third round but Cooper said no. He went out for the fourth and Clay was clowning around and dodging punches and Cooper caught him with an absolute belter towards the end of the round. Clay slithered down the ropes like a cartoon character. He said afterwards, "Henry hit me so hard he shook my ancestors in Africa." He got up after five seconds, which was probably a little bit too early because he was still very wobbly, but before Henry got a chance to finish him off the bell went. There were all sorts of shenanigans in the corner and accusations of gamesmanship being flung around but, crucially, there was a delay – and by the time they came back out, Clay had recovered. He went for it, opened up Henry's cut and that was it. Clay won it in the fifth round but seriously, what a fight. And when you consider what Clay went on to achieve as Muhammad Ali, how important historically.

3 BUFFALO BILLS v JACKSONVILLE JAGUARS (2015)

An American football game in London – who would have thought that would ever happen? The owner of the Jaguars – or *Jag-wahs*, as they insist upon pronouncing it – wanted to buy Wembley at one point, but this was a massive game. The score was Buffalo Bills 31, Jacksonville Jaguars 34. The Jags went 27-3 up, the Bulls came back to lead 31-27 and with three minutes left the Jaguars' quarterback, Blake Bortles, marched down the field and connected with a wide receiver, Allen Hurns, who provided the game-winning touchdown. It had fumbles, interceptions, running touchdowns and rushing touchdowns. Even though it was the ninth season of American football being played here, it's seen as the game where the Brits finally 'got' American football, when they finally understood the game. **AD: So we were all dimwits before that? Gotcha.**

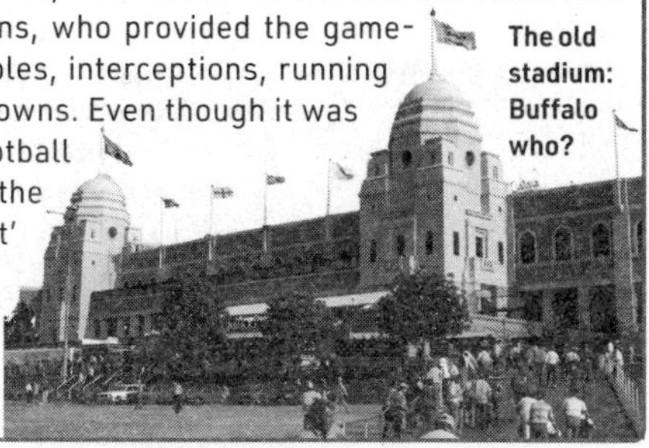

The old stadium: Buffalo who?

2 ENGLAND v WEST GERMANY (1966)

My number two is England winning the World Cup at Wembley in 1966. I really don't need to say anything more, other than that it's not my number one. **DG: That's thrown me.** Wait and see.

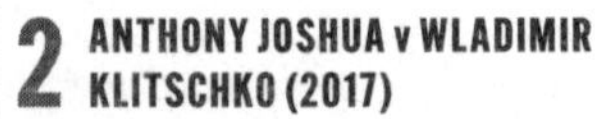

2 ANTHONY JOSHUA v WLADIMIR KLITSCHKO (2017)

This kind of sells itself as well. There were 90,000 supporters in the new Wembley for this. Klitschko had already lost against Fury and looked hungry. He was down in the fifth but got up to put AJ on the canvas in the sixth before Joshua came back to win on a TKO in the 11th round. Klitschko went off into the sunset after this, retiring a couple of months later. But it was a massive fight for Joshua and boxing magazine The Ring called it the fight of the year.

1 MANCHESTER UNITED v BARCELONA (2011)

My 'New Wembley' number one is football: Barcelona v Manchester United in the Champions League final. This had to be in because people still talk about that Barcelona team being the best club side ever and they certainly gave United a proper lesson here, winning 3-1. Just look at the team sheet: Valdes in goal, Alves, Pique, Mascherano, Abidal, Iniesta, Busquets, Xavi, Pedro, Messi, Villa; and on the bench they had Puyol, Afellay, Adriano, Thiago and Keita. Manchester United had no answers. Some of the football Barcelona played that day was just ridiculous! **AD: What a good shout that is.**

The new stadium: Phil who?

1 LIVE AID (1985)

There were 72,000 people there for my number one: Live Aid, on the 13th of July 1985. And, if you remember, the gig went on in Philadelphia afterwards. Phil Collins performed at both. So he played at Wembley, then flew on Concorde to New York and got a helicopter to Philadelphia and performed there. An estimated £150 million was raised by the concerts for famine relief in Africa. It was organised by Bob Geldof and Midge Ure. I remember it clearly. I played in a tennis tournament in the morning and we had a family barbecue in the afternoon. I remember my brother-in-law was a bit mad and was chucking petrol on the barbecue to get it going while we were all watching Live Aid. U2, David Bowie, George Michael, Elton John, Spandau Ballet... **DG: Queen and Freddie stole the show.** Yes. Amazing event and so Live Aid had to be my 'Old Wembley' number one.

Bono could have raised millions just by pledging to lose the mullet

TOP FIVE @ 5 OASIS SONGS

We put out a poll on social media to see which band or musician you wanted on the Top Five and we were overwhelmed at the response - it was Oasis by a country mile. As luck would have it, we had Noel Gallagher on the show and asked him about his Top Five. Here's what he said: "Don't Look Back In Anger, Supersonic, Rock'n'Roll Star, The Masterplan and Half A World Away. But I'd say we've got about 12 all-time classics so picking five ain't going to be easy." So modest. Let's see...

Only years later would Liam work out how to adjust a mic stand

5 SHE'S ELECTRIC

I know there are people around the country thinking, "Why on earth did you pick that?" - and I don't think Noel Gallagher likes it particularly - but let me explain my Oasis history very quickly. The second album, (What's The Story) Morning Glory?, was the only one I played over and over again. Now, from the other albums there were songs I liked, but it's predominantly that album you'll find in my Top Five. Some people hate it, I know, but I actually love it. In the middle of the global superstardom that Oasis found themselves in during the mid '90s, this track was just like a good, fun tune. And I've loved it ever since. it won't go down as classic but I like it. **DG: Yeah, you can sing along to it. There's nothing wrong with the song, it's a good start... but I can see why it's your number five and not your number one.**

Third Oasis album "Be Here Now" sold more than 350,000 copies on the day it was released, August 21st 1997. It is still the UK's fastest-selling album.

5 STOP CRYING YOUR HEART OUT

This is a great song, 2002. Only reached No.2 in the UK charts, but it's the video I originally liked - the way it starts: Noel on piano, Liam on the vocals, chewing gum. And it's absolutely brilliant. It's a bit slower than your normal Oasis song, came off their fifth album, Heathen Chemistry. It's not your normal Oasis up-and-at-'em but I had to put it and that was at the expense of Some Might Say, Roll With It and Cigarettes And Alcohol. **AD: I'll be amazed to see what else kept those three out. But do you know what I think about when I hear that song? Frank Lampard. The Leeds fans were singing it at him when he was the Derby boss.** You can sing along with all their songs, that's what makes them so brilliant.

4 WONDERWALL

This was brought out in 1995 and the reason I like this is that I'd just got into the England side, we went away on tour and this is what we'd be singing in the dressing room or on the bus. I bought a guitar, took it away with me and this is the first tune I learned to play on it. Look all around, no matter what age, most people can get stuck in with Wonderwall. It's a fantastic song and, although it's not their best, this is the one where people will know most of the words. **AD: Do you know what's interesting about this song? I've heard so many people sing it completely out of tune it's kind of ruined it for me a little bit. However, when you listen to the original, with these guys playing it, you remember just how brilliant it is. It missed my Top Five but, just listening to it again... imagine listening to that with them playing it live, the noise would be electric.**

4 THE MASTERPLAN

DG: Are you there, Adrian? Yeah, I was just waiting for the "Masterplan" bit to come in. Flipping heck. Why are we talking over the chorus? Do these people [*in production*] know the actual songs? It's The Masterplan, you have to listen to the chorus, that's the whole point of the song. Honestly, dear oh dear. Actually, I didn't know about this song for years after it came out, and then when I first heard it, which wasn't that long ago, I thought, "Wow, how did this pass me by?" It's just utter, utter genius. Absolutely love this song so much. It probably should be higher up my list. Powerful, solid sound, good hook, strong lyric. It's an Oasis anthem. In fact, I think it surpasses both Wonderwall and Don't Look Back In Anger as the most anthemic song they ever produced – and Noel still does it with his High Flying Birds. I've got this thing about Noel singing, I prefer him to Liam. Yeah, I do. Sorry. **DG: I think they're both great. Liam for that nasal sound when he sings and Noel just sitting there singing with his guitar – I've seen him do that with just been a few people in the room. You can't beat it. For all the qualities Liam has got you can't say he's a musical genius, but his brother is.**

3 LIVE FOREVER

Do you like this? **AD: I don't dislike it but it would never make my Top Five.** Released in 1994, the band's third single and first Top Ten hit in America. You don't like the way Liam sings when he delays and lengthens the lyrics but I absolutely adore it, that's what makes him different to everybody else. **AD: I just think it became such a cliché, "sunnnnshinnnnnne" and all that.** But that's part of it and part of him, and that's why people like it. It's all to do with his attitude. I told you I was sat opposite him on a train going into London, didn't I? He was there with his family and he was just a lovely family bloke, reading and doing puzzles with his kids, and when he got off the train he turned into a totally different animal because he became public space. He got the walk on and jokingly kicked his missus up the backside – he just turned on the popstar. He does make me laugh.

3 HALF A WORLD AWAY

This is the song Ed Sheeran wishes he'd written. It's actually a beautiful tune and a beautiful song. People will know it from The Royle Family but it deserves wider recognition than that. It's a very underrated song. There's something really special in Half A World Away. I love that song. **DG: They deliver, don't they?**

2 SOME MIGHT SAY

This could very easily have been my number one. From verse to bridge to chorus is a real big crescendo and you get swept along with it. I think, technically, it's a truly great song. It's arguably, technically, the best song Noel ever wrote. This is the one that really stuck with me when I first heard What's The Story.

2 ROCK'N'ROLL STAR

This is what it's all about: being in a band, being a rock'n'roll star. Noel talks about becoming this rock star and this is one of three songs that summed up everything he wanted to say in a song about being young, fulfilling your dream in a band. And this is what it's about. Absolutely brilliant from start to finish, a great tune well delivered by everyone in that band.

Noel and Liam, wondering about a wall

1 CHAMPAGNE SUPERNOVA

This choice might surprise a lot of people but I just love everything about this song. And I guess Noel must as well – didn't he use to live in a house called Supernova Heights in north London? This did well in the American charts in 1996. It starts off with these crashing waves that send you into a dream world, and then the guitar comes in and Paul Weller's on it. What more do you want from a song? Champagne Supernova. This is Oasis. Some people talk about the lyrics not making sense but that's what makes it for me. You make of them what you want. **AD: It's seven and a half minutes of greatness. What a way to end what has already been a brilliant album – just sends you into a trance.** I think they used to finish with this one live. **AD: Well, I Am The Walrus usually, but this would be the last of their own songs.**

1 DON'T LOOK BACK IN ANGER

Brilliantly written by Noel, perfectly sung by Noel, and this is him getting as close anyone has ever got to John Lennon. The lyrics are based on Lennon's own words, the piano at the start is reminiscent of Watching The Wheels, a Lennon song, and there are some intricate mini guitar solos throughout – but the one at the very end is so very Beatles. I think *this* is what Noel Gallagher was dreaming about when he said he wanted to be that rock'n'roll star. Even the video with the drumkit in the water is brilliant. **DG: We still talk about them and dream of them getting back together, but it ain't going to happen, is it? Just sit here and listen to the music.**

TOP FIVE @ 5 MARADONA MOMENTS

It was only when he passed away recently, aged 60, that many people paused to reflect upon the genius of Diego Armando Maradona. Here are our Top Fives from the many moments Maradona entertained, astounded and infuriated us all...

5 COPA DEL REY FINAL, 1984

Barcelona v Athletic Bilbao. This was a nasty game and Maradona wasn't happy going into it because he was coming face to face with the Butcher of Bilbao, Andoni Goikoetxea, who had broken his ankle the year before. He kind of knew what to expect and the game didn't disappoint – it was total carnage. It basically ended in disgrace with 22 players punching and kicking each other. Diego knocked somebody out with a knee, ended up being sold that summer and had to apologise to the King of Spain. **AD: Apparently, when he had that ankle broken, Goikoetxea had the boots he was wearing at the time framed like it was a prized scalp.**

4 PRE-MATCH WARM-UP, 1989

This is before the UEFA Cup semi-final second leg in 1989. It was Napoli v Bayern Munich. Music was playing and he was dancing and doing kick-ups with his laces undone, catching the ball on his neck and doing tap-ups on his head. He was just so chilled out and relaxed, and considering it was a big game it just showed how he could absorb all the pressure. **AD: The dancing footballer. For me it symbolises how comfortable he was with a ball at his feet on a football pitch. It didn't matter what was going on around him, he was just at home with the ball.** He got his teammates doing it too.

5 PRESS CONFERENCE IN SCOTLAND, 2008

There were so many things that made up the character that was Diego Maradona and, on that note, my number five is a little bit different. It's from a press conference that he did as Argentina manager. It was 2008 and it was his first game as Argentina manager – they won 1-0 at Hampden Park against Scotland. And at the start of the press conference beforehand a friend of mine, Carrie Brown, asked this question: "You are a proud Argentinian – I can only imagine, if you were in the position of being in a World Cup quarter-final and you lost to a hand goal, what your response would be? Can you understand the reaction of Terry Butcher in some manner?" And Maradona replied, "England won a World Cup with a goal, and it is plain to see by everyone that the ball never crossed the line so I don't think it's fair that anyone should judge me when stuff like that went on." At the end he looks like he caught a big fish. That's how far it wasn't over the line, is what he's saying. It's amazing that his first game is in Scotland and he knows he's on safe ground having a go at the English. But what a brilliant response to a question. And the face he pulls too. It's well worth checking out the video. **DG: He wasn't bothered what people thought.** He's got a point, though, hasn't he?

4 LAP OF HONOUR, 2010

My number four is another from when Maradona was managing Argentina. It was Argentina v Nigeria at the World Cup in South Africa. Maradona goes out 90 minutes before kick-off for a very slow lap of honour around the pitch. Everybody in the ground stands up, applauds him and can't get close enough to him. They can't love him enough. It was a magnificent spectacle. When Gabriel Heinze scored the only goal of the game he ran straight to Maradona. It wasn't just the crowd who loved him, the players loved him as well.

3 FAILED DRUG TEST, 1994

This was a huge scandal. This was supposed to be his comeback but he wasn't ready. He was overweight and he just didn't want to play football any more. Argentina, however, were desperate for him to play in this World Cup and he got in with a bodybuilder who got him on a crash diet, taking all sorts to get him in some kind of shape for the World Cup. Everybody remembers when he scored against Greece – he ran up to the camera eyes bulging in a 4-0 victory and everyone thought Maradona was back... but before the next game against Nigeria he picked up a cold, didn't he? So he was given an assortment of drugs to combat his sinus problems and help with his weight management, which was ongoing. He played the whole 90 minutes and got called in to give a urine sample at the end of the game. He failed the drug test and was sent home in disgrace. And it just goes to show that no matter who you are, you can be the best footballer in the world, if you get involved with the wrong sort of people and take shortcuts there is always a consequence at the end of it – and that's what Maradona discovered.

AD: That was Maradona's last World Cup but I'm going back to his first for my number three...

3 WORLD CUP RED CARD, 1982

This is Spain 1982; Brazil are beating Argentina 3-0. And, of course, Maradona is frustrated, he's fuming. He's angry and he can't calm down at all, he can't rationalise it at all. And he sees a high boot going into a teammate's head – it doesn't excuse him, but as an act of revenge he goes studs first into the groin of Brazil player Batista, and that challenge makes your eyes water. It's not for the squeamish. And it's a straight red, off he goes, and he ends that World Cup in disgrace as well... although he slightly made up for it in 1986, I have to say!

1994: "Nothing can possibly go wrong now!"

Yeah, that one was OK, s'pose

2 WORLD CUP FINAL, 1986

The way West Germany planned to solve the Maradona problem in order to win the World Cup final was to kick him from pillar to post for 90 minutes. The treatment of Maradona in that game was unreal, but he kept getting up after being kicked all over the place. He was man-marked for the whole game. But still, there were moments of brilliance in a turn here, a pass there... and his killer pass that led to the winning goal. He just let it run, opened up his body and slotted it through to Jorge Burrachaga to make it 3-2 with six minutes to go. Argentina won the World Cup and they had to, really, it had to be Maradona's World Cup. **AD: They would not have won it without him, that's for sure.** Some people say he didn't turn up in that final? Watch it again. He was all over the pitch and everywhere he went they were trying to kick him.

2 THE DOCUMENTARY

My number two is the brilliant documentary, called Diego Maradona, about his time at Napoli, directed by Asif Kapadia. If you haven't seen it you really should, just to appreciate how hard it was to be Maradona at this point in his life.

1 THE SECOND GOAL AGAINST ENGLAND, 1986

We've all seen it so many times before: the World Cup quarter-final in Mexico City. For those who can't remember it, Maradona receives the ball just inside his own half and is under pressure from Peter Reid and Peter Beardsley. He pirouettes out of danger and takes a heavy touch while driving towards goal. Reid can only jog behind him and looks like he's got a sack of coal on his back as Maradona bursts away with that speed. Terry Butcher then gives it a go as Maradona gets closer to the box but misses the tackle as Maradona cuts inside. What was he doing there? Terry Fenwick is the next up but Maradona knocks the ball past him as if he's a traffic cone, then dummies to take a shot and goes past Shilton before passing the ball into the back of the net. And he never once touched it with his right foot – all with his left foot. Who says you need to use both feet? **AD: Maradona's left foot was just ridiculous!**

1 THE HAND OF GOD

My number one is from the same game. What else could it be? Not everybody knew it was a handball immediately – the commentator certainly didn't. It wasn't until everyone saw that photo on the front of the papers the next day. It's one of the biggest headlines ever in World Cup history. So, whether you think he should be remembered as the brilliant footballer represented by the second goal that you described so well, or for the Hand of God, that's up to you. Either way, Diego Maradona was an absolute football God.

TOP FIVE @ 5 FAVOURITE NORDIC SPORT STARS

Initially we were going to go Scandinavian but then we thought we'd branch out a little to take in Iceland and go full Nordic. To begin with I had visions of skiing but I haven't gone there. **DG: I've gone for one, sort of.** Let's get on with it...

5 MORTEN GAMST PEDERSEN

When this Top Five came up, the first name I thought of was Morten Gamst Pedersen. People might think that's a little bit weird but I really loved watching him play. He had a magic left foot and played eight seasons in the Premier League... but quickly got forgotten, didn't he? I loved watching him, mainly because he used to have great fun while playing football and there's not many sport stars you can say that about. He played every single game with a smile on his face. You could tell he absolutely loved it, and that meant he had a proper connection with the Blackburn fans, but he was also flipping brilliant with that left foot and scored a couple of cracking goals. He's not one of the world's greatest players but he is one of my favourite Nordic sport stars.

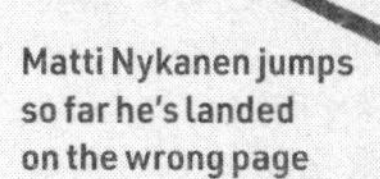

Matti Nykanen jumps so far he's landed on the wrong page

5 HENRIK STENSON

I've gone golf. At times this guy has been a superb golfer. He's played in five Ryder cups. European Golfer of the Year twice, in 2013 and 2016, the year he also won the Open; he even has an Olympic silver medal as well. He was world number two, didn't quite make it to number one, but being world number two with some of the golfers we have had over the last 20 years is remarkable. So Henrik Stenson has to be in it.

Stenson once tricked fellow pros at a tournament in China into using a pen that delivered electric shocks. What a card.

4 ZLATAN IBRAHIMOVIC

Iconic footballer and a great personality. He loves himself and that's why I love him. He's made loads of these Top Fives for different reasons, played for Ajax, Juventus, Barcelona, Manchester United and AC Milan, and he went to America and scored goals there. And now he's back in Europe. He's scored nearly 600 goals, more than 500 at club level. What more do you want from a great footballer?

4 JOHN CAREW

Let me take you back to 2001. Valencia were at their peak – they had just reached their first European Cup final the year before, and as they continued to build they brought in the godlike Norwegian John Carew up front. Arsenal were on course to win the Champions League that season when they came up against the man they called Little John: 6ft 5 of pure Norwegian manmeat. He swatted Tony Adams off like a fly as the cross flew in and got the most beautifully crafted glancing header that knocked Arsenal out. Valencia made their second successive final and took Bayern Munich to a shootout; Carew scored his but Valencia missed out. When Carew came to Aston Villa he had three full seasons with them and averaged one goal in three games in the Premier League. I thought he was terrific and probably should have played more for Villa – he was left out a few times. But since that goal against Arsenal he has been up there for me. **DG: That's a bit harsh.** Why? He swept aside England's centre-back, he made David Seaman look like a mug in goal. It takes a special talent to do something like that. He wasn't rapid but he was mobile.

3 MATTI NYKANEN

Here's the 'sort of skier': he's a Finnish ski-jumper and a controversial character. No longer with us, sadly. Matti Nykanen had problems in his life away from the sport but as a ski-jumper he was truly brilliant. He won four Winter Olympic golds and five World Championships golds, and he's the only ski-jumper in history to win all five of the sport's major events. This guy was out of this world. I tried it once. **AD: It looks petrifying to me.** I would never do it again. **AD: I would never do it in the first place.** I damaged ankle ligaments, hurt my knee and broke three ribs and I was still trying to jump! It's the only time in my life when I've had a mental block and just couldn't do it any more. I was only jumping 15 metres and these pros are jumping 100 metres! That's why when people take the mickey out of Eddie the Eagle, I'm like, he is one of the bravest men I know. **AD: I understand your ski-jumper was also a stripper.** He's been everything, married six times, been in prison. You don't want to look at what he got up to off the field. He's not a good role model in that respect. **AD: Did he ski-jump naked?** No, he didn't.

3 ANNIKA SORENSTAM

My turn to go golf, and arguably the greatest female golfer in history. Annika Sorenstam had some 90 tournament wins, ten majors, and is one of the biggest influencers of her generation. The profile and popularity of women's golf cannot be attributed to one person only but this Swede has definitely played her part. And here's something you may not know: Darren Gough prefers watching women's golf to men's golf, don't you? **DG: I like watching them for their skill and technique on the green; the men's game is more to do with power now.** I think as a gamechanger and as an individual, you have to admire what Sorenstam has achieved and what she's contributed to women's golf. Since she was a player, women's golf has taken off dramatically and she has left an incredible legacy.

2 BJORN BORG

What a talent! In the late 1970s Bjorn Borg absolutely dominated tennis before he decided to call it a day. Five back-to-back Wimbledon titles. I mean, how do you do that? In the Davis Cup he's got a record of 33 consecutive singles victories from 1973 to 1980. That's how good he was. He made tennis cool. He was handsome and he had the mental strength to compete at the highest level. It was just the US Open that eluded him – he lost four finals. His footwork, his agility, his speed around the court... and a wooden racket! No wonder he's still admired.

Borg: like Ikea, but in tennis form

2 MAGNUS CARLSEN

Before you say anything, I do believe chess is a sport. It's probably my favourite sport. Magnus Carlsen is only 30 but he's World Chess Champion, World Rapid Chess Champion and World Blitz Chess Champion. At age 13 he ran Garry Kasparov close in a game; Kasparov later became his mentor. He was born in Norway in 1990 and was world number one in 2010 – at the age of 20, incredible. He's been the best chess player in the world for a decade and, here's his crowning glory, in December 2019 he was the best Fantasy Football player in the world as well! He hit the top spot, ahead of seven million others Can you believe that? **DG: Surely there are only so many moves you can make in chess and everybody must know each other's moves?** It's strategy, that's what it is. It's thinking three or four moves ahead.

1 MICHAEL LAUDRUP

My number one is a Dane. In the 1986 World Cup Michael Laudrup was out of this world. He was fantastic, on another level. He made football look easy, an unbelievable passer of a football. When you talk about the great clubs, he played for some of the biggest: Juventus, Barcelona and Real Madrid. He was part of Cruyff's team at Barcelona that won the European Cup in 1992. In 1999 he was voted the greatest foreign player in Spanish football of the previous 25 years because he'd won five La Ligas. That's how good he was. An absolutely super player and he has to be my number one. **AD: And he won the League Cup as Swansea manager!** So he did.

1 PETER SCHMEICHEL

I've gone for a Dane too, and what more do you have to say? He was a legend, a great character and a brilliant goalkeeper. Peter Schmeichel is my number one.

TOP FIVE @ 5 TV THEME TUNES

Let me be clear, these are not our Top Five TV shows, just theme tunes, and mine aren't really in any order. **DB: Mine are in order, I did it properly.** How can you love one theme tune more than another? **DB: It's like songs, you love some more than others.** OK, good point, I'd not thought that through.

5 MASTERMIND

This brings back awful, awful nightmares. It's not a great tune but I had to put Mastermind in there because it's all anyone has gone on about since I went on it and failed. My specialist subject was James Bond. I got one point in that round and two points in general knowledge. The one I got right was "What bank did they rob in Goldfinger?" **AG: Was it the Midland?** It was Fort Knox. The presenter was John Humphrys. He's scary. Sitting in that chair was the most nervous and the worst experience of my entire life. It's that nerve-wracking. It's pitch black and all you can see is John Humphrys. You can't see that everyone is there looking at you. It's a lot worse than taking a penalty. **AG: I hope I never experience that.**

4 THE A-TEAM

This is a banger. This could quite easily have been my number one – it's a classic. When I listen to this, the first thing I think of is BA Baracus. Or Snickers. He does the adverts, doesn't he? He had all these necklaces and I'll tell you now, they never came off and they couldn't have come off. There are too many of them. **AG: Great show; nobody ever died in it. The thing I loved about the show was that they'd be stuck in a broom cupboard and had to create a tank from masking tape, washing-up liquid and some household bleach. You can have a point for that.**

5 CHEERS

"Sometimes you want to go where everybody knows your name." Do you know this? **DB: No.** How can you not know this? **DB: I didn't watch Cheers. This is not really a great theme song either.** I've got goosebumps. Great TV show, great tune. Look at everyone listening to this is in the gallery, they're happy, they've all got smiles on their faces. 1-0 to me, perfect.

4 GRANGE HILL

Goosebumps again. Why has that happened? Did you know the original Grange Hill theme tune is called Chicken Man? This makes me think of Tucker, Mrs McCluskey, Mr Bronson and a cartoon sausage flying through the room on a cartoon fork. Apparently they changed the Grange Hill theme tune to something that sounds like a sports quiz show at some point after I stopped watching it. Why'd anybody do that?

3 POWER

Have you seen Power? **AG: No.** You need to start, it's on Netflix. **AG: I think I saw it once, turned it off, bad acting.** I'm not saying anything. The acting is brilliant and the theme tune is great. Everyone has watched it! The name of the song is Big Rich Town. The singer is Joe Thomas but he goes by the name Joe. **AG: I bet it's about geezers with big arms who go to the gym.** Everyone knows that theme song. It's great, isn't it? **AG: It's not the best, but my next one is close to being the best...**

3 MINDER

Do you know who sang this? Dennis Waterman. I can picture them now walking around that Cortina, was it a Ford Cortina? [*It was a Ford Capri.*] George Cole was in it playing Arthur Daley – he had a great voice. They brought it back in 2009 with Shane Ritchie; it wasn't bad, but Minder was so brilliant that you don't want to ruin it. There are a lot of people driving now, tapping the wheel and going, "I love this tune! Great tune, Goldstein."

2 KNIGHT RIDER

Tune. David Hasselhoff was Michael Knight and the car was called KITT. What kind of car was it? It had the lights going across the front... was it a Corvette? [*It was a Pontiac Trans Am.*] It had a weird steering wheel. Hasselhoff, though. What a guy. He could have been in a couple of my top five. Baywatch was a great show. **AG: He was on the Berlin Wall when they pulled it down, singing.**

2 DALLAS

Dallas, fantastic show. Here's your question: Who shot JR? It was the biggest moment in TV at the time, 350 million people watched it worldwide when the would-be assassin was revealed. I'll give you a clue, it wasn't Bobby Ewing. **DB: I don't know, JR is the only character I can remember.** It was Kristin Shepard, his sister-in-law and mistress.

1 THE FRESH PRINCE OF BEL AIR

This is probably the most catchy theme song ever. Will Smith, obviously. The butler was called Geoffrey. The dad, the big fella, was Phil. There were two sisters and his cousins were Carlton, Hilary and Ashley. Big Phil's wife was Viv, Aunt V. Then they changed Viv to another one after, I think, season one or two. I preferred the first Viv. **AG: Who's your favourite Vivian out of all the Vivians in the world?** Viv Richards. **AG: I'm going for Vyvyan from the Young Ones.**

1 MOONLIGHTING

Goosebumps again, look! What a programme, what a tune. Monday night at 9pm, 1985. It had Bruce Willis and Cybill Shepherd, the company was the Blue Moon Detective Agency and every week they would solve a weird new case. **DB: Is it like CSI?** No! It would start with a person telling their story: "I think my husband is cheating on me" or something like that. Different story every week but the relationship between Bruce and Cybill was the thread. They had this thing but never got it on. Fantastic.

TOP FIVE @ 5 FAVOURITE BOXERS

We haven't just gone for the best boxers here - I've gone for entertainers. **DB: I've gone for genuine boxers – including one who, in my opinion, is the greatest sportsman ever to have lived. I've got a massive picture of him on my wall at home.** Let's find out who it is, then...

5 CANELO ALVAREZ

This Mexican has only been beaten once and that was by Floyd Mayweather. What a boxer Canelo Alvarez is! He was a light middleweight, then a super middleweight and up to light heavyweight. He's won titles at four weights - beaten Golovkin, Cotto and Shane Mosley. If he is fighting, whatever the time, I am setting my alarm clock and I am going to watch him. I think the fight he lost to Floyd just came too early for him. Floyd was really clever and thought, "I will get him now" because obviously he knew what he would go on to be.

4 LENNOX LEWIS

Lennox was the last undisputed heavyweight champion of the world, by the way: holder of the WBA, WBC, IBF and IBO titles. He won an Olympic gold, representing Canada unfortunately. And the people he beat when he turned pro! Wow! Vitali Klitschko, Mike Tyson, Evander Holyfield, Frank Bruno. He was a boxer, a pure boxer, I loved watching Lennox. Early on in his career when he was knocking people out he was really exciting, but he became more of a strategic boxer later on and I used to like the way he'd torture people with his jab. **AG: But then if he came up against somebody like Tyson it would become a mega power fight.**

5 PRINCE NASEEM HAMED

I adored watching my number five. Prince Naz was a southpaw, a cocky fighter. **DB: His ring entrances were something else.** He used to come in on a flying carpet! He'd jump the top ropes and stand there like a mini-Eubank. He was featherweight. He had one fight that he lost and that was against Marco Antonio Barrera. He had 37 fights and 36 wins – 31 of those were knockouts! **DB: He was never the same after that Barrera fight.** He only had one fight after that, for the IBO belt, which he won. There's a great documentary about the build-up to the Barrera fight, and they are filming with him in his camp in Vegas. And you can see the difference between the two fighters. One was completely focused on training and getting better, and the other one was enjoying life just a little bit too much! I used to watch his fights at Faces nightclub on a Friday night and we would all congregate around a massive TV. Everyone wanted to watch his fights because he was so exciting. The knockout power he had for his weight – you don't often see that. **DB: Were people watching him hoping that he'd lose?** Maybe, but he was wonderful to watch.

4 TYSON FURY

I like everything about this boxer, from the way he dresses to the way he talks. Tyson Fury wears his heart on his sleeve. Sometimes he says the wrong thing but I think he's aware of it. The Gypsy King is a 6ft 9in man-mountain, an absolute beast. His two fights with Deontay Wilder proved to everyone he is the best heavyweight on the planet. **DB: I agree.** That first fight where Wilder knocked him out and he was sparko... firstly, how the referee sees an unconscious boxer lying there without moving and doesn't just call the fight off straight away, I do not know. But then Fury opens his eyes and he's up, and then he jogs to the ref and says he's fine – forget Rocky, you can't write that. And then he schools him in the next fight. He embarrasses him. **DB: It was good refereeing in that first fight giving Fury the time to get up.** But not just coming back from that punch – when you hear about his struggles with his mental health and being massively overweight, from there to where he is now, it's incredible. And his fight against Klitschko – wow! The day he came back from that Klitschko fight I interviewed him. He was wearing sliders and his feet and toes were covered in cuts and bruises because they made the ring surface so bouncy and spongy. **DB: So in your opinion he is the best heavyweight on the planet by some distance?** Oh, without a doubt. If that fight happens between him and AJ I think there is only one winner. **DB: I agree.**

Wilder versus even wilderer

3 MANNY PACQUIAO

PacMan. Eight-division world champion. **AG: That is crazy.** He won 12 major world titles, 71 fights, 62 wins, and held titles in four decades from the 1990s to the 2020s. And if you think about some of the people he has beaten: Miguel Cotto, Oscar De La Hoya, Ricky Hatton, Keith Thurman, Timothy Bradley, Erik Morales... I love Manny Pacquiao, he goes to war. **AG: He's a great fighter but is he an entertainer?** Are you winding me up? Of course he is. He fights every minute of every round. Do you not remember what he did to Ricky Hatton? **AG: Which brings me rather neatly to my number three...**

3 RICKY HATTON

You have to remember the Hitman from when he beat Kostya Tszyu. In his prime he only got beaten by Pacquiao and Mayweather. **DB: He got absolutely annihilated by them both.** The referee for the Mayweather fight was embarrassing – an utter joke, I've no idea why Ricky's people didn't make a bigger fuss about it. Hatton used to take 10,000 people with him over to Vegas. For a British fighter that is unheard of. He may have been beaten by PacMan but he was far more entertaining. **DB: Not a chance!** Of course he was. **DB: Who was the better fighter?** I'm talking about him as an entertainer. He was explosive. His press conferences were incredible. I'm talking about the whole package you get as a boxer.

2 FLOYD MAYWEATHER

What a boxer – and if we're talking press conferences you're going to have to go some to beat Floyd 'Money' Mayweather. **AG: I'll give you that.** I love watching him. You could argue that in the ring he is sometimes a bit boring but technically I love watching him, nobody can hit him – he hasn't been punched for the last ten fights. **AG: He's been phenomenal in every way, but the fight with Conor McGregor ruined it for me.** You wanted him to lose, didn't you? **AG: No, I didn't, but he's not claiming a 50-0 record with that on it.** He destroyed McGregor. **AG: Of course he did. That's my point. He's also quite dull.** He used to be the knockout king earlier in his career but he's got brittle hands.

2 NIGEL BENN

My number two is the Dark Destroyer. A phenomenal middleweight, absolutely breathtaking. I used to love watching Nigel Benn – 48 fights, 42 wins. I've met the man, I've interviewed him and he is one of the nicest people you'll meet. He still thinks he could be middleweight champion of the world. **DB: He was supposed to box recently.** Yeah, and then he got injured and, thankfully, they stopped the fight. He had incredible fights with Michael Watson, Iran Barkley, Chris Eubank, and the brutal, horrific fight with Gerald McClellan. Just one of my favourite boxers to watch because you knew you were going to be entertained. You were going to get value. **DB: There were three of them at the same time, weren't there – Benn, Eubank and Steve Collins. I was always Eubank.**

1 MUHAMMAD ALI

Not just the greatest boxer of all time but the greatest sportsman ever to grace this planet: Muhammad Ali. **AG: You won't get an argument from me.** Olympic gold medallist – he won the light heavyweight championship in 1960. The Thrilla in Manila with Joe Frazier, the Rumble in the Jungle with George Foreman, his refusal to fight in Vietnam... I've got a picture of him on my wall at home – it's a treasured possession. **AG: He would have been my number one but we agreed to have different boxers, and that lets this guy in...**

1 MIKE TYSON

Here is my pound-for-pound most entertaining boxer. Mike Tyson was also the youngest ever heavyweight champion of the world at 20. He won his first 19 fights by knockout and 12 of those wins were in the first round. He was something we'd never seen before. **DB: Those black shorts and black trainers!** He was just like a brick wall. Frightening.

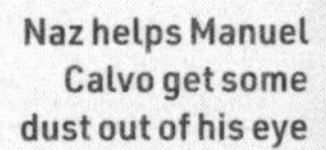

Naz helps Manuel Calvo get some dust out of his eye

TOP FIVE @ 5 FAVOURITE GOALSCORERS

We've ruled out Cristiano Ronaldo and Lionel Messi to make this more interesting. Mine are all Brits, and Darren is outraged that I mentioned having Andy 'Andrew' Cole as first reserve because he came so close – apparently that's not allowed. DG: Of course it's not allowed, it's a Top Five, the clue's in the name!

5 IAN RUSH

Started off at Chester City as a youngster and scored 14 goals for them, the most important of which for him was against Newcastle in the Cup when they won 2-0. That really brought Ian Rush to the attention of bigger clubs, Liverpool won the race to sign him and the rest is history. His numbers are insane. In six full seasons he had 30 or more goals five times, he won everything, and he cost only £300,000 – although that was in 1980. He scored a phenomenal number of goals over a long period. In between he went to Juventus and, although they say don't go back, he did... and still scored goals. What is indelible on my mind is his movement, his link-up with Dalglish and his finishing. Absolutely brilliant. **DG: So Andy Cole at six and Rushy at five, is there a number seven?** Moving on...

Henry: put the 'hi' in Terry

5 ZLATAN IBRAHIMOVIC

How can he not be on this list? He's out of this world and he's put the ball in the back of the net for every club he's played for - Juventus, AC Milan, Inter Milan, Barca, PSG, United, Ajax... he does it with absolute style, no matter which country he goes to or which league he plays in, and always delivers, even in America. And when he'd done it there he came back to Europe and started scoring again here. He just keeps doing it. At international level he has been Sweden's best player for many years and rattled in 62 at more than one every two games. He has to be in there. **AD: But when Malmo were relegated in his first season there, did you know he was going to go on and do what he did?** I never saw him at Malmo.

4 THIERRY HENRY

Not an out-and-out striker but he turned into that even though he could play anywhere. I really enjoyed watching him in the Premier League and when he was at Barcelona. People say he was average there but he scored 35 in 80 games for them. In his career, he got 290 in 600 games at club level and over 50 for his country. But it's not just about the stats: he scored some absolute pearling goals and he could also pass a ball. **AD: You could say he's got to be the best player the Premier League's ever seen?** As an all-round footballer, without a doubt. **AD: He was so easy on the eye in that winning Arsenal team. Can I have him as an honorary seventh on my list?** Yeah, put him down, mate.

4 WAYNE ROONEY

I feel very honoured and proud that I was actually there for his record-breaking Man United goal, a free kick at Stoke, and also his record-breaking England goal, a penalty. For more than 10 years running he had double figures for United – 34 in all competitions on two occasions. And to maintain a place in that team, playing different roles and with different players, you had to be top-drawer to survive under Sir Alex Ferguson year in, year out. Even though there was a time he was angling for a move away, and Ferguson was clearly rattled by that, it didn't matter because he still got in the team. There was no way Fergie was going to do without him. So Wayne Rooney – although there were times when Cristiano Ronaldo and Ruud van Nistelrooy were scoring more goals than him, he was just an amazing footballer who kept contributing goal after goal. If you're a double record-breaker for club and country, that says it all. **DG: I think his ability counted against him because he was versatile enough to play elsewhere – I think the same will happen to Harry Kane and he will end up playing deeper.** Kane's eighth on my list, by the way.

Before every match in the 2015-16 title-winning season, a double espresso and three cans of Red Bull helped Vardy "run around like a nutjob"

3 JAMIE VARDY

I've always said this guy is one of the favourites because he's gone from reject to non-league to Premier League winner, not to mention being in the England squad, being a bit bored on the bench and deciding he's not going to bother any more. I just think it's remarkable. Once Jamie Vardy had scored four in ten at the end of the 2014-15 season, then made his England debut, there was no looking back – and he's just proved his worth with over 100 goals in the top flight, a bona fide member of the 100 club. And guess what? The amazing thing I found out today – some people might say he hasn't proven himself with England but he has scored for his country against Spain, Germany, Holland and Italy. He's proven he could do it against the top sides in the world, so I think it's a waste that England never had him all this time. When you consider his career path and what he has achieved, he's just one of my favourite players.

3 ROBERT LEWANDOWSKI

Well, I've only actually picked five and Lewandowski's in it. A proper striker, whether it be for Poland or playing in the Bundesliga. Whichever team he plays in, he finishes top scorer. And let's just get it straight, he's still banging in goals, breaking records all the time – and how he's not won at least one Ballon d'Or I do not know. His goalscoring record for Bayern Munich is almost impossible to get your head around, almost a goal a game from over 200 appearances. **AD: Crazy, absolutely crazy.** The reason he's not number one is that he's not my favourite... but he is a brilliant, brilliant goalscorer. Who's your number nine?

2 IAN WRIGHT

My number two has not had a dissimilar career to Vardy, from non-league to the very top, and was another amazing goalscorer. What I really loved about Ian Wright was that he played and scored not just with a smile on his face but with a huge grin, if not a laugh, on his face. **DG: No arguments here.**

2 RONALDO

The Brazilian one, of course. **AD: Thought you were cheating there for a minute.** No, no, no. An absolutely brilliant footballer, Ronaldo at his peak was just unstoppable. He played for Brazil in the 1998 World Cup and won the Golden Ball as best player – and then, when everybody thought he was finished due to injury, he came back and blew everyone away in the Japan and South Korea World Cup of 2002. When it comes to his club career, he's done it in Italy with Milan and Inter and in Spain with Barcelona and Real Madrid, so he's got to be on this list. He scored 352 goals at club level from 518 games. At his peak he would be number one without a doubt.

Shearer: great at hailing taxis

1 ALLY McCOIST

Do you know what? Yes, he's part of the talkSPORT family, but he's here just for the goals. I can go through all the numbers if you like but anybody can do that. Here's the thing, here's the one line why Ally McCoist is my number one favourite goalscorer of all the Brits: Have you ever seen anyone enjoy their job more? Whether it was scoring goals, doing the breakfast show here, whatever it is, he just seems to love life, and what a fantastic message that is to send out to people. So he's my number one, who's yours...?

1 ALAN SHEARER

This guy is here because of his importance to the teams he played for, particularly Blackburn and Newcastle. And we're talking about being counted upon when it mattered. At Blackburn, he won two consecutive Golden Boots and the title in 1995. And then he went to Newcastle when all the big clubs wanted him – he went to his hometown club for a world record £15 million to become their main man. And how they relied upon his goals over the years. He has the most Premiership/Premier League goals with 260 from 441 appearances, with 11 hat-tricks in there. He was great in the air, amazing control, could hold the ball up, had a volley in him and was basically the total all-round centre-forward. He simply has to be on the list. **AD: He's not even in my top five Brits. A bit boring, Shearer, to be honest with you – the 'hand in the air' celebration and all that.** You've lost the plot.

TOP FIVE @ 5 VIDEO GAMES

We got such a great response from out Top Five old-school games – usually people rubbishing our choices – that it makes perfect sense to bring it up to date with computer, arcade and console games. DG: There are so many! From the ZX Spectrum to the X-Box, or even the games at the arcade when you were on holiday. Take it away...

5 TRACK & FIELD / DALEY THOMPSON'S DECATHLON

I'm going to go for Track & Field. It has to get in there purely because it was a gamechanger. You could play it at home in the arcade, which was a bit easier to do with the buttons, or on your home computer, which I used to do on the Spectrum 48K – that was Daley Thompson's Decathlon, which obviously had 10 events. Track & Field in the arcade had six and you got an extra life awarded for every 100,000 points. It had the 110m hurdles, the long jump, the 100m dash, the javelin, the hammer and the high jump. You used to have the sorest hands and fingers after having a go at that, pressing those buttons as fast as you can and then having to press the jump button when you went over the hurdles. Very, very difficult on the Spectrum as well. I always struggled with the javelin and the hammer. **AD: I remember repeatedly smashing those keys – so many memories.** The 1500m was the hardest one on the Spectrum, what a workout! It'd be easier to run it!

Who needs a social life anyway?

5 THRILLVILLE: OFF THE RAILS

There's nothing I like more than a Wii in the living room. And there's a couple of Wii games that are in my Top Five but this is one I don't think many people will know. There are various games in it but the one that makes it special is the main one: you build and ride your own rollercoaster. In your imagination you might come up with all sorts of ideas for rollercoasters but none of them are scientifically possible – chiefly due to gravity – but with Thrillville you can. I was just immersed in this game for weeks when it came out. I haven't played it for years, I've got to say, but it still remains one of my favourites.

4 DONKEY KONG

I'm going to go for Donkey Kong here. The old-school '80s original. Mario was Jumpman, climbing ladders to get to Donkey Kong. You must have played this? They're addictive, they're fun, and the music was quite cute as well. There are loads on YouTube, just videos of them, and it made me think how evocative that music of the mid-'80s is. Everybody played Donkey Kong. **DG: I took it on an England tour once when they had it on the Game Boy. I used to enjoy that game, it was one of the first. Good pick.**

4 PHOENIX

This is similar to Space Invaders. So you're at the bottom and you've got phoenixes coming down at you, one at a time. Sometimes there are three or four as it obviously gets progressively harder. Great music again. Eventually, after you've got through all the levels, you come to this spaceship, and then you have to shoot it to get at the alien that's in the middle. I preferred to play this at the arcade; and I preferred Phoenix to Space Invaders. **AD: Well, it's more sophisticated than Space Invaders. If I were looking over somebody's shoulder and they were playing Phoenix on a hand-held I'd be thinking, "I want a bit of that."**

The inventor of Tetris, Alexey Pajitnov, was employed by the Soviet government and did not make any money from the game until he moved to the US

3 TETRIS

I think you're going to think this is boring. I appreciate that Tetris is not everybody's cup of tea but I love it, even though I'm going to hold my hands up here and say I'm no good at it. As soon as it starts to get quick, I've had it. It's more mathematical than anything else. I've always struggled with maths generally so I can't really put my mind into working out where the shapes go and then moving them quickly enough, but it's a timeless game that will go on and on forever. **DG: It wasn't for me, but when you travel on the tube a lot of people still play that game on their phones – it's still very popular.**

3 FOOTBALL MANAGER

I went for Football Manager purely because, again, I used to take it on tour with England. It used to be Championship Manager when I first started playing it. This game has developed and stood the test of time. Now you're not only managing the team, buying and selling players, but training and everything else. So you've got a relationship with the players, you've got a medical centre now to help you prevent injury. It's so involved you can play it for hours. talkSPORT presenter Danny Kelly is obsessed with this game. **AD: Believe it not, I'm not interested in football games. FIFA, Championship Manager, none of them whatsoever. I love the real thing.**

2 CALL OF DUTY

The only reason this is not number one is that I find it very difficult to play. I've been to a couple of Call Of Duty launches and seen some amazing people play this game... but I'm not one of them. It came out in 2003 and since then it has had 18 different releases. It's a shooting game and the first one was set in World War Two. It was the start of something huge and has won so many awards; and the reason I find it difficult is that there are so many different buttons and I'm someone who likes to go on just for 10-15 minutes. Some people sit on that game for 10 or 11 hours a day. I don't get that. **AD: I've never been into shoot-'em-ups but I can see why people love Call Of Duty.** The launch days are crazy, all the Premier League footballers on 200 grand a week turn up just to get a free game.

2 PAC-MAN

This is one of those timeless games that everybody loves. One of the reasons I love Pac-Man is this: When you eat the big dot and you go chasing the blue ghosts, yes you get a phenomenal number of points, but just when you're about to eat one it turns back into a deadly ghost. And you've had it. You think you've just got enough time but it always gets you. It's so frustrating... as it is when you think you're going to power through a level and all of a sudden you can't. You're going for the cherries but you can't get them, and you're going for another big dot and you can't get there and you end up not getting to the level you know you should be achieving. Very frustrating but brilliant. **DG: It was so way ahead of every other game at the time. It was one of the best for graphics.**

Ask Google why they changed the name from Puck Man

1 OUT RUN

You go to the amusement arcade, you sit in a Ferrari, you put your money in and you're off. You feel the bumps, you feel the turns. It's the best driving game ever. When you get extended play you feel like you've won the lottery and it keeps going for another 10, 15, 20 seconds. And the music that goes with it is so cheesy it's brilliant. Outrun has to be number one for me. I was recently in South Africa with the cricket and we went to an amusement arcade and the first game I went on was Out Run. Brilliant. **AD: People might not know the name, but if they look it up I bet they realise they have played it at some point and loved it.**

1 MARIO KART

Just to contradict you directly, this is the best driving game there has ever been. On the Wii again, Mario Kart cannot be topped. This is the game we played more than any other when my kids were growing up so there's a sentimental attachment to it for me as well. My favourite racetrack by far is Rainbow Road, which floats in space. It has some really tough bends and jumps, but once you get the hang of Rainbow Road you can leave the rest behind. Toad's Factory is another great track. Mushroom Gorge. Do you think most people know what I'm talking about here? **DG: Most of the England lads on tour today stay in their hotel rooms and play on their computer games rather than go out. And most of them play Call Of Duty or FIFA against each other online. But there's one player who is obsessed with Mario Kart, and that's Joe Root. He's obsessed.**

TOP FIVE @ 5 QUEEN SONGS

We have to address the Bohemian Rhapsody issue before we go through our Top Fives. **DG: I think most people would include it but we've banned it here because it's too obvious.** It was never going to be in my list anyway. No apology. If you're upset about that, stick it in your own Top Five...

5 FAT BOTTOMED GIRLS

People might not like the title but it's an absolute beauty. It's in praise of women endowed with a large bottom, in case you were wondering. And the good thing about Fat Bottomed Girls is that it was released as a double A-side single along with a Freddie Mercury song called Bicycle Race, and radio stations would normally play them together because each song mentions the other. It only made No.11 in the UK charts and 24 in the US but I love it. **AD: Was this the one that had the big launch with a poster of a load of naked women on bikes?** Yeah, the artwork was actually deemed so offensive that it got banned so they had to change the artwork on the single cover.

Roger Taylor can be seen on a 1999 Freddie Mercury stamp even though the Royal Family are the only living people allowed to appear

4 IT'S A KIND OF MAGIC

I love a song with a distinctive bassline. And there is no doubt this has got a very distinctive bassline. This is from 1986, from the album of the same name. The drummer Roger Taylor wrote this. It reached number three. And the interesting thing is when you go into the detail of who wrote the song, Roger Taylor gets the writing credit, but that bassline and the middle eight section were actually written by Freddie Mercury. So Roger Taylor presented the basics of the song and they decided to leave the writing credit with him but the bit that I like - the bassline - Freddie Mercury wrote. How weird is that?

5 HAMMER TO FALL

Written by Brian May, from 1984. Not one of their best-known songs, not one of their biggest hits. It's a song about life and death, although some claim it's more of a political anthem about the Cold War. I don't care what it's about, it's just a really good song. It's one that stuck with me in the mid-'80s. It's on The Works album with Radio Ga Ga and I Want To Break Free. **DG: The music in all their songs is quality. There's not one bad one, and when it comes to delivery Freddie Mercury is one of the best.**

Now there's a man who knows how to adjust a mic stand

4 RADIO GA GA

I first fell in love with this song at Live Aid in 1985. When the audience gets involved in this it's absolutely fantastic. There's no one better than Freddie Mercury to get them on their feet during the chorus. This song was written in 1984. No.1 in 19 countries, No.2 in the UK, No.16 in the US. Another Roger Taylor track. It's a critique of radio stations becoming over-commercialised and playing the same songs over and over again. **AD: Playlisting started in the '80s. I was working in music radio at the time and it's very frustrating for the creative types in music radio.**

3 DON'T STOP ME NOW

The reason I like this song is that it has great memories for me: it was the closing number on the Strictly tour. Not the Strictly show, the Strictly tour. It was written by Freddie Mercury in 1978, at a time when he was doing lots of drugs and having sex with lots of men. It's been used in different films, including Shaun Of The Dead. It got to No.9 in the UK but it's just got better and better with age. **AD: I must admit, of all the Queen songs that haven't made it into my Top Five, this is the one that probably should have done. And it's kind of timeless, isn't it?**

2 KILLER QUEEN

This for me is real Queen: another Mercury song, from 1974. It got to No.2 and it's the first one that got them noticed abroad. It made the Top 20 in America, Canada and Germany. More Freddie Mercury piano on it. Like Fat Bottomed Girls and Bicycle Race this was a double A-side, and the other track Flick Of The Wrist was a Top Five contender for me but didn't quite make it. I've heard Brian May talk about this song and he loves it. He describes it as vintage Queen. And a little-known fact about this song is that it inspired Katy Perry to pursue a musical career, she loved it that much.

3 SEVEN SEAS OF RHYE

Oh, I love '70s Queen, the early stuff. Written by Freddie Mercury, Seven Seas Of Rhye was their first Top Ten hit, the first song they ever played on Top Of The Pops and the hit single that persuaded Freddie Mercury to go full-time with Queen and quit his job on a clothes stall at Kensington Market in London. That's how powerful this song was. What I like about Queen is that they were real musicians who wrote and played their own songs. All the band members contributed, although they didn't necessarily get the credit. Brian May gave this song its middle eight, for example, and Freddie played the brilliant piano on it as well. It's a song that highlights just how brilliant they were from virtually the very start. **DG: I totally agree. They stuck to the way they wanted music to be played and they became absolutely huge. And by the way, even without Freddie, who was an absolute genius, they've still sold out concert venues.**

2 WHO WANTS TO LIVE FOREVER

Brian May wrote this song for the film Highlander, which was released in 1986. And what I like about this song is that it shows off Freddie Mercury's unbelievable range. It's a moving song. It's performed with an orchestra when they play it live and it's totally different from their other tracks in my opinion. And that's what it makes it unique. **AD: Yeah, don't like it. I've never been able to stand that song. Amazing singing – the song just doesn't grab me in the way that it clearly grabs you.**

1 I WANT TO BREAK FREE

I had to have this – well, I said I'd go with whatever mood I'm in. This was written by bass guitarist John Deacon in '84. It's a great video with the band members dressing up in drag. It got to No.3 in the UK, No.45 on the US Billboard. It features at every single Queen concert and it has done ever since they wrote it. Lisa Stansfield sang this song really well at the Freddie Mercury Tribute Concert. **AD: I don't particularly like the song but the video is funny and I love the ideas behind it. It really took the world by storm.** When they played I Want To Break Free in Brazil with Freddie in drag, the audience threw objects at him and he thought it was because he was singing badly. It was because he was dressed in drag. So he took off his wig and they started cheering him straight away. **AD: Hopefully things have woken up a little bit over there.**

1 SOMEBODY TO LOVE

Freddie Mercury wrote this. It's inspired by his admiration for the songs of Aretha Franklin and that's why it sounds like a full gospel choir, but it's actually just three voices overlaid time and time again: May, Mercury and Taylor. The whole sound is so powerful and there's such a crescendo with the chorus. Another one from the '70s, I think it's about a man asking God why he can't find love. Of all the songs he wrote, this was actually Freddie's favourite. And I first heard it – I was only a little boy when it came out – when George Michael did it... and he did it so well. I almost prefer that version to this version. **DG: This was one of the 15 I had to knock down to five. Another one in there was Flash.** Not for me. I'm a bit Marmite with a lot of Queen songs. Crazy Little Thing Called Love was close for me, and Another One Bites The Dust wasn't far off my Top Five. But yes, there are loads of brilliant ones.

Now there's a man who knows how to adjust a bra strap

TOP FIVE @ 5 GANGSTER FILMS

I'm quite annoyed about some of the reaction to this when we tweeted out what Top Five we were doing today, because the responses have been so boring. Every single Top Five is The Godfather, The Godfather Part II, Goodfellas, Casino... what's up with you, people? Open your minds! I hope you've not gone down that route, Goughie. **DG: You'll have to see, won't you?** Let's go...

5 SAFE

Right, this is where I make a confession. Some people will already know this: I don't watch gangster movies. I've never seen any of those American films I just rattled off. I'm not interested. And then I realised one of my favourite actors, Jason Statham, has been in lots of gangster movies – so I rubbed my hands together and thought, "Here we go!" In Safe, Statham is a cage fighter. He's meant to take a dive in a fight but he gets it all wrong and so the Russian mafia are after him. Meanwhile the Chinese triads kidnap a ten-year-old maths genius to crack a code. There's some great action in this. Double bubble gangster trouble – and Statham and the girl who's been kidnapped take them all on.

4 LAYER CAKE

Daniel Craig is outstanding in this, and lots of people say it was his big audition to get the Bond gig. Tom Hardy and Sienna Miller are both in Layer Cake too, as is Michael Gambon. Craig is an unnamed London gangster who supplies cocaine on a grand scale because his plan is to make as much cash as possible as quickly as he can, because he wants to get out of the game; but it's not easy. He gets involved with some big hitters who give him two tough assignments, and on the eve of his retirement it all kicks off. Lots of fighting, lots of backstabbing, lots of betrayal. **AD: Do you know what? I actually turned it off halfway through because I thought was terrible. And I'm a big Daniel Craig fan.**

5 LOCK, STOCK AND TWO SMOKING BARRELS

I've gone for a classic from 1998 – it's a film that turned a footballer into a Hollywood star. It was a massive break for Vinnie Jones and your favourite Jason Statham. It's a Guy Ritchie film – this was the one that made him a household name – about a young lad who's good at cards but loses a lot of money to a big crime lord in a rigged game. And he gets desperate to pay off his debts, so he decides to rob a small-time gang. It's hilarious at times, and you've got to remember this was a really cheap film to produce and it made nearly $30 million. **AD: It's a terrific film, there's a nice Britishness about it. I love it when Vinnie says, "It's been emotional."** You'll be surprised how many films he's been involved with since then – he's been on an unbelievable ride.

Vinnie Jones: shinpads, check, boots, check, shotguns, check

4 SNATCH

This is a film with Brad Pitt, Jason Statham, Stephen Graham, Frank Butcher from EastEnders and Vinnie Jones. I mean, when all those guys are in it, that's just extraordinary in itself. Snatch is a good, fun film. There's a cute dog in it, and a twist at the end involving the dog. It's along the same lines as Lock, Stock... and it has Brad Pitt with maybe the worst Irish accent you've ever heard. Or is it actually him being in character? Just with that Irish accent? And can we even judge whether it's a bad accent or not? I don't know. He gets ripped for it, doesn't he? **DG: I thought it was alright. I thought he did well but didn't want to include two films that were so similar, so I only went for Lock, Stock.**

3 REVOLVER

Jason Statham again. **DG: Not again!** I know. This film will divide people, no question, but I'm amazed it's not my number one. I absolutely love this film. It's Revolver and it's a Guy Ritchie / Jason Statham classic. It's artistic, it's mysterious, there's beautiful cinematography. Statham plays Jake Green and the film is basically a two-hour therapy session inside his head. He plays the role superbly. I know he's not the greatest actor of all time, but in this he's brilliant. The film has to be followed closely and if you lose your way with it, then you're gone. But it's got everything, Ray Liotta's even in it. I think it's genius but I know a lot of people really hate it.

3 SCARFACE

I've gone there: I've chosen one of the ones you think is too obvious, Scarface. This had Al Pacino and Michelle Pfeiffer. Set in Miami, a Cuban immigrant takes over a drug cartel and succumbs to greed. That's the idea of these films: you look at all gangsters throughout the years, whatever they have, they want to make more and more money. Al Pacino as Tony Montana is not happy being a dishwasher in a local restaurant. He wants to work his way to the very top of the criminal underworld and nothing will stand in his way. It has so many memorable lines but the most famous is probably "Say hello to my little friend" as he starts shooting as many as he can before he's taken down.

2 SEXY BEAST

Ben Kingsley is genius in this film, arguably his best ever, and I include Gandhi in that. He's amazing. Ray Winstone is also on top form as a retired gangster and it's just a great film. It starts with a brilliant Stranglers song, Peaches, and it stays at the same quality level throughout. Winstone's character has retired to Spain with his wife. One day he's by the pool at his villa and a massive boulder rolls down the hillside from above and lands in the pool and stays there. There are also some lines that will stay in your head forever once you hear them. And this is one of those films where it actually frustrates me that all these people have got these Top Fives with Scarface and Casino and The Godfather. If they've not seen Sexy Beast then what's the point of them even trying to do a list?

2 CASINO

There's lots of action and Robert De Niro talks you through it. Robert De Niro, Sharon Stone, Joe Pesci. I mean, who else would you expect to be in these gangster films? It's got greed, deception, money, power, murder. Two best friends; one's a mafia enforcer, the other one runs the casino and they're competing against each other over that gambling empire. And these two guys are also fighting over the same girl, Sharon Stone. Of all the films you mentioned before that you don't think should be on anybody's Top Five, this is the one you should check out. **AD: Maybe I will give it a go. Joe Pesci, by the way, was filming that and Home Alone at the same time, which marks him down as one of the true greats if he managed to pull that off.**

1 GANGS OF NEW YORK

This has Leonardo DiCaprio, Cameron Diaz and Daniel Day-Lewis – who steals the show as Bill the Butcher. It's set in 1862 in New York, when there were lots of gangs based on religious and other lines. DiCaprio returns to the Five Points area in New York City intending on taking revenge against Bill the Butcher, who killed his father, the leader of another gang called the Dead Rabbits. And it's all based on actual gangs from the time. **AD: For me it was just too unnecessarily violent. And not enough of a storyline to it.** It's an amazing storyline! There's a love triangle, there's revenge. What more do you want? **AD: Nah, not for me. It's an excuse for violence, I need more than that. This is my number one...**

Lock, Stock And Two Smoking Barrels actor Dexter Fletcher plays one of the young boys "protecting" Harold Shand's car in The Long Good Friday almost 20 years earlier

1 THE LONG GOOD FRIDAY

Old London boozers, remote houses in the countryside where the loot is divided up, blokes with shooters, a powerful theme tune, Bob Hoskins and Helen Mirren looking the part as the main couple. This is a classic British gangster movie. It also has a very young Pierce Brosnan being chatted up by a gangster at a swimming pool. I watched it again this morning, absolutely love it. Like Sexy Beast, if you go with all these American ones and you haven't seen these two, you need to rethink.

Scarface: so-called because he's got an ace scarf (not pictured)

TOP FIVE @ 5 DRESSING ROOM GEE-UP TUNES

These are the tunes that get played just before a game to get everyone hyped up. I've never been in that situation so I've chosen five that I think would work. **DB: And I've chosen five that I actually used to listen to in the dressing room.** I took out Dancing Queen by Abba at the last minute – would that have worked for you? **DB: No, I'd put my headphones on.** Suit yourself...

5 I LUV U, Dizzee Rascal

What a tune back in the day. **AG: I've never heard of it. I thought the producer was messing with the mute button halfway through it.** The reason I put this in there is that, when I first moved back to the Premier League with Charlton, this was quite a big song at the time. I was a big Dizzee Rascal fan when I was younger and this used to get me in the mood. I'd play it at home before I left my flat, when I got to the ground with my headphones on. I like a lot of Dizzee Rascal's music, but this was one of my favourites. **AG: It's a bit stop-and-start.** My Top Five kind of changes over time. If my kids put this on now I'd be like, "Get that off, please. Too much noise." **AG: Good advice. Get this off.**

5 JUMP AROUND, House of Pain

Imagine this just before you go out and play Liverpool. **DB: It annoys me that you've picked this song because I love it. It reminds me of Mrs Doubtfire, when the little kids have a party and they're hanging from the light fittings and everything. Who is it?** House of Pain. I'm winning now, mine's better than yours.

4 BATTLE, Wookie

This is a classic garage song. Classic. **AG: It's a bit slow, though, isn't it?** How can garage be slow? Any garage-head out there will be bopping their head to this one. It's not slow. You're bopping your head! **AG: I'm shaking it in disbelief. It's a good tune, but it's not bang, bang...** Not all players need that bang, bang to get up for games. Sometimes I just needed something that's got a nice beat like this, that I can bop my head to, get my socks ready, get my tape on. **AG: No, it's too slow.** I love it.

A ghetto blaster: ask your great grandparents

4 IT TAKES TWO, Rob Base & DJ EZ Rock
It's a classic – I've done it again, you love it. **DB: Listen, it's a great song, but I'm not going to a house party back in the '90s.** You're getting geed up for a big game! **DB: No, no, this is a house party song, Wookie is better than this.** I've never even heard of Wookie, I think you've made it up. **DB: I've heard that Wookie song in 85% of dressing rooms at some point. I've never ever heard this in any dressing room I've been in.** Have you been in a league-winning dressing room? **DB: No, but I've been to loads of house parties.** That's probably why.

3 GABRIEL, Roy Davis Jr feat. Peven Everett
Again, it's a classic. **AG: Again, it's slow. When would you play this? Before you go out to play a frame of snooker?** What a tune, though! Roy Davis Jr. **AG: I thought the idea was that it was meant to gee you up.** This song did. I don't want something that's just going to make my heart beat out of my chest. I want something I'm comfortable with. **AG: Were you ever the DJ in the dressing room?** Not really, no. **AG: There's a shock.** I wasn't the DJ, but a lot of the tracks would be these ones you're hearing right now. Nice rhythm, ready to play. Football's about rhythm, not just about as much loud music as you can have. This was the kind of music being played at Soccer Aid. Remember? Oh no, you weren't there, were you? **AG: Oh, he's done that to me. Didn't want to play anyway.** Roy Davis Jr. A classic. Do you like it? **AG: It's alright, but I'd put this one on in the dressing room...**

3 JUMP, Kris Kross
Here we go, now that's a tune. **DB: Again, a '90s house party.** Respect your elders! Imagine this just before you go out. **DB: I've never heard it in any dressing room. I like Kris Kross; they used to wear their clothes backwards. I love this type of music. It's a great song, a classic, but wrong occasion.** Turn it up, just before you play Liverpool. Come on, lads! **DB: 16th birthday, house party, I'll call you as a DJ, 100%. When I'm going out to play football? No.** Did you play music when you were training? **DB: Not when we were training. We did in the gym, though.** Your type of music? **DB: Yeah.** No wonder you're putting on a bit of weight.

2 SKY'S THE LIMIT, The Notorious B.I.G.
I hope this is the clean version. **AG: This is a slow dance as well.** The Notorious B.I.G., Sky's The Limit. You've got to believe that the sky's the limit, that you can achieve your goal, which is to beat the opposition. **AG: Would you just crawl out of the dressing room on the floor?** No, just walk out ready to go. **AG: This would not gee you up for anything.** I'm telling you the truth. Listen, people are out there now bopping their head to this. **AG: If they're stuck in traffic. I don't believe it, who played this?** I would have played it, it would have been on my gameday playlist. Loved it. My number one is more mellow than this one, but it's how I evolved over the years. **AG: Embarrassing.**

2 SWEET CAROLINE, Neil Diamond

Imagine the whole dressing room reaching out, or arms in the air, touching me, touching you. Everybody in the Man United dressing room, come on, we're going to beat Liverpool. *Sweet Caroline, ba, ba, ba.* **DB: Good song for the boxing, love it when it comes on for Matchroom.** Getting you pumped up. **DB: But we're not boxing, we're going to play a match.** If it's good enough for a boxer...! When you're going out on the pitch, you cross that white line and you're supposed to be going into a war zone. With you, you're going into a slow dance. That's the difference. What's your number one, The Lady In Red by Chris de Burgh? This is a tune to get you going. **DB: Not for football. I've never heard this in any dressing room. There are footballers out there thinking, "Goldstein, what are you thinking about?"**

Neil Diamond: hope he went for a wee before he climbed into that

1 NIGHTS OVER EGYPT, The Jones Girls

Relaxed. **AG: Welcome to the jazz club.** The Jones Girls, Nights Over Egypt. Relaxed. Ready to go and play, not too pumped up. Focused, ready to go. **AG: Did you ever want to get into management?** No. **AG: Good choice. Imagine your speech before you get out there: "Lads, listen, let's just have a lovely, chilled day out there."** I don't need that headbanging music. I need that nice, calm, 'ready to go out and play', focused music. **AG: This is the FA Cup final, everyone – just chill. Do you want a soft drink with that, man? Some ice and lemon? This is terrible. What team did you go down with?** Fulham. **AG: Play this every week, did you?** No, never. **AG: This is terrible. What is it, have you got a little basket with a snake coming out? Listen. Who was in your dressing room, Indiana Jones? Let's see what beats it...**

1 COME ON EILEEN, Dexys Midnight Runners

This gets people up. **DB: I can promise you this has never ever been on in a dressing room.** You're winning the World Cup with this one. **DB: You're not. No team is playing this just before they walk out.** What a tune. Oh, yes. **DB: Oh no.** If you know Darren Bent and you're a professional footballer, text him which one you genuinely think is the best. **DB: I've already had one from Darren Ambrose and he says "Wookie. Bang".** This text says, "Darren Bent is on talkSPORT playing his pre-match songs. It's little wonder that Derby started off so slowly. They must have been half asleep." **DB: Another one, Jermaine Beckford: "Bent's playlist, 9/10. Goldstein's playlist, 6/10."**

TOP FIVE @ 5 FAVOURITE GOALKEEPERS

Let's just get this straight: my Top Five are not the greatest goalkeepers of all time, I would never say they are. There's no Peter Schmeichel, for example, who would surely be in most people's lists. **DG: That's absolutely fine, I'll start us off...**

5 DINO ZOFF

He was 40 when he won the World Cup in 1982 and pulled off some magnificent saves. People talk about that Brazil side as the best team to appear in a World Cup but not actually win it, and a lot of that was down to Dino Zoff. He was extraordinary in the final. He was also both captain and goalkeeper, which is pretty rare anyway but especially so in World Cups.

5 BOB WILSON

I never saw my number five play. I'm not even sure if I've ever seen any clips of him being a brilliant goalkeeper. **DG: So why is Bob Wilson one of your favourite goalkeepers?** Because he is genuinely one of the greatest men that I've met in the game of football. The work he's done for the Willow Foundation, his charity, is unbelievable. I've played in their golf days, hosted events for them and would do anything for Bob Wilson. There are some people who just don't waste a word. You know when you just listen to people and every word that comes out of their mouth is important or makes sense? That's Bob Wilson. He's just so eloquent. He's also a legend at Arsenal, of course – won the double.

4 PETER SHILTON

Look how many international caps this guy got over the course of his career. I think it was 125 – and this was when England didn't play as many games as today and he was in competition with Ray Clemence for years. But in 1990, probably coming to the end of his better years, Peter Shilton was outstanding in that World Cup. We only won one game in the group stages, didn't we? That was Egypt. And then we got that 120th-minute winner against Belgium. And then that quarter-final versus Cameroon, who battered us. And if you just go back and watch Peter Shilton in that game, you'll be blown away. **MR: Was he great in that? It's probably treason to say this but, because I'm a bit younger, I didn't see him at his peak or when he was the greatest goalkeeper in the world. But it's a very fair selection.**

Little did Bob Wilson know he'd one day be the subject of a Half Man Half Biscuit song

4 LIONEL PEREZ

Obviously we never had anyone famous, but Lionel Perez actually came to Cambridge United. Most people will remember him as the guy Cantona chipped for that amazing goal when he scored against Sunderland, but he pulled off some amazing stuff for us. I don't trust goalkeepers with short sleeves or tracksuit bottoms – don't say Casillas, I know there are exceptions. But Lionel Perez is a short-sleeved goalkeeper that I will accept. In our last game of the season, a season in which we had already been relegated from League 2 or League 1, I forget, we got a penalty and it was Lionel's last game for us. And the crowd were all yelling "Lionel! Lionel!" and the manager was John Taylor, who's our record goalscorer and he's sitting there in the dugout and eventually goes "Go on then". So right in the middle of the game, it's not the last minute, Lionel Perez steps up to take a penalty. He absolutely hammers it straight down the middle along the ground. It hits their goalkeeper in the ankle and flies over the bar and I think it breaks his ankle. There was a stoppage for like 10 minutes while the poor opposition goalkeeper was being helped off the pitch. I have no idea what happened to him but Lionel Perez is an absolute Cambridge United legend.

3 GIANLUIGI BUFFON

What can I say? Does he have any weaknesses whatsoever? I'm not sure he does. He was bought for €52 million way back in 2001. Think about that for a minute. That's how good Buffon is. He was a World Cup winner in 2006; he only conceded a penalty and an own-goal in that tournament. I think he was second that year in the Ballon d'Or, and you've got to give huge praise to a goalkeeper for that. The number of records he holds is unreal, including 176 caps for Italy. The Champions League is the only thing he hasn't won – and he tried to do it with Juventus and PSG but it just didn't happen for him. **MR: I interviewed Gigi Buffon once for the Qatar Airways guide to the World Cup 2014. We got a translator in. They chatted for five minutes in Italian. The translator then turned to me and said, "He's looking forward to the World Cup" and left. And that was it. I've still no idea what they were taking about.** I'm sure I've heard him do interviews in English...

Gianluigi Buffon started out as a midfielder and then striker before settling for becoming a keeper. His decision was inspired by Cameroon shot-stopper Thomas N'Kono.

3 JOSE LUIS CHILAVERT

Paraguayan goalkeeper, quite short, short sleeves again, so I'm a hypocrite. He played 617 games in his club career and scored 46 goals. Can only be Jose Luis Chilavert. He also played 74 games for Paraguay and scored eight at international level. Penalties, free kicks. **DG: He took free kicks as well? That's brilliant.** Total hero.

2 NEVILLE SOUTHALL

An absolute legend between the sticks. He played in a very good side at Everton and won trophies, but the reason I've got to put him in there is this. When he retired, I went to a dinner and in the middle of the venue there was an island with some nets. I turned up suited and booted, with proper shoes on, and they were asking people if they wanted to take a shot from a good 18 or 20 yards away against Neville Southall, who was in his full kit. Darren Gough had to try. I promise you I couldn't have hit my shot any better with the shoes I had on. Top left-hand corner, it was going in all the way. And he somehow – and Neville was not in his fittest state – pulled off an unbelievable save and tipped it around the post. It was the weirdest thing ever. **MR: Perhaps he's still there.**

1 PETER SCHMEICHEL

I already thought he was an absolute superstar but we were lucky enough to talk to him on *Drive* and it was a fascinating interview. He was passionate, honest, emotional at times. He talked about that time when Denmark were really good and won Euro 92 without qualifying and also, of course, about his brilliant time at Manchester United – the success he had there and then his regret in leaving in '99. But what a time to leave, when you win a treble! I love watching his son as well, he reminds me so much of his father because they have so many of the same traits. But Peter Schmeichel was in a different league as a goalkeeper. Unreal. If you're a defender and he starts shouting at you, you listen. He's a Viking! **MR: As the cliché has it, he definitely made himself big.**

2 JOHN VAUGHAN

Cambridge United from 1988 to 1993. He was with us as we went Fourth Division, Third Division, Second Division, almost into the Premier League; plus the quarter-finals of the FA Cup. I don't think he had any front teeth. He was about 5ft 9in at the tallest, barrel-chested, and he was the hero goalkeeper when I was growing up. He was a brilliant part of the team, a huge part of our success, and because John Beck was the manager he had to be able to kick it a long way as well.

Southall: also binmanned at the highest level

1 NEVILLE SOUTHALL

It's got to be Big Nev. **DG: So you've got him in as well!** You took the wind out of my sails a bit. Let me tell you, we played Soccer Six during the Soccer AM glory years and we came up against Babyshambles in the semi-final – and he was in goal for them. I hit a strike like Rivelino, caught it with the outside of the right foot and it was bending into the top left-hand corner. I don't think I've hit a ball better.... and Neville saved it. It was already in and he saved it. It blew my mind! And actually, what he does now – he's a footballer with a social conscience, doing good things, helping under-represented minorities and doing amazing work for them. As a man, brilliant; as a goalkeeper, second to none.

TOP FIVE @ 5 ROMANTIC COMEDIES

Are you romantic, Darren? Did you buy Valentine cards for girls at school? **DB: I honestly can't remember it as a kid.** What about when you were 18 or 19 and had proper girlfriends? **DB: There will have been the odd card, but I wasn't writing romantic letters like you.** There's nothing wrong with that, I'm a romantic man. Our Top Five romcoms coming right up...

5 HITCH

Will Smith and Eva Mendez. What a film! **AG: That's not a great film! I remember walking out of the cinema.** Are you winding me up? You obviously don't know a good film when you see one. This is a great romcom. **AG: No it isn't, it fills an hour and a half of your life up. So, this is the story where Will Smith is meant to be like this love guru and helps his mate out...** For someone who doesn't like it... **AG: Yeah, I walked out halfway through it.** No you didn't. **AG: I genuinely did, it's such a weak plot line. When did you last watch it?** About four weeks ago, it was on Sky. Great film, two good actors, great cast as well. **AG: When did it come out?** 2005. **AG: I was 19 then.** Mate, you were like 44 back then.

5 THERE'S SOMETHING ABOUT MARY

This is a great film from the Farrelly brothers. Cameron Diaz, Matt Dillon, Ben Stiller, Lee Evans is in it as well. **DB: So they just packed as many people as they could into it? I wouldn't say it's a classic but it's a good film.** This *is* a classic film. An absolute classic. You know, famous for that Cameron Diaz hair scene... It's very funny, very off the wall, very original. This is not a comedy about a bloke who has so much luck with women but can't get the one he wants – that was probably the promo for Hitch, 'The man who gets every woman but can't get the one he wants.' **DB: There are no superstars in this like Will Smith, then.** Cameron Diaz. **DB: I'll give you Cameron Diaz.**

4 THE PROPOSAL

Sandra Bullock. Came out in 2009. She's Ryan Reynolds' nightmare boss in a book-publishing company, but she's about to get deported back to Canada so she tells him he's got to marry her so she can stay in the country. He doesn't really want to but ends up taking her to meet his family. Spoiler alert! She ends up falling in love with him. Great film. **AG: Do they live happily ever after?** Yeah. But they're under investigation as well, because people think they're doing this deliberately for the visa. It's so funny.

Groundhog Day (see next page): good film but a bit repetitive

4 GROUNDHOG DAY

Do you know what film this is? **DB: What a film! Groundhog Day.** Do you know what film this is? **DB: Oh, I'm not falling for that one.** This is a wonderful film. I'm not the biggest Andie McDowell fan in the world, I think she's quite a wooden actress, but bizarrely she's in another one of my Top Five films. **DB: What's this one called?** Groundhog Day. When was the last time you saw it? **DB: Probably about 10 years ago.** When was the last time you saw it? **DB: Listen mate, I'm not going to fall for that one again.** What year do you reckon that came out? **DB: 1987.** No, miles off, 1993. What year do you reckon that came out? I could actually keep doing this joke until 7pm if I was allowed.

3 WHAT WOMEN WANT

Mel Gibson and Helen Hunt; came out in the year 2000. **AG: So, he becomes a woman?** No, he electrocutes himself in the bath and can suddenly hear what women are thinking – hence the name of the film. And all the women around him hate him. They all think he's horrible and doesn't like women, so he starts listening and becoming this perfect gentleman. But Helen Hunt comes in to take over his job, so he thinks he's going to plot against her, nick all her ideas because he knows what she's thinking, and get rid of her... but as he's doing it, he ends up falling in love with her and they get together. But then he loses the power, I think he tries to get rid of it by electrocuting himself again. **AG: Brilliant. My next choice is Groundhog Day, can we hear a clip of that? Oh, have we? Oh.**

3 FOUR WEDDINGS AND A FUNERAL

[*They listen to a clip of dialogue.*] Do you know who's in that clip? **DB: No.** Hugh Grant. What movie would that be then? I'll give you a clue, it's about four weddings and a funeral. Have you seen it? **DB: I've seen it but a long time ago.** You know, it's one of my favourite films of all time, not just romcoms. It's a Richard Curtis film. It's got Hugh Grant, Andie McDowell again, plus Kristin Scott Thomas, Simon Callow and Rowan Atkinson. **DB: Mr Bean?** Yeah, he's the vicar in it. He's not Mr Bean in this, that'd be weird. It's just such a beautifully made movie, it's so wonderful. It's about this group of friends who meet up at all these different events, hence Four Weddings And A Funeral. And it's the love interest between Hugh Grant and Andie McDowell, when they keep meeting at these events.

2 COMING TO AMERICA

Had to be very careful which clip they used there. **AG: Is that Coming To America? Didn't we include that in comedies?** No – and it is a romcom. Eddie Murphy is the Prince of Zamunda. He has an arranged marriage but he wants out of it so he goes to Queens and meets Lisa. Great movie. Coming 2 America is out now but the original came out in 1988. That's over 30 years, which is a long time to wait for a sequel. **AG: I'm sure there are other good examples. How about The Hustler, followed by The Color Of Money? There was a long time between them.** Obviously I'm going to watch Coming 2 America and it'll be funny. But 33 years later, really?

2 LOST IN TRANSLATION

Bill Murray and Scarlett Johansson. Have you seen Lost In Translation? **DB: No.** When it first came out in 2003, I didn't get it. And then I watched it again and just fell into it. **DB: That is your second Bill Murray film in the Top Five. Two Bill Murrays, two Andie McDowells. Are these your favourite actors?** You can immerse yourself in this movie. It's wonderful. Bill Murray is this very famous movie star who goes to Tokyo to film a whiskey advert, and he doesn't know anyone over there. And then Scarlett Johansson is the wife, the young wife, of a photographer who's out there doing fashion shoots. And obviously her husband's out working and so she's on her own, he's on his own, and they just hook up. **DB: Bill Murray? And Scarlett Johansson?** So she's like 24 in it, and he's like this old dude. They should never meet, that's the thing. They've got nothing in common. They shouldn't even find each other attractive. But because they're in Tokyo and away from real life, that's why all of a sudden they hang out and fall for each other.

1 JERRY MAGUIRE

Tom Cruise, Cuba Gooding Jr, Rene Zellweger. Can't argue with that cast. **AG: Phenomenal film.** Tom Cruise is an agent, Cuba Gooding Jr is a fading NFL star, and Cruise is trying to get him a new contract. And all these other clients are leaving Cruise – he gets fired from the company. But Gooding wants that last payday so stays with him, stays loyal. **AG: And Rene Zellweger is the PA at the company, isn't she? She's the only one who goes with Cruise when he leaves the company. There's a great scene in that where he's trying to sign that young kid up and the dad says his word is "stronger than oak"... then rips him off, doesn't sign with him.** Great scene. **AG: And your favourite romcom of all time is Jerry Maguire?** It was a flip-flop between that and Coming To America.

1 WHEN HARRY MET SALLY...

That is my favourite movie. Billy Crystal, Meg Ryan. I've watched that one a thousand times. He's amazing in it, she's wonderful in it. It's just such a romantic comedy, which is why it's top of my romcoms. It's just a perfect film. **DB: I don't know about perfect.** All your ones are like: He goes to work for a company, she needs a green card, they fall in love. But this is a classic. **DB: My Top Five was better.** Mine was better, but in the spirit of a romantic comedy why don't we just love each other and say they're both good? **DB: OK.** I won.

Jerry Maguire: nominated for five Oscars, including Best Lampshade

TOP FIVE @5 UNDERRATED CRICKETERS AND FAVOURITE RUGBY LEAGUE PLAYERS

We're doing something different today. You know, and most of the listeners know, that I love rugby league - but I'm also aware that it's a minority sport. It should be more loved and so there are no apologies here for indulging my passion for something so important in my life. **DG: But before you do that, I'm going to look at something that matters to me with my Top Five underrated cricketers.** Sounds fair enough, here we go...

5 SHIVNARINE CHANDERPAUL

I played against this guy a few times. Chanderpaul played 164 Tests for the West Indies, but the superstars in their illustrious history from Viv Richards to Brian Lara tend to dominate all the publicity. When he first made the team in '94 they were still number one in the world, before Australia's dominance, but he's got a weird, untidy technique and I think that goes against him. He was only the second West Indian to get 10,000 runs and was denied an opportunity to overtake Lara's haul when he was just 45 shy. He should have been given the chance but it was denied him. Later on, I criticised his signing at Lancashire in 2017 as a 41-year-old overseas player because I thought it was a bad move when the game needed to encourage young players to come through... but when you look at his average, he averaged over 50 in Test cricket. He was one of the first guys to wear warpaint under the eyes. But you'll never hear him get any of the praise given to the other guys who got runs because of that technique and the workmanlike style he had. He wasn't really ever fluent. **AD: I saw him in a T20 match. Yes, a weird technique, but he got a lot of runs off very few balls.**

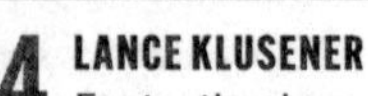

4 LANCE KLUSENER

Fantastic player. I played against him at Port Elizabeth and he smashed 160. Honestly, I was having nightmares for about three weeks after that. When I talk about bowling at Adam Gilchrist – which was hard work with a left-hander – this guy was another one. Now, for him to only have played 49 Tests I find quite remarkable. He smashed 102 off just 100 balls in 1997 versus India. He was nicknamed Zulu because he was fluent in the language. From those 49 Tests, he averaged 32 with a bat and 38 with the ball. The reason his bowling average is so high – it's a bit like Ben Stokes – is that he only bowled on flatties, because they had Jacques Kallis, Shaun Pollock and Allan Donald. They had so many great bowlers, so Klusener used to come on and bowl two or three or four overs, little cutters on flat pitches. Fantastic one-day cricketer, brilliant in the World Cups and he deserves to be on this list.

3 DAMIEN MARTYN

He made his Test debut way back in 1992. We'd met at international U19 level a few years earlier but when he was 21 he replaced the incredible Dean Jones. He was dropped in '94 because he played a terrible shot against South Africa, I'll never forget that. They didn't play him for seven years. Seven years! But such a stylish batsman. He didn't really come at you; he stood back in his crease and had great hands through the ball – 67 Tests, average 46.37. And he had a strange retirement. He'd just been Aussie Player of the Year in 2005, but started off a 2006 series badly and retired after the second Test. I thought he could have player another five years. He played over 200 ODIs, he was superb in one-day cricket. He was in the World Cup-winning team in 2003 and he got 88 not out in the final versus India. He was one of the best against spin. There were some great players in that Australia side, Ricky Ponting and all those guys, and that's why Martyn doesn't get the credit he deserves.

1 STUART MacGILL

The Aussies used to play two spinners back in the day. When I first started it used to be Tim May and Shane Warne but, for some reason, when MacGill and Warne were about they only played one. They did play together on a few occasions and performed well, but what an unlucky bloke to be around as a leg spinner at the same time as the greatest leg spinner the world has ever seen. I really feel for MacGill – what a competitor. Great bloke, great to play against – 44 Test matches, 208 wickets at 29. Strike rate of 48. That's the best for a spinner with at least 20 wickets in Test cricket. That's how good he was. Unfortunately for him, he was around with the great Shane Warne. If he had played 100 Tests, he would have got 500 wickets without a doubt. A great performer.

Glen Chapple, running from the England selectors

2 GLEN CHAPPLE

He was an ever-present for Lancashire over the years. When I consider some of the bowlers I played with for England, for this guy never to get a Test match in that period is unbelievable. I'm still gobsmacked. He managed to play a single ODI aged 32 against Ireland. I think they just gave him that because they were embarrassed they'd not picked him years earlier: 985 first-class wickets at an average of 26, and 39 five-wicket hauls. He got runs as well, six hundreds. He should have played for England in Test match cricket. It's ridiculous he didn't. **AD: He's a Yorkie, isn't he?** Yes, he is. **AD: Now I know why you've picked him. I'm joking, it makes total sense for him to be in your Top Five.** Considering some of the bowlers who played for England during that period, for him never to have played a Test match I find ridiculous.

5 LEE BRIERS

He started at St Helens and then quickly went to Warrington. If you ask Warrington fans – and they've had many great players down the years – a lot of them would say Lee Briers was *the* club legend. If I tell you his autobiography is called Off The Cuff, it tells you everything you need to know. I love a maverick rugby league player, somebody who does things that are unpredictable, and he is the epitome of that for me, a joy to watch and a winner as well with Warrington. Only played once for Great Britain. There's a little comparison with Kevin Pietersen, who also finished far too soon. GB coaches just didn't want to pick these mavericks. **DG: There is a lot of favouritism in selection.**

4 ANDREW JOHNS

I was trying to make it all GB but, even though he's an Aussie, you can't leave out Andrew Johns – an amazing player in the halves. I remember watching an NRL game and he actually broke his back and carried on. **DG: What?** It's an extraordinary thing that happened, but it's true. He got crunched in a tackle, carried on, and they later found out that he'd broken his back. That's a measure of the man. A very complicated character as well: his autobiography is called The Two Of Me.

3 CLIVE SULLIVAN

A boy from the Valleys in Wales who found himself in Yorkshire playing rugby league instead of union. Clive Sullivan had all sorts of problems physically as a young boy but won the Challenge Cup with both Hull clubs and then, in 1972, he scored that try in the Rugby League World Cup final that helped Great Britain become the world champions. A flying winger and a joy to watch. **DG: I love watching the old wingers.**

Flying winger Sullivan (pictured not flying)

2 GARETH ELLIS

For a massive bloke who was such a force as a forward, his skills with his hands, his movement and nifty footwork were amazing. He's an inspirational leader as well. He's won the lot. He also starred in the 2008 World Cup. An absolute winner, Gareth Ellis laid into anybody on the rugby league pitch but was a lovely bloke away from it.

1 PAUL COOKE

Now this is a very personal choice. When you travel miles and pay money just to watch one player play, that tells you everything. Cooke was another maverick – so much so that he decided to bin off the team I love to go to their arch-rivals, Hull Kingston Rovers. Even that didn't shake my joy in watching him. I wish he hadn't done it, but there you go. In the end we became pals and I wrote his book, so I couldn't really have anybody else at number one. **DG: I like that personal touch, but I thought Shaun Edwards, Martin Offiah, Garry Schofield, Mal Meninga and Ellery Hanley might have been in there.** Hanley was in the equation, but Schofield left for Leeds so I can't have him in.

TOP FIVE @ 5 BRAZILIAN AND ARGENTINIAN PLAYERS WHO PLAYED IN ENGLAND

I already feel we're going to come in for a lot of grief over this. I'm going to pick my Top Five Argentinian players to have played in England, and not just in the Premier League era. **DG: And I'm choosing the Brazilians.** One little matter of policy: No goalkeepers.

5 JONAS GUTIERREZ

This Argentinian had such an incredible career at Newcastle and still says the black and white shirt is his favourite. Jonas Gutierrez really fell in love with the club, and the fans fell in love with him. After scoring against West Ham to help keep them up – and remember, this is having come back from cancer, and having been informed that his contract wasn't going to be renewed – he peeled off his shirt, ran to the touchline, turned towards the directors' box and cupped his ears at Mike Ashley and Lee Charnley. At that moment he became a hero to the fans. He was just one of those players the fans love for his quality and his 100% commitment. **DG I totally agree. I didn't even think of him but, dear me, what a player.** I think he's the one of the best to have played in England.

5 DIEGO COSTA

Controversial one, this. Before anybody says anything, yes, we know he played for Spain. But Diego Costa was born in Brazil and in 2013 he played twice for the country of his birth. I was at the game when he played for Atletico against Chelsea in the Champions League. He wound Chelsea up the whole game. He dominated them... and then ended up playing for them. He's one of those players who's aggressive and confrontational. If you support the club he plays for, you think he's an absolute diamond. If you support another club, you can't stand him. But he has got serious quality. I think he's a superb player and he's got the trophies to back it up.

4 GILBERTO SILVA

He made 170 appearances for Arsenal, was part of the Invincibles team and won the World Cup. And yet, alongside all those other stars, Gilberto Silva probably doesn't get the credit he deserves. It was thanks to him that Patrick Vieira could bomb forward – he knew he would always be back there ready to clean up. A Brazilian magazine wrote that at the 2002 World Cup Gilberto Silva carried the piano for Ronaldo and Rivaldo to play their tunes. I think all Arsenal fans will tell you he was fantastic for them. **AD: They've already got in touch to say you're out of order only putting him at four. So you're in for some grief.** Wait until they see who I've got for the next three.

4 SERGIO AGUERO

You might think this guy is low down on the list but, as Darren just pointed out, wait for the top three. Sergio Aguero makes anybody's Top Five just for that particular moment when he scored the goal against QPR to give Manchester City the league title. It's such an iconic goal. I don't care what else he did, he could have left at the end of that season and it would still be *the* most iconic Premier League goal. **DG: I'm a massive fan. He just does what it says on the tin: Give me the ball and I'll put it in the back of the net. That's what you want from your striker.** He had to be in there.

Aguero (pictured very nearly flying)

3 ROBERTO FIRMINO

He doesn't score a lot of goals but I'm sure Jürgen Klopp wouldn't swap him with anybody, because what he does for Sadio Mane and Mo Salah by dropping deep and creating space for them is so important. And that's why they say Roberto Firmino is the best in that position and Liverpool fans absolutely love him. Many of them believe he's the best of the three, I'm not so sure but he deserves to be here. **AD: I do remember when he first arrived, you were waiting for him to come good and it took a little while, didn't it?** I think his game has developed massively since he came to Liverpool. Jürgen Klopp has obviously influenced him a lot. He's changed from someone who you could see just wanted to score 20 goals a season – he's not a selfish footballer now and that allows those around him to benefit.

3 RICARDO VILLA

His second goal in the 1981 FA Cup final replay against Manchester City was one of the greatest cup final goals of all time, in one of the greatest FA Cup finals of all time. It's a magical piece of art, isn't it? It's a little bit like the Aguero thing, for that goal alone Ricardo Villa has to be in my top five. **DG: Yep, absolutely fantastic goal. I've talked many times about how around '81 there were some players playing here who influenced the way I wanted to play sport and he was one of them.** I think Tottenham bringing over a couple of players from Argentina was such a bold move at the time. And then history meant that it all took a bit of a twist, but Villa by then had scored that wondergoal. It's gone down in Spurs folklore and he is one of their all-time legends.

2 FERNANDINHO

This guy is so important for Manchester City. And when Fernandinho does eventually leave them he will go down as an absolute legend. He is such a big part of the way they play – and Pep obviously rates him right up to the sky and back because he has so much to offer as a defensive midfielder. **AD: I remember when he signed in 2013 Jamie Redknapp said that, whoever else might arrive in the Premier League, this was the signing of the summer. And I was thinking, "Really?" Then of course he starts playing and you realise he's right. Fernandinho has held that midfield together defensively and I can see why he's so high on your list.**

2 OSVALDO ARDILES

I love the bit in that Chas & Dave song where Ossie says, "In the Cup for Totting-ham". Ardiles was magnificent, such a clever footballer. When they signed Villa and Ardiles we were all excited to see them play. They went and won the FA Cup, and then the Falklands happened and he had to go and play in France for Paris Saint-Germain, but he came back and helped Spurs win the UEFA Cup. He went on to play for Blackburn, QPR and Swindon, and of course he was also in management. He managed Spurs for a while, but what I remember most was watching his Newcastle team. In terms of league position and results they weren't particularly great but the football they played was sensational. So I think he had a big impact on English football and he's just a terrific guy.

1 JUNINHO

Look what Juninho did for Middlesbrough. **AD: He got them relegated.** Just think about it for a minute, swapping Sao Paulo for Boro in 1995. I mean, going to play in the North-East, he deserves a medal just for that. Most people choose the easier option, don't they? They like to play in London. He didn't. He went right up there to Boro and he was absolutely brilliant: 5ft 5in tall, Premier League Player of the Season in '97. Yes, they got relegated but they got to two finals. He cried on the pitch and this is why the fans love him – because he gave his heart and soul to the club. He left and then came back twice and he won the League Cup. And he said that meant more to him than winning the World Cup in 2002. What about that?

1 CARLOS TEVEZ

For a player involved in so much controversy, I still don't think he gets talked about enough. Carlos Tevez saved West Ham from relegation with that flurry of goals towards the end of the season. That was controversial. He goes to Man United for a couple of seasons, wins two titles and the Champions League and then goes to Manchester City – yep, more controversy – and in the first season he decides to score double the number of goals he'd scored at United the season before. And he wins the title with the Man City. I loved watching him and think he's underrated. Ossie could have been my number one, but when I was looking at it and thinking of the impact he had at three different clubs in the Premier League, two top clubs and another one at the other end of the table, I just thought, "Yeah, Tevez is the number one."

Juninho: when not playing for Boro, he made do with Brazil

TOP FIVE @ 5 MOTOWN SONGS

This is one of those where we literally can't go wrong, isn't it? **DG: Well, some people can be a bit precious about Motown acts that became a bit more souly or R&B as the years went on but I'm good. Motown gold never gets old.** OK, I'm not a big aficionado, I just like the music. Here are our Top Five Motown songs...

5 DO YOU LOVE ME, The Contours

This was a 1962 hit single for Motown's Gordy Records label. It was actually written by the CEO, Berry Gordy Jr, and was the band's only Top 40 single on the Billboard Hot 100 in the US – it peaked at No.3, and was also No.1 on the Billboard R&B chart. It was originally written, this is what I like about this song, for The Temptations... but they couldn't find them. They were at some other event. **AD: That would never happen now, would it?** Anyway, he bumped into some of The Contours in the hallway of the offices and they begged him to let them record it, he gave in and it got them on TV and Motown's very first tour.

5 I HEARD IT THROUGH THE GRAPEVINE, Marvin Gaye

This song had already been done before it got to Marvin Gaye, but he just hit the spot perfectly – and that's why this is the lasting rendition of it. It's the one that everybody remembers. Prince of Motown, Prince of Soul, call him what you want – Marvin Gaye had to be in my Top Five. If I hadn't picked I Heard It Through The Grapevine there would have been questions asked. **DG: It's a great song, mate. I would have had this if you hadn't.**

4 REACH OUT I'LL BE THERE, The Four Tops

Levi Stubbs' voice is something else and this showcases his vocal excellence better than any other song that he sang. When you listen to his voice he sounds like a man whose heart is genuinely hurting. He's just got that magic in his voice. You've got to listen to Levi Stubbs, you've got to admire Levi Stubbs, you've got to treasure Levi Stubbs. And a little story about this song: This seven-inch single, I found it in a bargain bin in a record shop when I was about 12 or 13. Bought it for about 10p. I've still got it and I absolutely treasure it. **DG: Again, this is another one I would have in my Top Five.** There's a little line towards the end of Reach Out I'll Be There where he says, "Just look over your shoulder" and he actually threw that in, that wasn't even meant to happen. It's kind of iconic now. But you're right, an absolutely brilliant song.

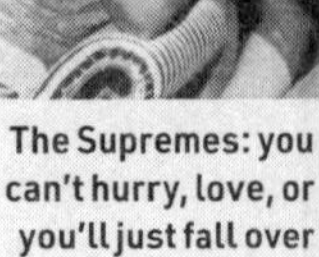

The Supremes: you can't hurry, love, or you'll just fall over

4 I CAN'T HELP MYSELF (SUGAR PIE, HONEY BUNCH), The Four Tops

What a title! Written by Motown's Holland-Dozier-Holland production team and delivered by The Four Tops. It peaked at No.23 in the summer of '65, then at No.10 in 1970 when they re-released it. It's Levi Stubbs and the rest of the group professing their love for a woman. That's what the song's about but it was such a big hit that, after it was knocked off No.1 by Mr Tambourine Man by The Byrds, it managed to climb back to the top spot again – where it was replaced by The Stones and (I Can't Get No) Satisfaction.

3 THE TEARS OF A CLOWN, Smokey Robinson & The Miracles

It's the start of this song that I love – you can nod along to this. It's about putting on a show of happiness when you're sad and is inspired by the clown in the Italian opera Pagliacci, who must make the audience laugh while he weeps behind his makeup because his wife has betrayed him. Stevie Wonder came up with the music with top Motown producer Hank Cosby. They released it on an album in 1967, Make It Happen; they didn't think it was going to work as a single at first, but when they released it three years later it made No.1 in the UK, their first hit over here. They released it in America shortly after and, guess what, it went to No.1 there as well. What a song, Smokey Robinson & The Miracles. **AD: We both had the Four Tops at number four. You've got Smokey Robinson & The Miracles at number three. So just take a listen to who I've got as my number three...**

3 LOVE MACHINE, The Miracles

I've always loved this song. Wham! did a great version of this but this is the one for me. **DG: I've never heard it.** I'm not kidding you, mate, this is the most-used song in Motown history. No.1 in the States, sold over 4.5 million copies and has generated $15 million in revenue. I mean, you can easily make the case and say this is the biggest song in Motown history. Just listen to the lyrics in this, they're outrageous. I'm sure the BBC would have banned them if they'd actually listened properly: "When I'm sitting next to you, electricity starts to flow and my indicator starts to glow." Let's quickly move on, it's a family show. Outrageous. Written by two of The Miracles, Pete Moore and the man who replaced Smokey, Billy Griffin. The growly vocal there is by Bobby Rogers. It's just magnificent.

2 YOU CAN'T HURRY LOVE, The Supremes

You mentioned Dozier, Holland and Holland – and they wrote this as well: You Can't Hurry Love, by The Supremes with Diana Ross. She left in 1970 to go solo, by which time Berry Gordy, Mr Motown, had fallen out with Holland, Dozier and Holland so they went their separate ways. The quality and the number of songs kind of suffered because of that, but this is an absolute classic... and I know what you're all thinking: "Oh, the Phil Collins version pales into insignificance next to this one." And you're right. **DG: I was going to have Where Did Our Love Go by The Supremes but they just lost out to The Contours on my list.**

2 NOWHERE TO RUN, Martha & The Vandellas

Released in 1965, this only made No.26 in the UK. Written by Motown's production team, as always, it's the story of a woman trapped in a bad relationship with a man she cannot help but love. So many people out there with exactly that same situation... it's a fantastic tune from a great group. Absolutely love it. **AD: It led to a few problems within Motown. Berry Gordy wanted it to be a big name plus the band. So originally it was Martha & The Vandellas, and then it became Martha Reeves & The Vandellas just as it was with Smokey Robinson & The Miracles. Thinking along the same lines David Ruffin, who was in The Temptations, wanted it to be David Ruffin & The Temptations. Berry Gordy refused by going against his own policy and that caused all kinds of grief. But yeah, this is a terrific tune as well.**

Stevie Wonder: in anyone else's hands it would have been just an OK stition

1 WORKING MY WAY BACK TO YOU, The Spinners

This is the one where people might question my choice because it was made popular by Frankie Valli And The Four Seasons in 1966. But this version of Working My Way Back To You is electric. It topped the UK singles charts for two weeks in 1980 and made No.2 in the US. It combines, and this where I am going to get out of trouble, the R&B of Motown with the late-'70s beat. Written by Sandy Linzer and Denny Randell, it's an absolutely great tune. **AD: But is it Motown?** It has little bit of that '70s beat to it but it's definitely Motown. **AD: The Spinners were also known as The Detroit Spinners and The Motown Spinners so I think that's settled in your favour.**

1 SUPERSTITION, Stevie Wonder

Stevie Wonder – we share the same birthday, the same kind of magic talent. Did you know he sang it, played the keyboards, the drums and the Moog synth bass as well? He was going to give the song to Jeff Beck and then Berry Gordy said, "No, don't do that, it's going to be a smash." It only got to No.11 in the UK. UK, what were you thinking? **DG: Ridiculous. This is as cool as.** When we decided to do this list, I thought Stevie's got to be in my Top Five – then I quickly realised he's got to be my number one. But we're bound to talk about Motown again someday because there are so many great tracks.

Stevie Wonder performed Superstition on Sesame Street in 1973. Many top acts would follow.

TOP FIVE @ 5 CLASSIC FOOTBALL SHIRTS

This is a tough one because there are lots. **DB: And we already know for a fact that we've missed out loads, but mine are the ones that immediately sprung to mind when I heard we were doing classic shirts so they have to be in there.** Let's get going...

5 LIVERPOOL 1995/6

This is Liverpool from the era of the 4-3 Newcastle game with Stan Collymore up front, 1995/6. I'm not a Liverpool fan but I absolutely love this kit. It's got the thick white collar and it just looks so comfortable. And for some reason that was always the one Liverpool kit I always liked. Red with little white stripes going down the sleeves. It's an iconic shirt, it's lovely. **MR: I'm really unhappy with their kit at the moment, the one that looks like it has been put on back to front; but the one you're talking about here about is not the Carlsberg one with three stripes on the sides?** No, just the Carlsberg in the middle on its own. But it's the thick collar that does it for me.

4 BRAZIL (AWAY) 2002

It's the Ronaldinho kit. Brazil, 2002, away, blue. Do you know what's good about this kit? I actually bought one and the detail in that shirt was incredible. There was even a bit of lining underneath for when you sweat. The whole kit was nice. White shorts, blue socks. **MR: The white detail down underneath the arms.** Brazil have always had really nice kits, haven't they? **MR: Well, here's my number four...**

Rivaldo: still decent in blue, unfortunately for England

5 ENGLAND 1986

I had to have an England kit. **DB: Why did you have to have an England kit?** I just felt I had to! And so I was really torn between several. There was the 1982 Admiral kit – we've actually got a framed one from Ray Wilkins, beautiful with the red and the blue on the chest. Then there was 1998, dark red with the crest in the middle. I thought about the light blue one from 1990, the third kit, do you remember that? **DB: Not really.** But eventually I went for the white Mexico 86 shirt. It wasn't a pure white shirt, it had these kind of lines down it – think Lineker with the broken wrist. England in white shirts and blue shorts is essential. In the quarter-final against Argentina in '86 we went light blue shorts and I actually didn't mind that turquoise on that day. But it's important, shorts make a big difference. You know that with the Man United zebra kit – the zebra kit with zebra shorts is ridiculous but without them you can just about get away with it.

4 BRAZIL 1982

That kit for me is so classic. I could watch the Carlos Alberto goal in the 1970 World Cup final against Italy over and over again, but do you know what? I've chosen Brazil 1982 – and you could equally have Italy or Germany from 1982 as well. They're absolutely lovely kits, it was a great era for kits. I wanted to get another international one in and I thought about Holland's from '88, the Van Basten volley kit. It's the orange with the kind of white little waves in it. It's a beautiful thing.

3 CAMEROON 2002-04

You must remember this kit! Between 2002 and 2004, with a young Samuel Eto'o up front, they had that Puma vest kit. They were obviously having a bit of a to-do with FIFA, so they kind of boycotted it and their kit was like a tanktop vest. The sleeveless kit was green; I can't describe the arms because there were no arms. **MR: There was a yellow trim on the vest. I think if you go Cameroon you've got to go 1990.** I think in the 2002 World Cup they had to wear the vest over a black top so it looked like it had black sleeves. To wear that kind of kit you've got to be in good shape. Have you seen that Cameron team photo of them wearing that kit? They're all absolutely ripped.

The famous 'vest kit' made its debut at the 2002 African Cup of Nations. After the row with FIFA they returned to defend their title two years later in a onesie.

3 TOTTENHAM HOTSPUR 1985/6

I'm a sucker for Hummel. This is the mid-to-late-'80s Spurs kit with the diagonal lines down the middle. It's so brilliant. Those lines are perfect. It reminds me of Hoddle and Waddle and that time when there were glorious victories for Tottenham and no trophies. It was absolutely perfect, exactly what a shirt should be. **DB: That kit is not for me. The logo in the middle of the shirt, it's like an arrow going in a certain way. The big sponsor's name as well, massive.** Look, I know fashion is in the eye of the beholder and I don't want to judge you, but I really think you need to study this again. I actually, genuinely think a bit less of you. **DB: You know what the problem is? There's too much chaos, there's too much going on with the shirt.** That's biased Arsenal talking. That is an absolutely glorious football kit.

2 PARMA 1998/9

Ooh, the yellow and blue home kit, Parmalat across the front. This is from the year Parma won the UEFA Cup. But never mind the kit for a minute, what a squad of players: Buffon, Crespo, Asprilla, Veron, Chiesa, Thuram, Cannavaro. Still, the kit is iconic as well. Do you know what it reminds me of? The old Gazzetta Football Italia show on Channel 4 with James Richardson. That was when Italian football was at its best. I loved it. **MR: Somebody's got in touch the with show to say, "Darren Bent's best kit must be Ipswich 2000/01: blue, white trim, touch of red."** Lovely kit but way too baggy. **MR: You played in an era of tents, didn't you?**

2 CAMBRIDGE UNITED 1990/91

This shirt will be forever associated with the 1991 FA Cup quarter-final where Cambridge battered Arsenal at Highbury and were robbed of a victory. David O'Leary should have been sent off for pulling back John Taylor; Dion Dublin scored. We had Howlett as a sponsor for the home games and Fujitsu for the away games. Made by Scoreline, it had a really good collar. **DB: What's with all these sponsors?** I always think of kits in terms of sponsors because you know when you're growing up and you have Panini stickers and you have, like, Oxford and Wang, Liverpool and Crown Paints, Arsenal and JVC... **DB: That's the problem with that Spurs shirt, there's so much going on you can't work out who the sponsor is.** Please text in or tweet if you think Darren Bent shouldn't work again.

1 ARSENAL 1992/3

Ian Wright, JVC, you said it. Arsenal home kit, 1992/3. The reason it's my number one is because it was the very first football kit I ever had – my dad bought it for me. Ian Wright on the back, number 8, nice big V-neck collar. The JVC is iconic as well. **MR: It's got a bit of black detail on the sleeve. I quite like the Arsenal yellow and blue as well, the "It's up for grabs now!" Michael Thomas kit – although Alan Smith never gets the credit he deserves for pulling the ball down and creating the assist for that goal.** They always have good kits, Arsenal.

1 DENMARK 1986

Another one from the 1986 World Cup – the Denmark kit. An absolute thing of beauty. You can just imagine one of the Laudrups sauntering around Monterrey or Guadalajara or wherever they played. It's Hummel again, it's got chevrons. I'm addicted to that type of kit. How do you feel about that one? Because you didn't like the Tottenham one... **DB: Yeah, this one's fine.** This one's OK? This is the best football kit ever made. It's not just fine. This is the best. **DB: I'm not sure.** I feel like I've missed a couple out. There are so many.

TOP 5 most lucrative kit deals in 2020:

1 Barcelona £135m (Nike)
2 Real Madrid £104m (Adidas)
3 Manchester United £78m (Adidas)
4 Paris Saint-Germain £75m from 2022 (Nike)
5 Manchester City £66m (Puma)

Wrighty wheels away in joy having learned that Darren likes his top

TOP FIVE @ 5 SONGS OF THE '80s

People either love or hate the music and culture of the '80s; I personally love it. Over the course of a week I'd say, at a conservative estimate, my Top Five has changed probably 30 times. **DG: It all depends what mood you're in. I've chosen ones I can sing out loud to.** We'd better get started, then...

5 TWO TRIBES, Frankie Goes To Hollywood

I must admit I've surprised myself with this selection. I really didn't particularly like Frankie Goes To Hollywood and I certainly didn't like the first single, Relax, which only became so massive because it got banned by Radio One due to the naughty lyrics. But this song, Two Tribes, has got that brilliant bassline and Holly Johnson sings well on it too. Politically it was live – it hit the spot in so many ways. I've put it in my Top Five because whenever I hear it I think 1980s. I don't think about anything else. I think this is so '80s probably because Frankie didn't really last beyond the decade. **DG: It is a terrific song but it just doesn't grab me.**

5 1999, Prince

I don't like his music whatsoever, but what makes this special is he's thinking ahead. When it first came out it in January 1983 it only made No.25 in the UK charts. Can you believe that? It was re-released when I was 15 in 1985 as a double A-side with Little Red Corvette and got to No.2... and charted again after he died. It's timeless, I guess. **AD: I've got to say it is a terrific song, you cannot dislike Prince and 1999 really is one of the best. I nearly had Prince in my Top Five.**

4 I'M YOUR MAN, Wham!

Do you know what this reminds me of? The school youth club on a Friday night. Don't get me wrong, it's not like I didn't chat to girls, because I did, but this was the first time I really danced and mixed with the opposite sex. And that was a dancefloor-filler. It got to No.1, of course. **AD: I loved Wham! Two young guys singing about having a good time.** And remember the big white T-shirts they used to have with the big black writing? Everybody had a Wham! T-shirt. Andrew Ridgeley is a massive rugby fan and I've been lucky enough to spend time in his company. I was really surprised how quiet he was, but what a nice man.

Frankie goes to an understocked charity shop

3 HOW SOON IS NOW?, The Smiths

I know you either love The Smiths or you hate them, and you either love Morrissey or you hate him, but I had to include them because I think they're an iconic band. They did four albums in the '80s and that was it, they were gone. Morrissey was very different, and I appreciate that some people don't like his voice, they don't like what he was singing about; but for me the guitar work by Johnny Marr, especially on this song, was on another level. I was always going to have a Smiths song, it was just a question of which one I went with. I'd just got to uni when I really discovered The Smiths and a lot of kids there were kind of struggling because they were away from home and they were very introverted, and they just wanted to listen to The Smiths and feel comfortable that they had a friend there. And this was the main song for us all back then. **DG: I get why people like them but that slow dreary voice is not for me.**

4 NEVER GONNA GIVE YOU UP, Rick Astley

It's one of those songs that you've just got to love. What a voice, what a song. This is Stock, Aitken & Waterman, the songwriters and producers who owned the 1980s. They had to be represented when we did this Top Five... and Rick Astley just sings it so well. It might be seen as uncool by some, but it's fundamentally a great song and deep down I think that literally everybody enjoys it. **DG: A mate of mine has just texted to say he loves the song but can we pause it while he goes into Tesco?**

3 THE WHOLE OF THE MOON, The Waterboys

The louder this song is, the better it is. It's great to sing along to. Wherever you are, you get into it. When you're at home, you tap your foot; when you're in the car, you tap the steering wheel. I'm doing it now! U2 have used it as a warm-up for their live shows, it's been in a movie, it's been in a TV show finale – The Affair. So it's still creating headlines to this day. When it was originally released it only reached No.26, which is mad. They re-released it in 1991 and it got to No.3. **AD: I would never have dreamed you'd put that in there. Fantastic choice.**

The name Frankie Goes To Hollywood comes from a headline in an American movie magazine about Frank Sinatra moving to LA. By the time the band played their first gig (at Pickwick's in Liverpool), they had just three original songs including "Relax" and "Two Tribes", which are now the 5th and 10th biggest-selling singles in UK history.

2 TOO SHY, Kajagoogoo
This is so '80s it's beyond belief. How many bands do you think have a No.1 with their first ever record? The Beatles didn't. Kajagoogoo did and it was with this one, Too Shy. I absolutely loved them and, of course, they were how I met my wife. We went to a Kajagoogoo reunion gig and we kind of made a connection after that. Too Shy was then our wedding dance song. We threw some really odd shapes to this! We both love it and it means the world to me, it could easily have been my number one. How many songs have a bass solo? That's how good Nick Beggs is on the bass.

1 TEARDROPS, Womack & Womack
This is going to surprise a lot of people but it's Womack & Womack with Teardrops. So sorry, Fleetwood Mac. Sorry, The Jam. Sorry, Van Halen, because Jump was great. Sorry, Billy Joel's Uptown Girl. Sorry, Cindy Lauper's Time After Time. Sorry, Wet Wet Wet and Wishing I Was Lucky. But I had to go for this for my number one. It's funky, it's disco, it's dance, it's got energy. I was 18 when this was released in 1988 and it's when I first started to go out. Legally I could go and have a pint, and this reminds me of going to Whispers nightclub with my mates. It holds terrific memories for me.

2 COME ON EILEEN, Dexys Midnight Runners
Another dancefloor-filler. Again, it's a band that I'm not actually over the moon about but this is one song I really like. It was a hit in the US and the UK, it won Best Single at the 1983 Brit Awards. When lads are together for some reason, this is the song that we'll all get up to dance to. **AD: It's interesting you say that, because there was a remake of this and I was part of it. talkSPORT did a song called Come On England for the 2004 Euros and we got to No.2. And I believe Kevin Rowland, the main man in Dexys, wasn't particularly happy that we'd twisted his song a little bit.**

Kevin Rowland, asking Eileen to give him a haircut

1 CARELESS WHISPER, George Michael
You just need the sax, don't you? The sax is incredible on this and it took them so long to get that sax absolutely right – and what I love about this song is it's written by George Michael and Andrew Ridgeley. Most of the big Wham! hits were just George, but I love that Andrew had the credit on this even though it was a George Michael solo record. I thought Wham! were really good fun, terrific songs I could listen to all day long. But this for me is on another level that takes it to that category of all-time classic. It reached No.1 in 26 countries and actually knocked Two Tribes off the top spot. **DG: I think we've both come to the same conclusion. There are so many great songs, you could have them in any order. I'm apologising because I missed out so many great songs.**

TOP FIVE @ 5 OSCAR-WINNING FILMS

This isn't a list of films that have won Best Picture at the Oscars – some have, but these Top Fives are brilliant films with some connection to the Academy Awards. So they could have won for Best Actor, Best Film Editing, Best Original Screenplay, Best Cinematography... you get the picture.

5 THE DARK KNIGHT (released 2008)

Heath Ledger won an Oscar for this. There's an argument that he could be the greatest baddy of any film ever. **AG: That's a big statement. I'm not saying no, but it's a hell of a statement.** How good is he, though? **AG: Unbelievable. Did it win the Oscar for Best Supporting Actor?** Yeah, it must have been. The main actor would be Batman. **AG: The best actor is Batman? "And the winner is... Batman!" It might have won for Best Screenplay.** I think it was Supporting Actor. **AG: "I think?" You've done your research, haven't you? On your little tablet...** Yeah, Heath Ledger, Best Supporting Actor.

4 NO COUNTRY FOR OLD MEN (2007)

How scary is Javier Bardem in this film? He's got that big gun thing that pumps out air or something. Josh Brolin has taken the money and it's got the tracker in it. He's wondering, "How can this guy keep finding me?" He works it out but by then it's too late. Great film. Oscars for Best Picture, Adapted Screenplay, Supporting Actor and Director, for the Coen Brothers. **AG: Is it called No Country For Old Men? I'm sure it's got rope in the title somewhere.** It's No Country For Old Men. **AG: There's no rope in that. No Country Rope For An Old Man? Have a look again.** I've looked. It's No Country For Old Men.

5 SEARCHING FOR SUGAR MAN (2012)

This won an Oscar for Best Documentary Feature. Have you heard of it? **DB: No.** It's an amazing story about this American dude called Sixto Rodriguez. He was a massive pop star in South Africa, huge like Elvis Presley, and then all of a sudden, overnight, no one heard any more of him. Rumours started circulating that he'd either had a heart attack and died on stage, or he was in a car accident, or he'd been murdered. So this documentary crew thought, "Well, let's go and find him." And they did, living back in America. He had no idea how big he was in South Africa. Eventually it ends – this is a documentary, all true – with him doing a concert in South Africa, one of the biggest concerts, to all the people who used to listen to his music. **DB: Had he been to South Africa before?** His last concert there had been 20 years earlier. He just thought, "I haven't really made it here" and went back to live in his tiny little house in America. And that was it. All of a sudden, this documentary crew turn up years later and say, "You know you're like Elvis to us?" And then they take him over there and it's like Elvis coming back.

4 PARASITE (2019)

This one from South Korea was the first non-English-language film to win Best Picture. Yes, it's a foreign film, so if we'd played a clip of it you wouldn't have understood it. **DB: But it would have been funny.** Have you seen the film Parasite? **DB: Not even heard of it. Subtitles, I'm guessing. I can watch it, but they take a bit of the concentration away.** It's about a poor family that hatches a scheme to all be employed by an incredibly rich family, one at a time. So, the son gets a job tutoring one of the kids, and then the dad gets a job becoming the limo driver... The rich family have no idea they're all related. But the ending of this movie is one of the most bonkers, barking endings and twists to any film I've ever seen. **DB: What happens? I'm not going to watch it, I promise.** I'm not going to tell you. There'll be people out there listening to this thinking they're going to watch it this weekend. **DB: No, they won't, they'll be too busy watching Justice League.** Parasite, amazing movie. I want you to watch it because the twist will blow you away, I'm telling you. Please watch it for me.

3 FORREST GUMP (1994)

Everyone always says "Life *is* like a box of chocolates" when they're quoting the film, but it's actually "My momma always said life *was* like a box of chocolates." **DB: Incredible film. I was close to putting it in my Top Five.** It won six Oscars: Best Picture, Actor, Adapted Screenplay, Director, Film Editing and Visual Effects. Forrest Gump is one of those movies where if you turn the TV on, wherever it is in the film, you'll watch the rest of it. **DB: The bit I always remember is when he's outrunning the truck and he ends up just running through the middle of a football pitch and then playing football for his school team. There's a big sign behind the stand: 'Stop, Forrest'.** You know Lieutenant Dan in the movie? He's obviously had both legs amputated, right? This is genuine, I wouldn't joke about this. The actor has his legs but in the film they've taped green from his knees down and then green-screened them out. **DB: I always wondered how they did that.** You should watch the making-of film. It's unbelievable. And that's probably why it won an Oscar for Visual Effects.

3 BEN-HUR (1959)

I've seen this film about ten times and it is one long film, by the way. There's even an intermission in the middle. **AG: I think there's been a mistake here. You've gone from Justice League to Ben-Hur?** It's my dad's favourite film. He got me to watch it a few times and now I love it. Charlton Heston. Him and his best friend kind of fall out and his best friend ends up taking him hostage and making him a prisoner. **AG: Is there a girl involved? Is that why it's her? Ben And Her?** No, it's not. That's his name, Judah Ben-Hur. Have you seen it? **AG: I've seen the bit where they run around in the chariots.** That's actually one of the best parts of the film. **AG: They did it with mirrors, magnets and a bit of smoke.** I don't believe you. **AG: What did it win?** It won Best Picture and 11 other Oscars. You have to stop watching films in French or whatever it is and watch Ben-Hur.

2 TRAINING DAY (2001)

Denzel Washington on top form. **AG: Great film, great soundtrack.** Very good soundtrack. Denzel won Best Actor for Training Day. He's a horrible copper, though. **AG: Is this the film where Ethan Hawke is going to have his head blown off in the bath?** Yeah. There are some scary scenes, like the one where they're playing cards and then Denzel leaves him there... and when Ethan's character goes back to Denzel's area. Great movie. **AG: They're all going to be great movies from here on in...**

1 GLADIATOR (2000)

I've put this in here because it won Best Picture but Russell Crowe must have won Best Actor, he's brilliant in this. **AG: I've got this mixed up with Ben-Hur. It's this one where they used mirrors to film the chariot races.** You're all over the gaff. Gladiator is a great movie. **AG: It is, in fact I think it's one of the very few movies I actually went to the cinema to see twice. It was that good.**

2 THE DEPARTED (2006)

An incredible cast. You've got Jack Nicholson, Leonardo DiCaprio, Matt Damon... It won four Oscars: Best Picture, Adapted Screenplay, Director and Film Editing. The Departed. **DB: You know, I've never seen it.** Oh my! **DB: I know, it's unbelievable. But for whatever reason, I've just never watched it.** It came out in 2006. That's on my Sky+ player. Whenever I've got an hour or half an hour to kill, I'll just watch that. **DB: DiCaprio's only won one Oscar, hasn't he? And that was for The Revenant. And he's made so many better films than that.** The Wolf Of Wall Street was unbelievable. That's on my Sky+ player too, I'll watch it whenever.

1 GOODFELLAS (1990)

Everyone on the planet knows this film. Have you seen Goodfellas? **DB: Probably, yeah. I'm not really big on the mafia-type films if I'm honest.** Joe Pesci, Best Supporting Actor. 1990, over 30 years ago! **DB: I like Joe Pesci in everything that he does.** How could you not have seen Goodfellas? You should be ashamed of yourself. If they edit it so Joe Pesci is played by Wonder Woman, would that be better for you? **DB: If they could fly and there are more capes I'm watching it.** If Joe Pesci can melt Ray Liotta with his eyes, you're going to watch it! Good Top Five, I enjoyed it. **DB: Mine was better, though. Gladiator is the best.**

Training Day: "And will we get a certificate at the end?"

TOP FIVE @ 5 FAVOURITE LONG-HAIRED FOOTBALLERS

The inspiration for this is my new, longer hairstyle. The producer said it looked really nice when he saw me with it on the TV and it made him think of footballers with similarly distinguished barnets. **DB: Your hair looks better long than it does short.** Do you find me attractive? **DB: Number five...**

5 JAMIE VARDY

People are going to go, "What? Jamie Vardy doesn't have long hair!" But in 2013 he got cornrows, didn't he? And it just looked funny. **AG: That was a holiday haircut he left in. It was like a mohawk braided down the middle. Why have you put that in your Top Five?** Because it was one of my favourites. I like his hair like that. **AG: You don't like that, no one likes that hair. You showed me a picture and we laughed.** I would have my hair like that but it will not grow long enough. I'd have to have extensions. It's taken me 37 years to get to this. It doesn't grow that fast. It takes ages. Jamie Vardy, number five.

4 GABRIEL BATISTUTA

Great haircut, wavy and full. **AG: Batistuta's got the kind of hair that looks better in the rain.** He has it slicked back. When he scores a goal or hits a shot, it seems to go everywhere. Great footballer, great hair. **AG: Yeah, he looks a bit like Iggy Pop, doesn't he?** I don't know who that is. **AG: He's got that sort of hair, sings without a top on, very skinny, must be about 70 now.** No... I like Batistuta.

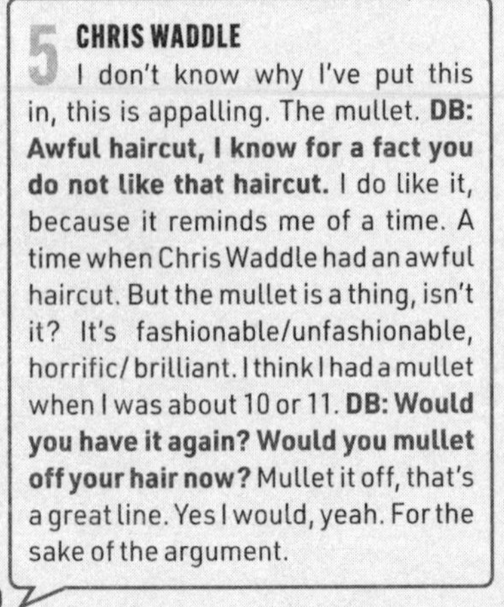

5 CHRIS WADDLE

I don't know why I've put this in, this is appalling. The mullet. **DB: Awful haircut, I know for a fact you do not like that haircut.** I do like it, because it reminds me of a time. A time when Chris Waddle had an awful haircut. But the mullet is a thing, isn't it? It's fashionable/unfashionable, horrific/ brilliant. I think I had a mullet when I was about 10 or 11. **DB: Would you have it again? Would you mullet off your hair now?** Mullet it off, that's a great line. Yes I would, yeah. For the sake of the argument.

Waddle: this is actually short hair, but on fire

4 DAVID BECKHAM

I had to have this fella in. I Googled how many haircuts David Beckham has had. **DB: He had cornrows as well, didn't he?** Yeah, he did. It came up with 25 of his best haircuts. We've got blond, bald, braids, mohawk, greased back, combover with a parting, highlights, stuck up, a number one all over, the Elvis, the short on the sides and long on the top... it just goes on and on and on. He has had some wonderful haircuts, Becks. **DB: He's had some awful ones as well.** The long hair he had when Fergie accidentally kicked the boot in his face – he had his hair in an Alice band, that was when his hair looked really cool. He can do anything. I saw him once with a holster for a phone on his belt, which is a no-no, and I even thought that was cool. I've only met him a couple of times. I think the first time was when his autobiography came out and I just couldn't believe how beautiful he was. He's like a waxwork, isn't he? **DB: I don't know about a waxwork. He's just got that aura, hasn't he? When I got in the England squad, my first ever squad, and met him... I was just looking, thinking, "Whoa, it's Becks!"** I bet you'd tell him he's attractive but not me. **DB: No, I'd say he's got great hair.**

3 PAOLO MALDINI

He speaks for himself. **AG: Amazing hair... beautiful, shiny.** Immaculate. **AG: Yeah, proper Italian hair.** It's not just his hair, it's the way it's styled as well. **AG: Again, another man who could just wear a white shirt with the top button done up and look amazing.** Maldini had to be in here.

3 RUUD GULLIT

In the final of the Euros in 1988, the Netherlands played the Soviet Union – and that's when the world kind of took notice. **DB: Was that the header he scored? Great goal.** Yeah, and his hair went absolutely everywhere. Great hair, and it's quite an iconic hairstyle he had. Obviously he was also an iconic person at that time but that was an amazing, amazing haircut. And that kit, that Holland kit – the whole package.

2 CARLOS VALDERRAMA

Unbelievable big blond hair. **AG: Was that a great haircut? It was just a big ball of mess, wasn't it?** Carlos Valderrama, Colombia. **AG: You can't go out like that, you'd just look stupid. You can't wear a hat. I bet he could never put a cap on.** OK, he probably can't put a cap on, but his hair is cool. People know him by his hair. **AG: I know they do, but they know Edward Scissorhands by his hands but that doesn't mean you want them.** That's real life, is it? **AG: No, that's not a documentary. But I'm just saying, just because people know you for something, doesn't mean it's cool.** That's great hair. **AG: I don't know, would you want to go out clubbing with that hair?** Would you want to go out with a mullet? **AG: Loads of people did go clubbing with a mullet back in the '80s.** Loads of people went out with an Afro like he's got. **AG: No, no one's got a Valderrama haircut.** It's great, loads of blond hair. Proper blond. **AG: Why have you put that in? You would not want that.** I would!

2 DAVID GINOLA

He had wonderful hair. The thing I love about Ginola's hair is that, when he used to run, it used to sort of flow on its own. It looked as beautiful as him when he used to run with the ball. And, of course, he had something that I should have soon, which is a shampoo advert. You remember his catchphrase? Remember who the advert was for? L'Oreal. The catchphrase was: "Because I'm worth it." **DB: I think he had good hair, yeah, but it wasn't standout hair.** Oh, mate, come on. Ginola's hair is legendary. So legendary, in fact, apparently it had a paper round. **DB: Really? I know you're lying.** Of course I'm lying, how could hair have a paper round!? **DB: Listen, I think he's got good hair, but it's not outstanding.** You just talked about Valderrama, he looks like he's fallen in a pot of paint. **DB: If you said to me "Valderrama", I'd say, "Oh, the geezer with the hair."** I don't understand why you think just because you can recognise someone because of a... **DB: He's got great hair.** Ginola's hair is 10 times better. Valderrama's looks like a joke-shop wig. **DB: Do you know what Ginola's hair looks like? Yours.** That's one of the best compliments you've ever given me. **DB: It isn't.**

1 RONALDINHO

Great hair. **AG: It was awful hair. I tell you now, if Ronaldinho came over to my house and asked if he could kip the night, I wouldn't be happy because he'd ruin the pillow.** Because of the Jheri curl? **AG: Yeah. He would just slide out of that bed. Whoosh. Where's Ronaldinho? He's on the floor.** You know we spoke about Ruud Gullit, when he scored that header and his hair went everywhere? When Ronaldinho dribbled with the ball, his hair did the same thing. **AG: But awful hair.** Great hair. **AG: When we do this and I go back home and look through Insta, loads of people are like, "What's Benty thinking with his Top Five this week?"** You've got a mullet in yours. You've got a guy who's got hair like everyone else, Ginola. Normal hair. Valderrama, world-class hair. Ronaldinho, world-class hair and footballer. **AG: Would you be happy putting your hand in Ronaldinho's hair?** Yeah. **AG: You'd never find it again. Let's find out the real winner...**

1 ANDREA PIRLO

He has to be top of the pops. **DB: I'll give you that, but you've only put him in because you think your hair looks like his.** I don't think people stop me in the street and go, "Oh, I thought you were Pirlo" when I turn around. I looked back at pictures of Pirlo when he was younger. He still has the beard and the hair. My understanding is he was born like that. He popped out and they went, "You've given birth to a legend, Mrs Pirlo." **DB: He's probably the only one on your list I'd go with. Maybe Beckham. The rest of them no.** How about Gullit? **DB: No.** I think out of all of them you'll give me the fact that Pirlo has the best hair. **DB: No, Valderrama.** Come on. **DB: Or Ronaldinho.** Ronaldinho's hair is horrible. Sometimes he wore it in a big ponytail as well, didn't he? Did he ever wear an Alice band? **DB: Yeah, of course he would have done.**

TOP FIVE @ 5:
MOST DIFFICULT OPPONENTS...

TOP FIVE @ 5 MOST DIFFICULT OPPONENTS: ANDY TOWNSEND

Andy, this is from a career where you played top-flight and World Cup football so I imagine there are going to be some serious names here...

5 FRANCO BARESI

He was an outstanding central defender, such a brilliant organiser. Franco Baresi was *the* superior central defender in the late '80s and early '90s. Everywhere in world football, he was the one everybody wanted to have in their team. I was standing next to him in the tunnel as we were about to walk out onto the field at the Giants Stadium for our opening group game against Italy in the 1994 World Cup. He started wagging his finger at me. I'm looking at him and he's looking at the kit I've got on. We have got white/green/white and unfortunately they have white/blue/white. So I started wagging my finger back at him but one of us had the wrong kit on and, of course, it was us! Big Jack screamed at our kitman, Little Charlie. I can't repeat what he said but the gist of it was if we lost the game it would be Charlie's fault. Thankfully we went out there, Ray Houghton got the goal and we won!

4 LOTHAR MATTHÄUS

I played against him a couple of times. He was unbelievably quick across 10 yards. Ridiculous pace. He could get to the other side of you very quickly and easily. There was a spell for four or five years where Matthäus was considered to be the ultimate central midfield player. I played against him in a friendly for the Republic [*of Ireland*] in Hanover once, or 'Hangover' as it became known after the match, and we actually won. He wasn't quite so unbelievable in that match but he was always a player I genuinely liked watching and was a brilliantly consistent operator for the Germans.

3 MARCO VAN BASTEN

The ultimate predator at one point. One of the few players I've looked at in the tunnel before a match, and this was in the '90 World Cup, and thought, "Oh dear, if he turns up and plays like he can we might have a spot of bother this evening." But it didn't quite pan out that way: we didn't lose, we drew. I always joke that big Mick McCarthy man-marked Mark van Basten for the last 10 minutes of the game just to swap shirts with him at the end! But he was an amazing player, a phenomenal goalscorer... and to have to retire almost at the very height of his powers must have been very difficult for him. **AD: So far we've had Baresi, Matthäus and Van Basten... I'm guessing there are not going to be any players from your time at Weymouth.**

2 ROBERTO BAGGIO

He was a proper player. Not only was he good – he looked good. Baggio was the darling of the Italian team, the focal point. I remember in the '90 World Cup, he skipped past me on the halfway line and I had a chance to have him up in the air. I could have just fouled him... and I should have done, because the ball ended up being knocked out wide to Donadoni who shot, Packie Bonner saved it but Schillaci banged in the rebound. Great player.

1 BRYAN ROBSON

When I was a young lad striving to be a footballer and wanting to play professionally, Bryan Robson was always the benchmark. He was the original 'everything midfielder'. Nowadays we pigeonhole players. You're a 'sitter' or an '8' or a '10', but Robbo was all of those. He could get up and down and he scored goals and he was brave. He was a warrior as well as a top-class player. **AD: How is Gazza not on your list?** I think he was at his very best at Rangers, but I didn't play against him then. But what a talent.

Andy pays tribute to his idol Robbo by shoving him in the back

TOP FIVE @ 5 MOST DIFFICULT OPPONENTS: JAMIE CARRAGHER

Friend of the show, former Liverpool and England defender – and we don't need to go back into when he quit international football and I commented on it, as we've been through that before. Let's get on to his most daunting opponents...

5 PAOLO MALDINI

Along with Franco Baresi, one of the two I always looked to as defenders. I played against Maldini in the Champions League Final in 2005, and I'll never forget he did an interview before the game and he mentioned me in his interview. I was like, "Oh my god, Maldini knows who I am!" I have actually got his shirt from that game. They left everything in the dressing room after the game – the shirts, the medals, everything. We had a lot of young lads on the trip so they went in there and raided it.

4 JOHN TERRY

He was the best centre-back of the Premier League era, just ahead of Rio Ferdinand. **AD: This choice surprised me because, of all the brilliant attacking players you have played against...** John Terry was my type of player. He was basically a better version of me, if I'm being honest, and I think his football ability is massively underrated. He was two-footed and could ping the ball 40 or 50 yards with his left. I also wanted to get an English player on my list so I went for him because there's no way I could put Stevie [*Gerrard*] in.

Jamie Carragher has a nice sideline as the king of the put-down on social media. El Hadji Diouf: "The difference between me and Carragher is that I am a world class player and he is a sh*t." Carragher: "The other big difference is he has scored less goals for LFC in the Premier League than me (not counting OG's!!)" Ouch.

3 XAVI

Love him. He's the greatest midfield player I can think of. Xavi was player of the tournament in World Cups and Euros when Spain dominated, and that's before you think about what the Barcelona team did. I've interviewed him once and it was a great honour for me to speak to him because for me he's number one in terms of midfielders. He took what he did, running games, to the super-elite level at World Cups and nobody could stop him doing it. He played his part at every level, not just club football.

Jamie Carragher paying extra close attention to Thierry Henry. Reinforcements on the way

2 LIONEL MESSI

I played against Messi when he was a young lad. He certainly wasn't the Messi of the Pep era, but we played against the Barcelona team who were reigning European champions in 2007. Messi was on the right wing, Ronaldinho was on the left and Samuel Eto'o was up front, so it was some front three. We beat them in the Nou Camp 2-1 and then lost at home 1-0 but went through on away goals. So we came up against Messi and did OK, but he's just an absolute god; there's no way I could not put him in my Top Five.

1 THIERRY HENRY

I think he's the greatest player to ever play in the Premier League, and I still say that the Arsenal team of that era is the best team I ever played against – that includes Milan, Real Madrid and Barcelona – although it did underachieve in terms of the Champions League and never quite got one. I was on a shopping trip in London with my wife once, I was carrying all the bags and stood on the side of the road and there was traffic everywhere. A taxi driver stopped in front of me and went out of his way to fetch a piece of paper and write 'THIERRY HENRY' in block capitals before hanging it out of the window. I just thought, "Oh my God, I can't get away from this fella." He drove away laughing but, listen, Henry was fantastic. Definitely the toughest player I ever came up against and the best in the world for a year or two.

TOP FIVE@5 MOST DIFFICULT OPPONENTS: DEAN ASHTON

From Crewe Alexandra to West Ham United, via Norwich City, to England recognition and an all-too-early retirement aged 26 due to an ankle injury sustained while on international duty, these were your Top Five most difficult opponents along the way...

5 SEAN GREGAN (Preston/Leeds)

Not many people may have heard of him but he was tough. I was 16 or 17 years old and had just got into the side at Crewe, and those first couple of seasons were when defenders could still leave a tackle on you if they wanted. I had blond tips in my hair because my mum was a hairdresser – and as soon as we kicked off Gregan was on at me, talking about my hair and saying, "You won't fancy this today, you're in for an absolute lesson." First challenge, he just steams in and elbows me right in the side of the head. And when I was on the floor he said, "Today's going to be my day." **AD: There was no VAR then.** No VAR! That was a wake-up call. I was just a boy playing against men and football was their livelihood.

4 ALAN STUBBS (Everton)

This man is made of granite – as I discovered when I played against Everton for Crewe Alexandra in the FA Cup. This was my first taste of coming up against two top defenders in David Weir and Alan Stubbs, and the latter was just so physically strong... but also, out of anyone I've ever played against, he was the best organiser I've ever heard. So vocal. It makes it quite hard as a striker to know where to go. Another eye-opener for me.

3 JOHN TERRY (Chelsea)

It was one of the first seasons I was in the Premier League and we went to Stamford Bridge. I wanted to be able to grab hold of defenders and physically know where they were and be able to manoeuvre them. And John Terry loved that. He was happy to oblige. I remember, we had a free kick out wide and I just grabbed his arm and yanked him into one of his own players. And as we were walking back he just went, "I'll let you have one. And that's it. You don't ever do that to me again." And I thought, "I'll do whatever it takes to try and score a goal"... but he was fuming at the fact that I'd cheated him.

2 VINCENT KOMPANY (Manchester City)

It was when he first got to Manchester City that I played against him. He played the first half as a defensive midfield player and the second half at centre-back. **AD: That's not easy.** No, and it was like having two players in one. He was just so good. He played midfield and was silky on the ball; and then he drops to centre-back and he is just as good in that position. You then try to run him but you can't because he's got the pace to adjust. He was big, so he was great in the air. He had so many attributes – you could see then that he was going to go on and be their captain and do great things. He was outstanding.

1 RIO FERDINAND (Manchester United)

I scored against him twice in the games I played against him but he's the one player I've always felt useless against. Terry and Kompany want to get in a physical battle but Rio wasn't interested. He would stand about a yard off me, and when I tried to put my arm back to grab, he wasn't there. When he did step out he would start their attacks, so then I was getting grief for not getting hold of the ball. I won some headers and I scored a couple of goals against him, but I always felt like he just had me in his pocket. **AD: So you scored arguably the greatest goal of your career against the guy who was your toughest opponent?** It was the first time he didn't anticipate what was going to happen before I did.

Ashton and Kompany (or Ashton & Ko for short)

TOP FIVE @ 5 MOST DIFFICULT OPPONENTS: TROY DEENEY

Troy has based his choices on how well these players have done against Watford when he's been on the pitch. And that's as good a set of criteria as any. Let's go...

5 MESUT ÖZIL

Why are you looking so astounded? **AD: Mesut Özil? Is this a joke?** The question was, who are the most difficult players you've played against, and there have been times when we were playing Arsenal when I thought this guy was an alien. He's ridiculously good. **AD: When was this?** A couple of years ago, he hasn't really played since. I just think he is immensely talented. I like people who can see the game differently. They're not only great on the ball but can see other people's runs and make other players better. In the games we played against Arsenal, certainly in the 2017-18 season, he was so good – and when Ronaldo is saying he was the second-best player in Spanish football, after himself, that's high praise. **AD: Are you OK? Something is not quite right here. Am I being set up for something? Mesut Özil in your Top Five? My mind is blown.**

4 DAVID SILVA

My number four is along similar lines, another player who is on a different wavelength. David Silva's had the longevity, obviously, but the biggest thing about him for me is that when Manchester City bought all these superstars along the way he was never really replaced.

3 VIRGIL VAN DIJK

This guy is probably changing the way that centre-halves will be built for the next ten years. Big Virgil van Dijk. **AD: Were you saying this when he was still at Southampton?** Yes. **AD: Fair enough.**

2 SERGIO AGUERO

Every time he plays against us he scores. It's probably the same for everyone, to be fair. Sergio Aguero is that good. And it's not just tap-ins – there have been different kinds of finishes every time he has played against us for Man City over the last four of five years. **AD: I was there for the 6-0 at Vicarage Road and he was unbelievable that day. The whole team was. It could have been about ten! And Watford didn't even play that badly.** When you play against those elite teams, they have to be playing at 7/10 and you have to be at 11/10 to just make it a fair game. **AD: Let's get to the big one...**

Deeney attempts to get past
Van Dijk by taking flight

1 KEVIN DE BRUYNE

People will be asking what about Harry Kane and Paul Pogba, and players like that who would normally make these kinds of list, but I can only go off the players I have played against. This was quite a tough one because I could have gone for Wayne Rooney, who was also consistently good against us, but I chose Kevin De Bruyne in the end because he just plays a completely different game. It's like we are all playing checkers and he is playing chess. Plus, his hard work off the ball doesn't get highlighted enough. **AD: Great line-up, although Özil seems like a bit of an odd one out...**

Troy Deeney puts down his big break to his mum. "She kicked me out of the house because she wanted to clean up. So I went and played football." He scored four for Chelmsley Town, a scout saw him and offered him a trial at Walsall.

TOP FIVE @ 5 MOST DIFFICULT OPPONENTS: GABBY AGBONLAHOR

Former Aston Villa and England striker Gabby Agbonlahor has come up against some of the very best defenders in the world. Here he tells us which five gave him the most problems...

5 GERARD PIQUE

We played against each other when we were younger, in a reserve-team game when he was at Manchester United, and I scored a hat-trick. It was a cold, frosty night and after 60 minutes the referee called the two captains over to say he might have to call the game off. I was the Villa captain and I said, "You'd better not – I've just scored a hat-trick and this might get me into the first team for the weekend." And so we ended up finishing the game. This certainly wasn't the Gerard Pique we came to see at Barcelona – the guy man-marked me out of the game when England took on Spain. He was so composed on the ball, he would get there before you and then dribble out with the ball and start off the attacks. An outstanding defender.

4 JOHN TERRY

For me he is one of England's, if not one of the world's, best ever defenders. John Terry is up there with the top three or four. He was outstanding to play against and we had some great battles over the years. Even when he came to Villa we would have battles in training. He was a really tough player to play against, really clever. If he knew there was space behind he would not come tight to you – he would always give himself that yard so if you made a run in behind he could get there and cover. And he was a great passer, he could switch the play so easily. A great defender all round.

3 VINCENT KOMPANY

He is up there with the great Premier League centre-halves. I used to have nightmares about the games in which I played against him. I've never known a defender to be so physical – you got the ball played in to your feet and he was there, he was pushing you on the floor, throwing you about, and after the game you had marks all over your body from Kompany. If you ran in behind he was as quick as you, if not quicker. And he was so good on the ball as well. He proved his worth with everything he won with Manchester City.

Celebrity Villa fan and world famous violinist Nigel Kennedy: "When someone like Gabby is born a mile from the Villa ground, then he's my player. I've worn his shirts so much they stand up by themselves."

2 LEDLEY KING

Anybody who has played against this guy would admit he was a real handful. Obviously he had his injury problems but, when Ledley King was fit, he had everything. He had the speed, the aggression, and he was another one who was great on the ball. Every time I played against him he basically shut up shop. I just feel sorry for the injuries that hampered his career, but he was so tough as an opponent.

1 RIO FERDINAND

Similar to Pique and Kompany: not only would he get to the ball before you, he would dribble the ball past you... but he's not just going to play it off somewhere, he's going to have some fun. He's running up the pitch with the ball and so I end up chasing him back towards my own goal – the job that he was meant to be doing to me. Rio Ferdinand was unbelievable for Manchester United, he was unbelievable for England. The best all-round Premier League centre-half. No question.

Pique manages to tackle Gabby even during his mid-game nap

TOP FIVE @ 5 DARREN GOUGH MOMENTS

Ahead of Goughie's 50th birthday we surprised him with his very own Top Five @ 5 collection of golden moments from his time at talkSPORT. He pretended he didn't want any fuss but he loved it really...

5 IL CANTO DEGLI ITALIANI

This was Darren singing the Italian national anthem on live radio. This happened quite early on in his time at the radio station. And I remember afterwards I thought, "He will do for me! This is going to work out just fine." If he can take the mickey out of himself like this, no problem at all.

4 FOOD, GLORIOUS FOOD

Food – he talks about nothing else. But this is also about a moment we had in Leeds. We'd been to an awards do and Goughie kept going on about this kebab shop. We ended up in a bar in the early hours and I lost him. I thought he must have gone to that kebab shop so I headed in that direction and, sure enough, there he was ordering himself a kebab. So I got one too... and it was the best kebab I've ever had. **DG: That was the night we had to put our producer to bed. He had one too many, but he's not very tall and shouldn't have tried to keep up with us.**

3 PART-TIME COMMENTATOR

People forget you were actually quite good at cricket. The Gough style of commentary is funny and intelligent, and who can forget you calling Roston Chase a part-time spinner live on air, just as he claimed an England wicket? That was hilarious. **DG: I love doing the commentary – getting to see great cricket being played all around the world. And talkSPORT delivered, didn't we? We won an award for best live broadcast for our commentary.**

2 I PREDICT A RIOT

Euro 2012. Warsaw, Poland v Russia, and about 5,000 Russian fans were marching through the streets. When they got to the stadium they met with the Polish fans and it all kicked off. There were fans fighting, 11 people were hurt, over 120 arrested. And we were watching it from the studio when all of a sudden Goughie says, "I'm going out there." And he just walked out into the middle of it and started broadcasting. **DG: I felt the danger but wanted to be part of it. I'd never done that sort of broadcasting before. I knew it had calmed down when these three blokes walked past me in fancy dress. One of them was Darth Vader, I think another was Chuck Norris.** As indeed you informed the listeners.

1 KP NUTS ABOUT GOUGHIE

My number one is your interview with Kevin Pietersen in 2014. KP has always been box-office but this interview sticks in my mind. **DG: That was an emotional interview.** He was wobbling a bit when he was talking about going to visit Andrew Strauss and apologising. He dissected his own character, and showed he had the ability for self-analysis. **DG: He realised that, whatever happened at the end of his career, it took away at least 30 Test matches from him. He could have been England's top run-scorer of all time.** Great interviews. Thank you for those, Darren Gough, and for everything else over the last few years.